Aprovecho

A Mexican–American Border Cookbook

THE HIPPOCRENE COOKBOOK LIBRARY

Aprovecho

A Mexican-American Border Cookbook

Teresa Cordero-Cordell & Robert Cordell

HIPPOCRENE BOOKS, INC.
NEW YORK

Paperback edition, 2008.
Copyright © 2004 Teresa Cordero-Cordell and Robert Cordell.

Book and jacket design by Acme Klong Design, Inc.

For more information, address:
HIPPOCRENE BOOKS, INC.
171 Madison Avenue
New York, NY 10016

ISBN 13: 978-0-7818-1206-1
ISBN 10: 0-7818-1206-2
Cataloging-in-Publication Data available from the Library of Congress.
Printed in the United States of America.

This book is dedicated to the sons and daughters of the Southwest who have moved all across the United States. We hope this book gives you a taste of home and that you and your family continue to enjoy and share the culture that you left behind.

A special dedication to our son, Michael, and our daughter, Lily, with all of our love. We hope you pass this on to your children.

We would also like to gratefully acknowledge all of those who submitted recipes, as well as Caroline Garland and Kat Kalman for their invaluable help, Lily and Jennifer for the help they gave with their computer expertise, Mike and Jenn and all of the friends of Aprovecho who helped with preparation, and tasting of the recipes. Thanks to you all.

Hola. Bienvenidos a Aprovecho, The Mexican Kitchen

Greetings from El Paso, Texas, the largest American city located directly on the Mexican border. How close is Ciudad Juárez, Mexico to El Paso? Well, you can go to downtown El Paso and walk over the bridge to Avenida Juárez in a couple of minutes or drive to one of the bridges and take your car into Juárez. The influence that these sister cities have upon the politics, the people, and the culture, including the food, of one another is enormous.

Aprovecho is dedicated to the food of the Southwestern border. Some of the recipes have been handed down from mother to daughter, from kitchen tables in the *barrio*, to phone calls across the country. With the ever-increasing Hispanic population in the United States, the availability of the ingredients listed in these recipes has increased and more Americans are enjoying meals that we eat here on a daily basis. Some of the best and most authentic eateries in El Paso are the small mom and pop restaurants where the closely guarded recipes are known only to family members.

We've asked some fellow El Pasoans to submit a recipe to this book, along with a shared thought about what it was like to grow up on the border. Also included are some stories, legends, and interesting facts about Border life. Please, try the recipes, read about our Border culture and, most of all, enjoy the food!

You can also visit our website at www.aprovecho-themexicankitchen.com and, if you have a suggestion, leave us a message as to how we can make the site and this book even better.

¡Aprovecho! Sus amigos de El Paso, Bob y Tere.

What Is Border Food?
Two Perspectives

We want to tell you what Border food is, but even we don't always agree. So, we decided it would be best to tell how each of us views this book and the recipes that it contains. Here goes.

Bob's Border Story

I remember my first encounter with Border food very well. We moved to El Paso from New Jersey when I was ten years old and we were living in a motel. There was a local restaurant chain, Pancho's Mexican Buffet, right next to the motel. Our first night here, my father walked us over to Pancho's and my brother, my sister and I walked down the buffet line looking at all the weird, colorful food not knowing what anything was. We were all greatly relieved to find fried chicken at the end of the line, but I did try a taco.

My mother, originally from Boston, didn't do much Border cooking, but when I would go over to a friend's house for dinner I'd always try whatever was put on the table. I wouldn't ask what was in it until after I'd eaten it. That's how I slowly came to be familiar with Border food. I loved enchiladas, cheese or chicken. It surprised me that there were so many different varieties of *tacos*; *al carbon* and *barbacoa* were my favorites. What finally got me to eat onions were fajitas, beef please. The thing about Border food that really hooked me, though, was the spicy flavors. In El Paso, they asked you if you wanted jalapeños on your hamburger. This was in the late sixties, way before fast food places discovered tortillas and chipotle sauce.

El Paso is seventy-five percent Hispanic and the flavor of the people is everywhere. If you go to downtown El Paso, you can cross over a bridge, by foot, and be in Juárez, Mexico in a couple of minutes. I once asked a friend from Juárez how many really authentic Mexican food restaurants she'd found in El Paso and her answer was, "None." Border food is a mixture of the two cultures, a blend of ingredients that are Mexican or American that make their own wonderful tastes. Now that many Mexican spices and foods are available in most of the United States, anyone can make Border food.

In the seventies, I spent four years in the Army, most of that time in Germany. The food there was good, but also very meat-and-potatoes. When I came back to El Paso in 1977, and I've been here since, I couldn't wait to get a chile verde burrito and *borracho* beans. The thing I missed most about Germany was the beer, but Mexican beer compares very favorably with any European beer (see the section on Mexican beer, page 196).

I married Tere in 1988 and my appreciation of the food and culture of the Border region blossomed. Tere, obviously, is a wonderful cook. My own first experience cooking Border food took place in the kitchen of our first house. Tere made chile con queso and I liked it so much that I wanted another batch the following weekend. She said, "You make it," and she showed me how. Since then, I've learned how to make everything from enchiladas to tamales.

Border food is the best of the Mexican and American ways of cooking. The ingredients come from both sides of the Border and together form unique, delicious flavors. Try some of these recipes, mold them into what you like and fall in love with Border food.

Tere's Border Story

My family came to El Paso from Chihuahua, Mexico in 1915, when my mother, Maria Luisa, was five years old. My grandmother, Annie, and her husband and three other daughters settled in the Segundo Barrio of El Paso, also known as the Second Ward. A *barrio* is simply a neighborhood that Hispanics, usually of low income, share. When I was growing up there, I guess I was like any child in that I didn't know what we didn't have. My two older brothers and I all went to the same schools, and we all graduated from Bowie High School, proud Osos (Bears). Bowie has a huge, loyal alumni association with members all over the country.

I learned to cook from both my mother and my grandmother. Since she'd moved to the United States, Annie had to find substitutes for some of the ingredients she couldn't find in her new home. Maybe that's how Border food really began, with Mexicans coming to America and adapting their traditional dishes to the foods and spices available here.

The influence of Juárez on El Paso, and El Paso on Juárez is felt throughout both cities. In El Paso, as you head downtown, the closer you get to the Rio Grande and the Santa Fe Bridge that spans it, the shops and billboards are almost exclusively in Spanish. When you walk over the bridge into Juárez, the majority of signs are bilingual and most of the Mexicans speak at least some English. Mexicans come to El Paso to purchase things at all the regular stores, while El Pasoans head to Juárez for everything from groceries to dentists (cheap) to prescription drugs (really cheap). You can also head to the Market for all sorts of Mexican spices and foods.

Mom was a cook for the El Paso school system, but she was her own kind of cook. If she didn't think that a meal was good enough for the kids, she'd add her own spices and ingredients. She wrote down many of her recipes and they ended up with me and my two brothers. Our website and our cookbook began as an effort to record the recipes handed down for generations along the Border. We asked many of our relatives to send their favorites; we asked friends and fellow El Pasoans, from musicians to our Congressman, to contribute. You'll find their submissions in this book, and we thank them all.

If you travel thirty miles up the road into New Mexico, the "Mexican" food tastes different than it does here on the Border. It's also prepared in quite a different manner. Border food is found all along the U.S.-Mexican Border, not just in Texas. Sometimes it is referred to as Tex-Mex but you can also find it along the Mexican boundary in New Mexico, Arizona, and California. The best way to describe it is a mix of American ingredients with those that are truly from Mexico. These Mexican foods and spices are available in almost every grocery store here, and what you can't find can be purchased on a twenty-minute trip into Mexico or online. The simplest fare can become Border food. If you pour some chili powder over an ear of corn you have an *elote*, and there are *elote* stands at most outdoor events in El Paso. Take an American dish, send it down to the Southwest for some spices and ingredients, and you have a Border dish.

There's something in *Aprovecho* for every taste and every occasion. From the lightest salad to the most extraordinary main dishes, you'll find that the taste of Border food is truly unique. Not every dish has to burn your tongue off, though some might if you're not careful, but they are fun to prepare and they are authentic. We believe in making every recipe your own, so try them, have fun and, most of all, eat!

Table of Contents

Breakfast

Proverbs
Dichos

One man's gravy is another man's poison.
El piso de uno, es el techo de otro.

Birds of a feather flock together.
Cada quien con su cada cual.

First come, first serve.
Para el primer costal, nunca falta harina.

Forbidden fruit is sweetest.
La fruta prohibida es la mas deseada.

Be forewarned.
Hombre prevenido vale por dos.

Breakfast Burrito

Burrito del Desayuno

1 serving

One of the tastiest, and easiest, Southwestern breakfasts is the burrito. The basic recipe is to take a flour tortilla, warm it up, and fill it with egg and anything else that you want. Among the suggestions for added ingredients are chorizo, ham, bacon, sausage, cheese, onion, mushrooms, or just about anything you might put in an omelet. Cook all your ingredients, warm the tortilla, either on the stove or in the microwave, and shovel everything into the tortilla. The amount of each ingredient is up to your hunger at the time. For added zest, you can put salsa, green chile strips or some jalapeños in your burrito. Pile it on and enjoy!

---

2 slices bacon   **1 flour tortilla, warmed**
1 egg   **Grated cheese**
1 teaspoon chopped onion **2 tablespoons chopped**
Salt and pepper, to taste   **green chile or taco sauce**

Fry the bacon and set aside to drain on paper towels. Break the egg into the bacon grease. Break the yolk and stir slightly. Sprinkle with the onion and salt and pepper to taste. Flip the egg and fry until firm. Line the center of a flour tortilla with the grated cheese. Place the hot fried egg on top of the cheese. Spoon the chile onto the egg and top with bacon. Fold the tortilla sides over, wrap in foil, and warm in the oven.

Breakfast Tortillas

Tortillas del Desayuno

This is a Border-style French toast, without the syrup. It's basically a fried breakfast burrito, with a buffet of ingredients and condiments that you pile on to the tortilla. It's quite filling.

4 eggs	**CONDIMENTS**
1 teaspoon salt	**Bacon**
1 tablespoon milk	**Grated cheese**
3 tablespoons butter	**Diced avocado**
8 flour tortillas	**Taco sauce**
	Chopped green chile

Beat the eggs, salt, and milk together. Melt the butter in a large frying pan over medium heat. Dip the tortillas in the egg mixture, one at a time, allowing excess egg mixture to drip back into the bowl, and fry in the butter until golden brown. Serve hot. Pass the condiments and allow each person to create his own dish.

Margarita French Toast

4 servings

Now we're talking my kind of breakfast! Actually, I would probably make this special French toast for a midnight meal. You don't have to use French bread, but it seems to make the dish a little more special.

¹/₄ **cup milk**	**Pinch cinnamon**
1 tablespoon tequila	**4 large or 8 small slices of**
1 teaspoon Grand Marnier	**stale French bread**
4 eggs, well beaten	**2 tablespoons butter**
Pinch salt	**Lemon juice**
Pinch nutmeg	**Confectioners' sugar**

Mix the milk, tequila, and Grand Marnier into the eggs and stir in the salt, nutmeg, and cinnamon. Place the bread in the mixture and let it absorb the liquid, turning 2 or 3 times. Melt the butter in a large frying pan and sauté the bread on both sides until lightly browned. Sprinkle lemon juice over the hot toast and sift a generous amount of confectioners' sugar on top.

Chorizo

8 to 10 servings (2^1/$_4$ pounds)

You can always go to the grocery store and purchase prepared chorizo, but if you truly want to enjoy the Border cooking experience, homemade chorizo is a must. Who knows? You might never go back to buying it pre-made. Chorizo can be stored in the refrigerator for seven to 10 days and can be frozen for six to eight weeks.

---

5 or 6 dried New Mexico chiles (about 3 ounces)
^{1}/$_2$ cup red wine vinegar
^{1}/$_2$ medium onion, quartered
2^1/$_4$ pounds ground pork
4 cloves garlic, minced

1^1/$_2$ teaspoons salt
2^1/$_2$ teaspoons dried oregano
^{1}/$_2$ teaspoon ground cumin
^{1}/$_2$ teaspoon ground red pepper or cayenne

Soak the chiles in the vinegar until soft, about 3 hours. Remove the stems and seeds. Place the chiles, vinegar, and onion in a blender and whirl until smooth.

Combine the chile puree, pork, garlic, salt, oregano, cumin, and ground red pepper in a large bowl and mix well. Cover and refrigerate for at least 2 hours or overnight.

Crumble the pork mixture into a frying pan over medium-high heat. You may have to do this in batches. Cook, stirring, until browned, about 7 minutes. Drain off any fat. Or shape the mixture into patties or links and cook until no longer pink inside, about 10 minutes.

Hard-cooked Eggs
with Avocado Sauce

Huevos con Salsa de Aguacate

4 servings

Pour the avocado sauce right over the hard-cooked eggs. It's an amazing taste sensation. Serve with sliced *Bolillos* (page 140) that have been toasted under the broiler and brushed with melted butter. This breakfast will fill you up.

---

2 tablespoons butter or margarine

2 tablespoons minced onion

1 (4-ounce) can chopped green chile

1 tablespoon flour

$^1/_2$ cup milk

8 hot hard-cooked eggs

2 avocados, pitted, peeled, and cut into chunks

Salt

Melt the butter in a medium pan over low to medium heat. Cook the onion in the butter until soft. Add the chile, flour, and milk and cook until thick. Peel the eggs and keep them warm in hot water. Whirl the avocados in blender until smooth. Stir into the hot milk sauce, season with salt, and pour over the hot sliced eggs.

Ranch-style Eggs

▼ ▼ ▼ ▼ ▼ ▼

6 servings

This breakfast dish is a big hit with a wide variety of people. The chile con carne's warm smoky heat is reminiscent of Old West chuck wagon cooking. No doubt, even our resident cowboy-rancher, Mr. Jimmy Bowen, would enjoy this dish for breakfast when out on the range herding his cattle. It is a fine hearty breakfast to get you going in the morning.

---

1 (19-ounce) can of chile
  con carne (without beans)
$^1/_2$ medium onion, chopped

6 eggs
2 ounces grated longhorn
  cheese, $^1/_2$ cup

Preheat the oven to 325 degrees. Mix the chile con carne and onion in a saucepan and heat slightly to soften the onions. Pour the chile mixture into a shallow 1½-quart casserole. Make 6 holes in the mixture. Crack the eggs and drop into the holes. Sprinkle the cheese over the top of the casserole. Bake for 15 to 20 minutes, or until the eggs are set.

Huevos Rancheros

6 servings

Remember, you can always customize your preparation of this dish to suit your individual taste. That's what's so great about doing your own cooking.

---

1 recipe Salsa Fresca
   (page 68)
Spiced Tomato Sauce
   (recipe follows)
6 to 12 fried tortillas
   (6-inch) (recipe follows)
6 to 12 fried eggs

GARNISHES
Sliced avocado
Fresh cilantro sprigs
Radishes
Shredded lettuce
Chopped green onions,
   including tops
Shredded Monterey jack or
   cheddar cheese
Lime wedges

Prepare the Salsa Fresca, cover, and refrigerate. Prepare the Spiced Tomato Sauce and fried tortillas and keep warm. Arrange the garnishes in separate bowls.

For each serving, place 1 or 2 tortillas on a plate; top with 1 or 2 fried eggs and about 1/2 cup of the tomato sauce. Accompany with garnishes and salsa.

Spiced Tomato Sauce

 **Makes about 3 cups**

---

2 large onions, minced

1 large green bell pepper,
seeded and minced

3 tablespoons vegetable oil

1 (14-ounce) can roma
tomatoes

1 (14$^{1}/_{2}$-ounce) can
chicken broth

1 (10-ounce) can red chile
sauce

$^{1}/_{2}$ teaspoon dried oregano

$^{1}/_{2}$ teaspoon cumin seeds

Combine the onions, bell pepper, and oil in a wide frying pan and cook, stirring often, over medium heat until the onions are soft, about 10 minutes. Add
the tomatoes and their liquid, the broth, red chile sauce, oregano, and cumin
seeds. Break the tomatoes up with a spoon. Bring to a boil and cook, uncovered, stirring often, until reduced to about 3 cups.

Fried Tortillas

Heat a $^{1}/_{2}$ inch of vegetable oil in an 8- to 10-inch frying pan over medium-
high heat. When the oil is hot, add the tortillas, one at a time. For soft tortillas, cook, turning once, just until softened, about 10 seconds total. Drain on
paper towels. For crisp tortillas, cook, turning once, until crisp and golden
brown, about 45 to 60 seconds total. Drain on paper towels.

Scrambled Eggs
with Chorizo

4 servings

Want to make a McDonald's breakfast burrito at home? Here you go. Nothing compares to authenticity and that really good, fresh homemade taste. The fast food burrito is usually made with sausage and green peppers. This homemade burrito is made with hot and spicy chorizo and green chiles.

$^1/_2$ **pound chorizo or pork sausage, crumbled**	**1 tablespoon butter or margarine**
$^1/_2$ **cup chopped green chiles**	**4 corn tortillas, heated to crisp**
2 tablespoons finely chopped onion	$^1/_2$ **cup thick and chunky salsa, bottled or homemade**
8 eggs	
$^1/_4$ **cup milk**	$^1/_4$ **cup sour cream**

Combine the chorizo, chiles, and onion. Cook over medium-high heat for 5 to 8 minutes, or until the sausage is well browned and the onion is tender, stirring occasionally. Remove the mixture from the skillet and drain on paper towels. Combine the eggs and milk in a large bowl and mix well. In the same skillet, melt the butter over medium-high heat. Add the egg mixture and cook until the eggs just start to set, stirring occasionally. Add the sausage mixture and mix well. Cook until the eggs are set, stirring occasionally.

Spoon one quarter of egg mixture onto each tortilla and top with salsa and sour cream.

Texas Eggs

What can I say? We do everything bigger in Texas. Why else would you use a whole dozen eggs? Even if this recipe is made to serve 6, you can set it out on a buffet table and allow people to serve themselves as much or as little as they prefer.

3 to 4 jalapeños, or fresh green chiles, roasted and peeled	1 (4-ounce) can chopped green chiles, drained
2 tablespoons butter	1 (2^1/$_2$-ounce) can sliced olives
1 large onion, diced	1 teaspoon salt
1 bell pepper, diced	^{1}/$_4$ teaspoon pepper
1 dozen eggs	
1 large tomato, diced	
4 ounces grated cheddar cheese, 1 cup	

Seed and chop the jalapeños. Melt the butter in a skillet and when hot, brown the onion and bell pepper. Remove from skillet and set aside. Beat the eggs until frothy. Pour into the skillet and cook until soft and very wet. Add the onion and pepper, along with all other ingredients and serve.

Mexican Omelet

Torta de Huevos Mexicanos

1 serving

We enjoy this dish with Monterey Jack while our daughter prefers it with asadero cheese. The amount of any ingredient can be adjusted to what you like.

2 eggs	**2 tablespoons chopped**
2 tablespoons milk	**green chiles**
$^1/_2$ teaspoon dried oregano	**$^1/_4$ cup thick and chunky**
$^1/_4$ teaspoon salt	**salsa**
Dash pepper	**Sour cream (optional)**
1 tablespoon butter or	**Chopped fresh cilantro**
margarine	**(optional)**
2 tablespoons shredded	
Monterey Jack cheese	

Mix the eggs, milk, oregano, salt, and pepper with a fork just until the whites and yolks are blended. Heat the butter in an 8-inch skillet or omelet pan over medium-high heat. As the butter melts, tilt the skillet in all directions to coat completely. When the butter just begins to brown, the skillet is hot enough.

Quickly pour the eggs all at once into the skillet. Rapidly slide the skillet back and forth over the heat and, at the same time, stir quickly with a fork to spread eggs over the bottom of the skillet as they thicken. Let the eggs stand over the heat for a few seconds to lightly brown the bottom. Do not over-cook; the omelet will continue to cook after folding. Tilt the skillet and run a fork under the edge of the omelet, then jerk the skillet sharply to loosen the eggs from the bottom of the skillet. Sprinkle with cheese and chiles. Fold the portion of omelet nearest you just to the center. Grasp the skillet handle and turn the omelet onto a warm plate, flipping the folded portion of the omelet over so the far side is on the bottom. Tuck the sides of omelet under if neces-sary. Top with salsa, and sour cream and cilantro, if desired.

Omelet with Mushrooms and Avocado

Torta de Huevos con Hongos y Aguacate

 **4 servings**

Now we're getting fancy: a super breakfast omelet with mushrooms and avocado. Some tastes just seem to go together, and avocado and mushroom rank right up there.

8 eggs	**2 medium tomatoes,**
1 1/2 teaspoons salt	**peeled and chopped**
1/4 teaspoon pepper	**Pinch garlic powder**
1/4 cup cream or milk	**1 avocado**
3 tablespoons butter	**Salsa (optional)**
1/2 cup chopped mushrooms,	
such as cremini (also	
called Italian brown	
mushrooms)	

Beat the eggs slightly, just enough to mix. Add 1 teaspoon of salt, 1/8 teaspoon pepper, and the cream. Heat 1 tablespoon of the butter in a small saucepan and sauté the mushrooms and tomatoes for 4 to 5 minutes, then season with 1/2 teaspoon salt, 1/8 teaspoon pepper, and garlic powder. Peel, pit, and dice the avocado and add to the mushrooms and tomatoes, but do not cook. Heat the remaining butter in a skillet and make omelet as usual (see page 15). When almost cooked, sprinkle the vegetables over half the omelet and fold. Serve with salsa, if desired.

Chile Cheese Soufflé

▼ ▼ ▼ ▼ ▼ ▼ ▼

You can't go wrong with chile, cheese, and eggs for breakfast. Be sure to have some of your favorite salsa and tortillas or *Bolillos* (page 140) to serve with this dish.

$^1/_4$ cup ($^1/_2$ stick) butter or margarine	1 (4$^1/_2$-ounce) can chopped green chiles, drained
$^1/_4$ cup all-purpose flour	
1$^3/_4$ cups milk	1 teaspoon salt
3 ounces shredded sharp cheddar cheese, $^3/_4$ cup	6 eggs, separated

Preheat the oven to 400 degrees. Grease 9 individual soufflé dishes or 6-ounce custard cups.

Melt the butter in a heavy saucepan over low heat. Add the flour, whisking until smooth. Cook for 1 minute, whisking constantly. Gradually add the milk and cook over medium heat, whisking constantly, until thickened and bubbly. Add the cheese, chiles, and salt, stirring until the cheese melts.

Beat the egg yolks with an electric mixer at medium speed until thick and pale. Gradually stir about one fourth of the hot mixture into the yolks, and then add to the remaining hot mixture, stirring constantly. Bring to a boil and remove from the heat.

Beat the egg whites at high speed until stiff but not dry. Gently fold into the cheese mixture. Pour the mixture into the prepared dishes. Seal with aluminum foil and freeze up to 1 week.

Unwrap the soufflés and place in a 13 x 9 x 2-inch pan. Add 1 inch of hot water to the pan. After for 10 minutes, reduce the oven temperature to 350 degrees, and bake 25 additional minutes or until puffed and golden. Serve immediately.

Chiles Rellenos
with Red Sauce

▼ ▼ ▼ ▼ ▼

If you're up for making chiles rellenos the old fashioned way, here's a great recipe to go by. The red sauce is excellent and makes a tasty accompaniment to the chiles.

8 canned whole mild green chiles (about four 4-ounce cans) or 8 fresh poblano or Anaheim chiles	$^1/_4$ teaspoon salt
	$^1/_8$ teaspoon pepper
	4 eggs, separated
	Vegetable oil
1 (8-ounce) package Monterey jack cheese with peppers	Red Sauce (recipe follows)
	Store-bought tomatillo salsa (optional)
$^3/_4$ cup all-purpose flour	Fresh cilantro (optional)

If using canned chiles, rinse the chiles and remove the seeds. Pat the chiles dry with paper towels. If using fresh chiles, place on a baking sheet. Broil the chiles about 5½ inches from the heat for 5 to 10 minutes on each side, or until the chiles look blistered. Place the chiles in a zip-top plastic bag and let them stand for 10 minutes. Peel off the skins and remove the seeds.

Cut the cheese into 8 crosswise strips. Place a strip of cheese inside each chile. (If the chiles tear, overlap the torn sides. The batter will hold the chiles together.)

Combine ½ cup of the flour with the salt and pepper in a shallow bowl and set aside. Beat the egg yolks until thick and pale. Beat the egg whites in a large bowl at high speed with an electric mixer until stiff peaks form. Gently fold the yolks and the remaining ¼ cup flour into the beaten egg whites.

Pour 2 inches of oil into a Dutch oven and heat to 375 degrees. Dredge each stuffed chile in the seasoned flour and then dip in the egg batter.

Fry the chiles, a few at a time, in the hot oil until golden, turning once. Drain on paper towels. Serve warm with Red Sauce and tomatillo salsa, if desired. Garnish with cilantro, if desired.

Red Sauce

▼ ▼ ▼ ▼

Makes 2 cups

---

¹/₄ cup (¹/₂ stick) butter or margarine

4 cloves garlic, crushed

¹/₄ cup all-purpose flour

1 cup beef broth

1 (8-ounce) can tomato sauce

1 tablespoon chili powder

1 teaspoon ground sage

1 teaspoon ground cumin

Melt the butter in a medium-size saucepan. Cook the garlic in the butter over medium heat for 3 minutes, stirring constantly. Add the flour, stirring until smooth. Cook 1 minute, stirring constantly. Gradually add the beef broth and tomato sauce, stirring constantly. Add the chili powder, sage, and cumin and cook, stirring constantly, until the mixture is thickened and bubbly.

Chiles Rellenos Casserole

8 servings

Don't like the mess and the time it takes to make traditional chiles rellenos? Try this casserole. It's great for breakfast or a weekend brunch.

1 (7-ounce) can whole green chiles	3 eggs
8 ounces shredded Monterey Jack cheese, 2 cups	3 cups milk
	1 cup biscuit mix
	Seasoned salt to taste
8 ounces shredded sharp cheddar cheese, 2 cups	Salsa

Preheat the oven to 325 degrees. Split the chiles, rinse them, and remove the seeds. Dry the chiles on paper towels and arrange them on the bottom of an 11 x 7 x 1½-inch baking dish. Top with the cheeses. Beat the eggs in a bowl and add the milk and biscuit mix. Blend well and pour over the cheese. Sprinkle the casserole with salt. Bake for 50 to 55 minutes, or until golden brown. Serve with salsa.

Egg and Chile Casserole

Cazuela de Huevos con Chiles

6 to 8 servings

This wonderful breakfast casserole dish goes great with some Jalapeño Cornbread (page 136). You'll be amazed at how good a nice, mild green chile tastes in the morning.

2 or 3 (7-ounce) cans whole green chiles, seeded	8 eggs
4 corn tortillas (6-inch), cut into wide strips	1/2 cup milk
1 pound shredded Monterey jack cheese, 4 cups	1/2 teaspoon salt
1 large tomato, seeded and sliced	1/2 teaspoon pepper
	1/2 teaspoon ground cumin
	1/2 teaspoon garlic powder
	1/4 teaspoon onion salt
	Paprika

Preheat the oven to 350 degrees. Lay half the chiles in a well-greased 9-inch-square baking dish. Top with half the tortilla strips and half the cheese. Arrange the tomato slices on top. Repeat layers, using remaining chiles, tortillas, and cheese.

Beat the eggs with the milk, salt, pepper, cumin, garlic powder, and onion salt and pour over the tortilla mixture. Sprinkle with paprika.

Bake, uncovered, until puffy and set in the center, about 40 minutes. Let the casserole stand for about 10 minutes, and then cut into squares.

Three Cheese and Chile Casserole

Cazuela con Chile y Tres Quesos

8 servings

The use of three cheeses is what gives this casserole its great taste. As with most Border dishes, feel free to substitute, or add, jalapeños instead of the chopped chiles.

---

8 eggs, lightly beaten
$^1/_2$ cup all-purpose flour
1 teaspoon baking powder
1 (16-ounce) carton
   small-curd cottage
   cheese
8 ounces shredded
   Monterey jack cheese,
   2 cups

8 ounces shredded cheddar
   cheese, 2 cups
2 ($4^1/_2$-ounce) cans
   chopped green chiles
$^1/_4$ cup butter or
   margarine, melted
$^1/_2$ teaspoon garlic powder
$^1/_2$ teaspoon chili powder

Preheat the oven to 325 degrees. Lightly grease a 13 x 9-inch baking dish. Combine the eggs, flour, and baking powder, stirring well. Stir in the cheeses and remaining ingredients. Pour the mixture into the prepared pan. Bake, uncovered, for 35 minutes.

Green Chile Quiche

▼ ▼ ▼ ▼ ▼ ▼ **4 servings**

Quiche is a must for any good brunch. For a special treat, try this one. If you like, switch chorizo for the sausage or jalapeños for the green chile. That's Border style.

$^1/_2$ **pound ground beef or sausage**	**2 eggs, lightly beaten**
$^1/_2$ **cup finely chopped onion**	$^3/_4$ **cup milk**
$^1/_2$ **cup chopped green chile**	$^1/_8$ **cup unbleached flour**
4 ounces shredded cheddar cheese, 1 cup	$^1/_4$ **teaspoon salt**
	$^1/_8$ **teaspoon pepper**

Preheat the oven to 350 degrees. Lightly grease a 2-quart casserole. Brown the meat and onion over medium heat. Drain on paper towels. Layer the meat and onion mixture, green chile, and cheese in the prepared dish. Mix together the eggs, milk, flour, salt, and pepper. Pour the egg mixture over the layers. Bake for 45 minutes.

Tex-Mex Quiche

6 servings

Another quiche to consider. Try them all until you find the one you like the best, then experiment and make the recipe your own.

1 teaspoon chili powder	3 eggs, lightly beaten
One 9-inch unbaked pie shell	1^1/$_2$ cups half-and-half
4 ounces shredded cheddar cheese, 1 cup	1 (4-ounce) can chopped green chiles, drained
4 ounces shredded Monterey Jack cheese, 1 cup	1 (2^1/$_2$-ounce) can sliced olives, drained
1 tablespoon all-purpose flour	1 teaspoon salt
	^{1}/$_4$ teaspoon pepper

Preheat the oven to 325 degrees. Sprinkle the chili powder over the inside of the pie shell. Combine the cheeses with the flour and place in the pie shell. Combine the eggs, half-and-half, chiles, olives, salt, and pepper. Pour over the cheese. Bake for 45 to 55 minutes, or until a knife inserted in the center comes out clean. Cool for 10 minutes before cutting into wedges.

Mexican Quiche
with Guacamole

This quiche recipe is topped with guacamole. This guacamole is not too creamy, but rather a little chunkier so you can enjoy the texture of the avocados.

---

6 (6-inch) corn tortillas
2 tablespoons milk
$^1/_2$ pound chorizo or hot
  pork sausage
$^1/_4$ cup finely chopped
  onion
1 tablespoon chile powder
1 teaspoon ground cumin
3 eggs, lightly beaten
1 ($4^1/_2$-ounce) can
  chopped green chiles,
  liquid reserved

$1^1/_2$ cups half-and-half
$^1/_2$ teaspoon salt
$^1/_8$ teaspoon pepper
6 ounces shredded
  Monterey Jack cheese,
  $1^1/_2$ cups
Guacamole (recipe follows)

Preheat the oven to 350 degrees. Pour 2 inches of water in a large skillet. Bring the water to a boil, then remove from heat. Dip each tortilla in the water to soften and drain on paper towels. Place the tortillas in 6 lightly greased 10-ounce custard cups and set aside.

Cook the sausage, onion, chile powder, and cumin in a skillet over medium heat until the meat is browned, stirring until it crumbles. Drain and set aside.

Combine the eggs, half of the green chiles, half-and-half, salt, and pepper in a large bowl. Stir in the sausage mixture.

Spoon half of the egg mixture into the tortilla shells and sprinkle with half of the cheese. Pour the remaining egg mixture over the cheese. Bake for 20 minutes. Sprinkle with the remaining cheese and bake 5 additional minutes. Remove from the oven and let stand 5 minutes. Remove from the custard cups and sprinkle with the remaining green chiles. Serve with Guacamole.

Guacamole

Makes 1$^{1}/_{2}$ cups

---

1 avocado, mashed
1 tomato, peeled, seeded,
  and chopped
1 clove garlic, minced

1 to 2 tablespoons fresh
  lime juice
Salt to taste

Combine all the ingredients in a small bowl.

Jalapeño Cheese Pie

▼ ▼ ▼ ▼ ▼ ▼ ▼ **12 servings**

A tasty treat for a lazy weekend outdoor breakfast or brunch. Serve with fruit and Mexican coffee to make a complete meal. For those who prefer a milder taste, chopped green chiles can be substituted for the jalapeños.

---

1 (11$^{1}/_{2}$-ounce) jar whole
  jalapeño chiles, drained
16 ounces shredded
  cheddar cheese, 4 cups

6 eggs, lightly beaten

Preheat the oven to 350 degrees and lightly grease an 11 x 7 x 1$^{1}/_{2}$-inch pan. Cut the jalapeños in half lengthwise, and remove and discard the seeds. Rinse the jalapeños with cold water and drain on paper towels. Mince the jalapeños. Sprinkle half of the cheese in the prepared pan. Top with the chiles and the remaining cheese. Pour the eggs over top. Bake for 30 to 40 minutes, or until lightly browned and set. Cool for 5 to 10 minutes and cut into squares.

Tortilla Pie

This tortilla pie is prepared in layers, almost like a lasagna. It's great not only for breakfast, but for any meal. You can add ground beef, chicken, or anything else you think you'd like.

1 (16-ounce) can refried beans	1 (8-ounce) package shredded Mexican cheese blend
1 teaspoon chili powder	Cilantro sprigs, for garnish
1/2 teaspoon ground cumin	Sour cream
8 (8-inch) flour tortillas	
1 cup chunky salsa	
1 cup guacamole	

Preheat the oven to 350 degrees. Combine the beans, chili powder, and cumin in a small bowl. Set aside. Place 1 tortilla in a lightly greased 9-inch round cake pan. Spread with half of the salsa and top with another tortilla. Spread with half of the guacamole and top with another tortilla. Sprinkle with half of the cheese and top with another tortilla. Repeat layers with remaining salsa, guacamole, and cheese, ending with cheese. Cover with aluminum foil and bake for 20 minutes, or until thoroughly heated. Cut the pie into wedges and garnish with cilantro and sour cream, if desired.

Tortilla Rolls with Pork and Pumpkinseed Sauce

Taquitos de Puerco y Pipián

6 to 8 servings

This dish is more of a traditional Mexican-style breakfast. I'm sure it can be found in some of the more gourmet-style Mexican restaurants, but it would probably be served with black beans. While this is all fine and good, Southwestern Border cuisine usually serves pinto beans, not black beans, but either one is great.

2¼ cups Pipián Sauce
  (page 89)
2 cups chicken broth
1 pound ground pork
8 hard-cooked eggs,
  peeled and chopped

12 flour tortillas
  (7- to 9-inch diameter)
2 tablespoons melted
  butter or margarine
Tomato Sauce (page 92)
Fresh cilantro

Preheat the oven to 350 degrees. Prepare the Pipián. Combine the sauce and broth in a 2- to 3-quart pan, stirring to blend smoothly. Bring the mixture to a boil, stirring, and keep warm.

Crumble the pork into a 10- to 12-inch frying pan and cook, stirring, over medium heat until browned and crumbly, about 10 minutes. Remove from the heat and drain off the fat. Stir in the eggs and 1½ cups of the pipián sauce.

Spoon the pork mixture down center of each tortilla, then roll up to enclose the filling. Place the tortillas, seam side down, in a 9 x 13-inch baking dish, brush with butter, and drizzle with the remaining pipián sauce. Cover and bake until hot, 20 to 25 minutes.

Meanwhile, prepare the Tomato Sauce. To serve, drizzle the tortillas with sauce. Garnish with cilantro.

Tripe

Menudo

▼ ▼ ▼   10 to 12 servings

Menudo is often served in the southwest as a breakfast food after a night of partying. There are several establishments in El Paso that remain open until midnight or open by 6:30 in the morning to serve those who have been out all night. As with many of the dishes presented in this book, there are different ways to prepare tripe. Which one you choose depends on you and your taste. As for me, they are all great, even the one with pig's feet!

3^1/2 pounds beef tripe, rinsed well and cut into 1-inch squares	**CONDIMENTS**
	3 limes or lemons, cut into wedges
3 to 3^1/2 pounds beef shanks	^{1}/2 cup fresh oregano leaves
2 medium onions, chopped	1 cup fresh cilantro sprigs
10 cloves garlic, minced	1 medium onion, chopped
2 teaspoons ground cumin	^{1}/4 cup crushed dried hot red chiles or 5 fresh serrano or jalapeño chiles, stemmed, seeded, and thinly sliced
Chile Puree (recipe follows)	
3 (29-ounce) cans white or yellow hominy, drained	
Salt	

Combine the tripe, beef shanks, 10 cups water, onions, garlic, and cumin in an 8- to 10-quart pot. Bring to a boil over high heat, then reduce the heat, cover, and simmer until tripe is very tender, 6 to 7 hours. Meanwhile, prepare the Chile Puree and set aside.

Skim and discard the fat from the liquid. Remove the beef shanks from the pan and discard bones and fat. Cut the meat into chunks and return to the pan with the chile puree and hominy. Season to taste with salt. Bring the mixture to a boil, then reduce the heat, cover, and simmer for 30 minutes. If making ahead, cool, cover, and refrigerate for up to 2 days; reheat before serving.

Arrange the garnishes in separate bowls. Pour the soup into bowls; offer condiments to add to individual servings.

Chile Puree

Makes 2 to 2^1/$_2$ cups

Discard the stems and seeds from 9 large dried red chiles (either New Mexico or California) in a bowl with 3^1/$_4$ cups warm water. Let stand until softened, 20 to 30 minutes. Discard all but 1^1/$_4$ cups of the liquid. Puree the chiles with the liquid in a blender or food processor until smooth, scraping sides of container once or twice.

Did You Know?

▼ ▼ ▼ ▼ ▼ ▼ ▼

LEGEND OF JUAN DIEGO

Canonized July 31, 2002

Juan Diego, born in 1474, was an Aztec tribesman who converted to Christianity. He was a meek and humble man; married to Maria Lucia, who had also been baptized in the Christian faith. Juan Diego was known to be a deeply devoted and religious man. He walked fourteen miles from his village of Cuauhtitlan to Tenochtitlan (now Mexico City) to receive instruction on religious doctrine. In 1529, Maria Lucia died and Juan Diego moved to Tolpetlac, which was nine miles closer to Tenochtitlan.

Every weekend he walked, barefoot, the nine miles to hear mass. (Only the higher social classes wore sandals.) To keep warm on the long chilly walks to church, he wore a mantle or *tilma*, made with fibers from the maguey cactus. (Cotton was also used only by the upper class.)

One day during his long trek to the church as he approached the foot of Tepeyac Hill, he heard music and a voice calling to him, "Juanito, Juan Diegito, the humblest of my sons ..." Juan Diego, startled, but drawn to the voice, went up the rocky hill. As he looked up, he found himself face to face with a beautiful lady. Her garments shone brightly in the early morning rays of the sun. She beckoned him and as he approached, he fell to his knees in veneration. She asked him where he was going and he told her he was on his way to mass. She smiled and told him that She was the Virgin Mary, Mother of the True God. She asked him to tell the bishop that it was her desire that a temple be built at the very spot where she stood.

Juan Diego immediately went to the city and relayed the message to the bishop. The bishop listened politely and soon dismissed him. Juan Diego returned to Tepeyac Hill and told the Virgin. She once again very kindly instructed him to return and tell the bishop of her wishes. Juan Diego once again returned to the bishop, who told him that he would need a sign from Heaven for his story to be more convincing.

When Juan Diego returned to the Lady and explained what the bishop wanted, She smiled tenderly at him. On the morning of December 12, She asked him to gather flowers growing at the top of the hill. She told him to take them to the bishop as the sign that the bishop had requested. When Juan Diego returned to the bishop, he opened the *tilma* to uncover the flowers that the Virgin had told him to deliver to the bishop. For the longest moment, everyone's eyes were on Juan Diego and his *tilma*. As the flowers dropped from his mantle, a replica appeared on the cloth, an exact replica of the Virgin herself as she had first appeared to Juan Diego at Mount Tepeyac.

The tilma, despite its age of over four hundred years, still exists and is at the Old Basilica of Guadalupe in Mexico City.

Appetizers

Proverbs
Dichos

There are none as deaf as those that won't hear.
No hay peor sordo que el que no quiere oir.

When one door shuts, another opens.
Cuando una puerta se cierra, otra se abre.

You can't have your cake and eat it too.
Soplar y sorber, no puede ser.

Worrying to death.
Sustos y disgustos matan a muchos.

There's nothing lost to civility.
La palabra honesta mucho vale y poco cuesta.

Spiced Peanuts

Cacahuates Picantes

20 servings (7 cups)

Peanuts (*cacahuates*) are found in many Mexican dishes, but they're also delicious eaten on their own. Here's one appetizer that's hot and spicy and will keep people coming back for more.

20 small dried whole red chiles	**2 pounds salted peanuts**
4 cloves garlic, minced	**1 teaspoon coarse or kosher salt**
2 tablespoons olive oil	**1 teaspoon chili powder**

In a wide frying pan, combine the chiles, garlic, and oil. Cook over medium heat, stirring constantly for 1 minute. Add the peanuts and stir over medium heat until slightly browned, about 5 minutes. Sprinkle with salt and chili powder. Mix well. Let cool, then store in an airtight container for at least 1 day or up to 2 weeks.

Cheese Fondue
with Tequila

▼ ▼ ▼ ▼ ▼ ▼ ▼   **4 cups**

This is one fancy chile con queso recipe. The use of chipotle chiles and tequila makes it an elegant way to get your guests ready for an evening of pure Border delight. Feel free to substitute your favorite cheese.

1 large round of garlic-flavored bread	1 jigger tequila
1 cup (2 sticks) butter	$1/2$ teaspoon pureed chipotle chile
1 clove garlic, minced	Salt and pepper
$2/3$ cup Roquefort cheese	1 medium-size baguette
7 ounces cream cheese, cubed	
5 ounces Monterey Jack cheese, shredded	**GARNISH**
	1 sprig parsley
2 tablespoons sour cream	1 red pepper, finely chopped

Cut a large hole in the top of the garlic bread and scoop out the insides without breaking the crust.

Melt 1 teaspoon of butter in a saucepan, add the garlic, and cook until soft, about 1 minute. Add the Roquefort cheese, cream cheese, Monterey Jack cheese, sour cream, tequila, and chipotle chile and stir until the mixture is well blended. Add salt and pepper to taste and pour the cheese mixture into the hollowed-out bread round.

Cut the baguette into 1-inch cubes and brown in the remaining butter a few pieces at a time.

Garnish the fondue with the parsley and red pepper and serve with the bread cubes.

Guacamole Dip or Salad

**8 servings as a dip or
4 servings as a salad**

This guacamole goes well on *gorditas*, *flautas*, or *tortas* (the traditional Mexican sandwich). We like wrapping our fajitas in a warm tortilla and dipping them in guacamole. Try it!

2 ripe avocados, peeled and pitted	2 tablespoons grated onion
1 tablespoon fresh lime juice	$^1/_2$ teaspoon salt
4 canned green chiles, rinsed, seeded, and chopped	6 tablespoons picante sauce
1 clove garlic, minced	Pepper
$^1/_2$ teaspoon ground coriander	1 large ripe tomato, skinned and finely chopped
	Tostada chips (optional)
	Lettuce leaves (optional)

Mash the avocados to a smooth pulp. Add the remaining ingredients. Serve accompanied by tostada chips as a dip or on lettuce as a salad.

Chile, Feta, and Walnut Bundles

▼ ▼ ▼ ▼ ▼

15 bundles

These bundles make an impression on any border buffet table. They may be a little fussy to make but are well worth the compliments. Look for phyllo pastry sheets in your grocery near the frozen pie crusts.

1 large egg, lightly beaten	2 green onions with tops,
8 ounces feta cheese,	minced
crumbled, at room tem-	1/4 cup walnuts, chopped
perature	1 teaspoon dried oregano
1 New Mexico or Anaheim	1 pound phyllo pastry
green chile, seeded and	sheets, thawed
minced	1/2 cup melted butter

Blend the egg and feta cheese together until smooth. Stir in the green chile, green onions, walnuts, and oregano. Place 1 phyllo sheet on smooth work surface (keep remaining phyllo covered with damp cloth). Lightly brush the phyllo sheet with melted butter. Cover with a second sheet and brush with butter. Using a knife cut the phyllo stack lengthwise into 4 strips, 3½ inches wide. Cut the strips crosswise into 3½ inch squares.

Place 1 teaspoon of filling in the center of each square. Gather the edges together over the center, twisting them slightly to form a frill. Transfer to 2 large greased baking sheets, placing bundles 1 inch apart. Brush the tops with melted butter. Repeat using remaining phyllo sheets and cheese mixture. Refrigerate at least 1 hour before baking.

Preheat the oven to 350 degrees. Bake until crisp and golden brown, about 20 minutes. Cool 5 minutes before arranging on serving platter. (Bundles can be made up to 1 day ahead, covered with plastic wrap, and refrigerated.)

Green Chile Pinwheels

18 to 24 pieces

These little pinwheels are so cute; they make an excellent addition to any buffet table.

8 ounces grated cheddar cheese, 2 cups	$^1/_2$ cup (1 stick) butter, melted
1 cup all purpose flour	2 (4-ounce) cans chopped green chile
$^1/_2$ teaspoon salt	

Preheat the oven to 350 degrees. Lightly grease a baking sheet.

Combine the cheese, flour, and salt, then add the butter and mix until thoroughly blended. Roll out into a rectangular shape, 6 x 8-inches, about $^1/_8$-inch thick. Spread the dough with chopped green chile and roll up like a jellyroll. Chill.

Cut the roll into $^1/_4$-inch slices, just as you would refrigerator cookies. Bake for about 10 minutes.

Stuffed Jalapeños

▼ ▼ ▼ ▼ ▼ ▼ **6 to 8 pieces**

Jalapeños are not for the faint of heart, but they sure are good, especially stuffed. And, it wouldn't be a complete Border meal without chile. The combination of cream cheese and jalapeño may sound odd, but try a stuffed jalapeño and you'll see what we mean.

1 (11-ounce) can pickled jalapeño chiles	**Sour cream (optional)**
1 (8-ounce) package cream cheese, at room temperature	**Onion salt**

Drain the chiles, slit each down 1 side, and remove the seeds. Soften the cream cheese (with a little sour cream if needed) and season to taste with the onion salt. Stuff each chile with the cheese, press closed, and chill until firm.

Variation: Jalapeños are also delicious stuffed with shrimp paste made by blending finely chopped shrimp with a little sour cream or cream cheese. Any good seasoned softened cheese may also be used.

Jalapeño Cheese Squares

Makes about 64 squares

These are great for a potluck or fiesta. Make them according to the instructions and they make a great dish. Or, improvise and add other ingredients, like sausage or chorizo, to make this appetizer a little heartier. This recipe uses canned jalapeños for the sake of convenience, but you can certainly use fresh roasted jalapeños instead.

---

1 pound shredded cheddar cheese, 4 cups
4 eggs, lightly beaten
1 teaspoon minced onion

4 canned jalapeño chiles, seeded and chopped

Preheat oven to 350 degrees. Grease an 8-inch square pan. Combine all the ingredients, stirring well. Spread in the prepared pan. Bake for 30 minutes. Cut into 1-inch squares.

Jalapeño Pepper Jelly

▼ ▼ ▼ ▼   **Makes approximately 4 pints**

Prepare this during the holidays to give out as a gift with a bag of tortilla chips and your friends will be impressed. Don't forget to include the recipe with the gift or you'll be called on to make more often.

---

1 large green bell pepper
2 fresh jalapeño chiles,
    stemmed, seeded, and
    ribs removed
6$^1/_2$ cups sugar
1$^1/_2$ cups cider vinegar

Half (6-ounce) package
    liquid fruit pectin
Several drops green food
    coloring (optional)

Finely chop the green bell pepper and jalapeño chiles. Combine the chopped peppers, sugar, and vinegar in a 4$^1/_2$-quart saucepan. Bring to a boil, and then reduce the heat. Cover and simmer, stirring often, about 15 minutes, or until the pepper mixture turns transparent.

Stir in the pectin and add the food coloring, if using. Return the mixture to a full rolling boil. Boil, uncovered, 1 minute, stirring constantly. Remove from the heat. Skim off any foam with a metal spoon. Immediately pour into hot, sterilized half-pint jars; seal, using metal lids or paraffin. Serve with cream cheese and assorted crackers.

Pickled Jicama

Jícama en Escabeche

Escabeche, meaning to pickle, requires the use of vinegar. In this dish, carrots, jícama, and chiles are pickled to create an incredible Border-tasting sensation.

3 to 4 carrots	**3 to 4 bay leaves**
1 cup vinegar	**1 (4-ounce) can jalapeño**
$^1/_2$ cup olive oil	**chiles**
3 onions, sliced	**2 large jícama, peeled and**
6 cloves garlic	**sliced**
1 teaspoon salt	**Crackers**
2 teaspoons dried oregano	

Cut the carrots into small chunks and cook in salted water until tender. Drain and cool. Combine the vinegar, 1 cup water, oil, onion, garlic, and salt in a large frying pan. Cook until the onions are tender. Add the oregano and bay leaves. Boil and let cool. Add the jalapeños, carrots, and jicama. Let the vegetables sit for several hours. Store in the refrigerator. Serve as an appetizer with crackers.

Mixed Tostadas

Tostadas Compuestas

Makes 6 tostadas

Tostadas, like tacos, *gorditas*, and burritos, can be topped with just about anything you can imagine. In this recipe, chicken and beans make up a tasty delight. They also make a quick and easy after school snack.

> 1^1/2 cups refried beans
> 1^1/2 cups salsa
> Vegetable oil
> 6 (6-inch) corn tortillas
> 2 cups cut-up cooked
>   chicken
>
> 3 ounces shredded Monterey
>   Jack cheese, ^{3}/4 cup
> 3 cups shredded lettuce
> 1 avocado, peeled, pitted,
>   and cut into 12 slices
> Sour cream (optional)

Preheat the broiler. Heat the beans and salsa separately. Heat ⅛ inch of oil in an 8-inch skillet over medium heat just until hot. Cook the tortillas, one at a time, for about 1 minute, or until crisp. Drain the tortillas on paper towels. Spread each tortilla with ¼ cup of the beans. Top with 2 tablespoons of salsa, ⅓ cup of chicken, and 2 more tablespoons of salsa. Sprinkle each tortilla with 2 tablespoons of the cheese. Place the tortillas on a rack on a broiler pan. Broil 2 to 3 inches from the heat, about 3 minutes, or until the cheese is melted. Top with ½ cup lettuce, 2 avocado slices, and sour cream, if using.

Quesadillas

6 servings

This is your basic quesadilla recipe. Cut into wedges, quesadillas make a simple appetizer. Folded over, taco fashion, they can be served as a main dish. The quesadilla, a Mexican-style grilled cheese, can also be customized to suit your family's taste buds. Add chicken or beef, even shrimp, and you'll have your very own family favorite.

---

8 ounces shredded cheddar or Monterey Jack cheese, 2 cups

6 (6-inch) corn or flour tortillas

1 small tomato, seeded and chopped (about ¹/₂ cup)

¹/₂ cup chopped green onions

2 tablespoons chopped canned green chiles

Chopped fresh cilantro

Preheat the oven to 350 degrees. Spread ¹/₃ cup of the cheese evenly over half of each tortilla. Sprinkle the tomato, green onions, chiles, and cilantro over the cheese. Fold the tortillas over the filling. Sprinkle with cilantro, if desired. Place the quesadillas on an ungreased baking sheet and bake for about 5 minutes or just until cheese is melted. Serve quesadillas whole, or cut into 3 wedges.

Refried Bean Pâté

▼ ▼ ▼ ▼ ▼ ▼ **Makes 48 pâté slices**

Here's another appetizer that my husband likes while watching his sports on TV. Give him a platter of these and some Dos Equis and he's in high heaven.

1 dozen large *Bolillos* (page 140)	1 teaspoon cayenne pepper or hot red pepper flakes
$^1/_2$ cup (1 stick) butter, melted	Salt
2 cups cooked pinto beans with 1 cup cooking liquid reserved	$^1/_2$ cup bacon drippings or lard or butter
$^1/_2$ pound ground beef, browned and drained	4 ounces shredded soft cheese, such as asadero, blanco, or Monterey Jack, 1 cup
1 medium onion, minced	Jalapeño Chiles, sliced (optional)
1 teaspoon ground cumin	

Preheat the oven to 350 degrees. Cut the ends off of the bolillos. Slice the center portions of the bolillos into $^1/_4$-inch slices. Brush each slice lightly with melted butter. Place on a baking sheet and toast the slices in the oven for 10 to 15 minutes, or until crisp. Combine the beans, ground beef, onion, cumin, cayenne pepper, and salt to taste. Working in batches, puree the mixture in a blender until smooth. Puree will be thick, so periodically scrape down the sides of the blender. Then, heat the bacon drippings in a large skillet. Add the bean mixture to the skillet and fold in the cheese. Slowly add the reserved liquid from the beans to prevent the beans from refrying too quickly and burning. Stir frequently over medium heat until the drippings are absorbed and the pâté is hot.

Serving Options:

1. Spread the bean pâté on bolillo slices. Sprinkle with additional cheese and broil for 2 to 4 minutes. Arrange on a platter with a small bowl of jalapeño slices as optional garnish.

2. On a large platter, arrange the bolillo slices, a bowl of hot bean pâté, a bowl of jalapeño slices, and a bowl of cheese. Allow guests to create their own appetizers.

Nachos

No get-together for my kids and their friends is complete without a full platter of nachos. The jalapeños are usually set in a separate bowl for those who don't especially like the heat. Again, this is the basic recipe, toss on whatever you like.

6 (6-inch) corn tortillas	**8 ounces grated cheddar**
Vegetable oil	**or longhorn cheese,**
$^2/_3$ cup refried beans	**6 tablespoons**
	3 pickled jalapeño chiles,
	cut into eighths

Cut the tortillas into quarters. Heat the oil and fry until crisp. Drain on paper towels. Spread the tortillas with refried beans, sprinkle with cheese, and top each with a jalapeño chile. Place the nachos on a baking sheet and broil until the cheese melts. Serve hot.

Shredded Pork Nachos

Makes 4 to 6 servings

There are one hundred ways to prepare nachos, all according to your own particular taste. Half the fun of cooking is turning a basic recipe into your own favorite. Experiment! There are even Italian nachos, but we won't go into that.

---

1 container (2 pounds)
fully cooked shredded
pork with barbecue sauce
1 (7-ounce) can Mexican-
style corn, drained
1 (4$^{1}/_{2}$-ounce) can
chopped green chiles,
drained
$^{1}/_{4}$ cup chopped fresh

cilantro
1 bag corn tortilla chips
8 ounces shredded cheddar
cheese, 2 cups
2 green onions, sliced
1 (2$^{1}/_{2}$-ounce) can sliced
black olives

Preheat the oven to 400 degrees. Spoon 2 cups of the pork into a medium bowl. Reserve the remainder for serving on buns for another meal. Add the corn, chiles, and cilantro to the pork. Spread half the corn chips on a baking sheet. Spoon half the pork mixture over the chips. Top with 1 cup of the cheese. Sprinkle with half the green onions and olives. Repeat with the remaining chips, pork, cheese, green onions, and olives. Bake for 8 minutes, or until the cheese has melted. Serve hot.

Shredded Pork Empanadas
with Chipotle-Barbecue Sauce

 **Makes about 30 appetizer empanadas**

The combination of chipotle chiles and barbecue sauce in these *empanaditas* (turnovers) is a truly Southwestern taste. You can make extras and freeze them for reheatable meals or snacks.

FILLING	DOUGH
2^1/2 **pounds boneless loin of pork roast**	**2 cups all-purpose flour**
Salt and pepper	**1 teaspoon salt**
1 to 3 canned chipotle chiles in adobo sauce	**^{1}/2 cup plus 2 tablespoons butter, cut into small cubes**
1 cup barbecue sauce	**^{1}/3 cup cold water**
1 cup beef broth	**Egg white mixed with a little water, for egg wash**

Preheat the oven to 300 degrees. Season the pork roast with salt and pepper, and wrap tightly in aluminum foil. Bake for 3 hours. Shred the meat while warm and set aside. In a blender, puree the chipotle chiles, barbecue sauce, and beef broth. Makes 2 cups.

Mix the shredded pork with 1 cup of the chipotle-barbecue sauce in a large frying pan over low heat. Simmer for 15 minutes to allow flavors to meld. Remove from the heat and set aside.

To make the empanadas, preheat the oven to 325 degrees. Combine the flour, salt, and butter in a food processor. Mix until the ingredients become like coarse meal. Add the water and pulse to form a dough. Roll out dough ⅛-inch thick. Using a 3-inch round cookie cutter cut out empanada circles. Place 2 teaspoons of shredded pork filling in the center of the dough. Moisten the edges with a little water and fold the dough over to seal. Crimp the edges and brush with egg white to gloss while baking. Bake the empanadas for 8 to 10 minutes.

Shrimp Salad Empanaditas

▼　▼　▼　▼　▼

**Makes approximately
30 appetizer empanadas**

Another great appetizer, this one prepared with shrimp. Add a little cumin and red pepper (or cayenne) and you could swear you're in the heart of Texas, or at least along the border.

SALAD	EMPANADA PASTRY
2 pounds cooked baby shrimp, chopped	$^3/_4$ cup ($1^1/_2$ sticks) butter, cold
3 hard-cooked eggs, diced	$2^1/_4$ cups flour
$^1/_2$ cup minced celery	$^1/_2$ teaspoon salt
$^1/_4$ cup minced onion	$^1/_4$ teaspoon baking powder
$^1/_4$ cup minced fresh cilantro	$1^1/_2$ (3-ounce) packages cream cheese, cold
1 teaspoon hot red pepper flakes	2 tablespoons ice water
$^1/_4$ teaspoon cumin	1 tablespoon cider vinegar
Lemon juice	Egg white mixed with a little water, for egg wash
Salt and pepper	

Combine the shrimp, eggs, celery, onion, cilantro, red pepper flakes, and cumin in a large bowl. Mix gently. Add 5 to 6 drops lemon juice. Season with salt and pepper to taste.

To prepare the pastry, place a medium-size mixing bowl in the freezer to chill. Cut the butter into ¾-inch cubes. Wrap in plastic and refrigerate for at least 30 minutes.

Place the flour, salt, and baking powder in a medium bowl and whisk to combine. Add the cream cheese and rub the mixture between your fingers to blend the cream cheese into the flour until it resembles course cornmeal. Spoon the mixture, together with the cold butter, into a re-closable gallon-size freezer bag. Expel any air from the bag and close it. Use a rolling pin to flatten the butter into thin flakes. Place the bag in the freezer for 10 minutes.

Transfer the flour mixture to a chilled bowl, scraping the sides of the bag. Set the bag aside. Sprinkle the mixture with the water and vinegar, tossing lightly with a rubber spatula. Spoon it back into the plastic bag. Seal the bag and knead the dough through the bag, making sure the bag stays closed. Refrigerate the dough in the plastic bag for 1 hour.

Preheat the oven to 325 degrees and grease a baking sheet. Remove the dough from the plastic. Divide the dough into 4 pieces. Roll each piece between lightly floured pieces of wax paper. Using a 3-inch round cookie cutter cut out circles of dough. Place 1 tablespoon of shrimp salad in the center of each pastry round. Moisten the edge of the pastry round with a little water. Fold pastry round in half and seal. Continue cutting and filling the pastry rounds until done. To glaze the empanaditas, brush the tops lightly with egg wash. Bake the empanadas for 10 to 12 minutes.

Chicken Hash

Salpicón

About 10 servings

This dish goes great on a buffet table. You can substitute shredded brisket for the chicken if you like. Whichever you use, remember that the taste will be enhanced by the use of the jalapeño chiles. If you want to make it less hot, use green chiles instead.

3 chicken breasts, poached	$^1/_2$ cup white vinegar
6 fresh jalapeño chiles, chopped	$^1/_4$ cup olive oil
2 tomatoes, seeded and diced	1 teaspoon salt
	1 teaspoon pepper
$^1/_2$ onion, chopped	2 avocados, peeled, pitted, and quartered
$^1/_4$ cup chopped fresh cilantro	1 head iceberg lettuce

Slice the chicken into thin strips and mix with all the ingredients, except the lettuce. Serve the hash on a bed of lettuce.

Southwest Jerky

Machaca Picante

This *machaca* recipe gives new meaning to the words beef jerky. It is a great snack, along with a cool Mexican beer, while watching the game.

1 to 1$^{1}/_{2}$ pounds boneless beef top round, partially frozen (for ease in slicing)	2 cloves garlic, minced
	$^{1}/_{8}$ teaspoon cayenne
	1 teaspoon ground cumin
2 tablespoons Worcestershire sauce	1$^{1}/_{2}$ teaspoons chili powder
1 teaspoon salt	

Trim and discard fat from the meat. Slice the meat in strips $^{1}/_{8}$-inch thick and as long as possible. In a bowl, combine 2 tablespoons water, Worcestershire sauce, salt, garlic, cayenne, cumin, and chili powder. Stir until well blended. Add the meat strips and mix thoroughly. Cover and marinate for at least 6 hours or overnight.

Preheat the oven to 200 degrees. Shake off any excess liquid. Arrange strips of meat close together, but not overlapping, on racks set on 2 rimmed, foil-lined 9 x 13-inch baking pans.

Dry the meat in the oven until it has turned dark brown and feels dry, 5 to 6 hours. Pat off any beads of oil. Let the meat cool. Remove from racks and store in an airtight container for as long as 2 to 3 weeks to maintain the freshness of the taste.

Mexican Meatballs

Albóndigas Mexicanas

Makes about 2 dozen meatballs

Meatballs, *albondigas* in Spanish, were a staple in our house while my brothers and I were growing up. Mom could make lots of dishes with meatballs, but ultimately, this recipe has always been a favorite.

MEATBALLS	SAUCE
1 pound ground beef	1 tablespoon oil
1 teaspoon salt	$^1/_4$ cup chopped onions
1 teaspoon pepper	1 (8-ounce) can tomato
$^1/_2$ teaspoon garlic powder	sauce
$^1/_2$ cup bread crumbs	2 cups hot water
$^1/_2$ cup chopped onions	$1^1/_2$ teaspoons
1 small green bell pepper,	Worcestershire sauce
chopped	Garlic powder
	Salt and pepper
	Minced fresh cilantro
	(optional)

Mix all the meatball ingredients together. Shape into 1-inch balls. Heat the oil and brown the meatballs and chopped onions. Add the tomato sauce, hot water, Worcestershire sauce, and garlic powder, salt, and pepper to taste. Add cilantro, to taste if you like. Cook for 20 minutes. Add a small amount of water during cooking if necessary.

Tequila Meatballs

Albóndigas Tequila

6 to 8 servings

Another *albóndiga* recipe, this one made with tequila. Whoever thought the agave cactus (which tequila is made from) could taste so good! Use these meatballs in a sandwich, soup, or whatever strikes your fancy.

---

1 egg	1 teaspoon black pepper
1/2 cup tequila	1 pound ground beef
1 teaspoon Worcestershire sauce	1 cup bread crumbs
	1/2 cup Parmesan cheese
1 tablespoon minced fresh cilantro	3 to 4 tablespoons vegetable or olive oil
1/2 teaspoon celery seed	Lettuce leaves
1 teaspoon red chile powder	Tequila Salsa (page 91)

Whisk the egg with the tequila, Worcestershire sauce, cilantro, celery seed, chile powder, and pepper. Combine the mixture with the ground beef, bread-crumbs, and Parmesan cheese. Form into small (1-inch) meatballs. Heat the oil in a large frying pan and sauté the balls, turning to brown all sides. When cooked through, place on paper towels to drain. Serve on a lettuce leaf-lined platter accompanied with Tequila Salsa.

Chorizo Nuggets

Makes about 48 nuggets

Our son was hooked on sausage balls until Tere came up with this variation to give an old recipe a new kick. They're quick and easy to make. The taste is truly Southwestern.

1 pound chorizo, store bought or homemade	**2 cups baking mix, such as Bisquick**
1 pound asadero cheese, shredded	

Preheat the oven to 350 degrees. Crumble and cook the chorizo in a large skillet over medium heat until browned. Drain the chorizo on paper towels. Mix the chorizo in a medium bowl with the cheese and baking mix. Form the mixture into ½-inch balls and arrange on a large baking sheet. Bake for 10 to 15 minutes, or until golden brown.

Savory Ceviche

Ceviche Sabroso

If you like sushi, you'll love ceviche, although the fish is actually cooked by the acid in the lemon juice. The additional ingredients give this dish a unique flavor and make it an excellent beginning, or addition, to any meal. The ceviche can be served on individual plates or set out on a buffet table for guests to enjoy as a dip.

---

2 pounds any firm fish, such as cod or salmon (if frozen fish is used, use cod)
Lemon juice to cover fish (approximately 1 cup)
$^1/_2$ cup olive oil
1 large onion, chopped
2 ripe tomatoes, peeled and chopped
1 to 15 stuffed green olives, chopped
1 ($2^1/_2$-ounce) jar capers, drained
$^1/_4$ cup chopped fresh cilantro
1 fresh manzano chile (yellow banana chile), veined and chopped
2 medium avocados, peeled, pitted, and cubed
Salt

Bone the fish and chop into $^1/_2$-inch cubes. Cover the fish with lemon juice and let stand refrigerated for 4 to 5 hours, turning so that the juice permeates all parts. When the acid has cooked the fish (it will start to change color), pour off the lemon juice. Add the onion, tomatoes, olives, capers, cilantro, and olive oil, adding the avocados last. Add salt to taste and sprinkle the chile over the fish (the chile gives an excellent flavor even for those who cannot take much chile). Serve with crackers for scooping.

Cilantro-Lime Shrimp

Makes about 24 hors d'oeuvres

Shrimp (*camarónes*) make an excellent appetizer prepared in a variety of ways. Here is one. Cilantro's strong aroma and taste makes all the difference in this dish, but keep tasting it as you add the cilantro so you'll know how much you like. El Paso has a very close-knit Asian community and as a result, several restaurants have opened offering delicious Chinese and Japanese cuisine. This recipe incorporates some of the tastes of the Orient and some from the border to offer a dish that has been influenced by both Asian and the border cultures.

1/2 cup fresh lime juice	1 tablespoon soy sauce
1/4 cup orange marmalade	1/2 teaspoon hot red pepper
3 large cloves garlic,	flakes
minced and mashed to a	Salt and pepper
paste with 1 teaspoon	1 pound large (21 to 24)
salt	shrimp, shelled and
1/2 cup finely chopped	deveined, leaving tail
fresh cilantro	shell section intact
1/4 cup olive oil	4 or 5 cilantro sprigs

Whisk together the lime juice, marmalade, garlic paste, chopped cilantro, 3 tablespoons of oil, soy sauce, red pepper flakes, and salt and pepper to taste in a measuring cup. Combine the shrimp with the mixture, reserving 1/3 cup for dipping, in a large sealable plastic bag and marinate, chilled, tossing occasionally to coat shrimp, about 45 minutes. Drain the shrimp and pat lightly between paper towels. Heat 1 1/2 teaspoons of oil in a large nonstick skillet over medium-high heat until hot but not smoking. Sauté half the shrimp until golden brown and cooked through, about 1 1/2 minutes per side. Sauté the remaining shrimp with an additional 1 1/2 teaspoons oil in same manner. Place on a warmed platter and garnish with cilantro sprigs. Serve with dipping sauce.

Did You Know?

▼ ▼ ▼ ▼ ▼ ▼ ▼

EL MARIACHI

There are varying opinions as to the origin of the word mariachi. One is that the word comes from the French word *mariage* meaning marriage, where strolling musicians were hired to play and entertain. The word also refers to strolling musicians going from restaurant to restaurant or walking down the street playing their music. In researching the word, I also found that the Coca Indians (1500s) of Mexico used the word mariachi to refer to any person engaged in musical activities. Whatever the origin, the best definition for the word mariachi is a Mexican folk musician.

Early in the history of the mariachi, before the 1930s, these musicians wore workmen's clothing, white shirts and pants (*calzones de manta*), sandals (*huaraches*), and straw hats. They traveled around from hacienda to hacienda looking for work. After Gaspar Vargas, founder of Mariachi Vargas, went from Jalisco to Mexico City, mariachi music became much more popular in urban areas, and the costumes changed. The players could now be seen wearing the typical *traje de charro*, a Mexican horseman's outfit. This outfit consisted of a waist-length jacket; tightly fitted pants open slightly at the ankle to fit over short riding boots called *botines*, a wide-rimmed sombrero, a large bow tie and a wide belt. The jacket and pants were and still are decorated with beautiful embroidery and silver buttons.

Historically, the instruments used by the mariachi were those introduced by the Spaniards. These consisted of guitars, *vihuelas* (violas), harps, and violins. With their widespread popularity, mariachis chose to expand their use of instruments to include the trumpet.

Mariachi music has its roots in the countryside. These strolling musicians played for fiestas including weddings, birthdays, religious and patriotic holidays, and sometimes even funerals. "*Las Mañanitas*" is a traditional tune played at birthday celebrations and on saint days. Mariachis were often hired to play *serenatas* (serenades) during the rites of courtship, conveying messages of love. Mariachi music has also been incorporated into the Roman Catholic mass.

After Gaspar Vargas went to Mexico City with his mariachi group, mariachis could be found playing for legendary songwriters and singers like Pedro Infante, Miguel Aceves Mejia, and Lola Beltran. Soon mariachi groups were contracted for motion pictures, giving rise to their popularity. Radio and television played their music of *sones* (like the *sone* from Jalisco, "*La Negra*") to *zapateados*, *jarabes*, and polkas.

Salsas & Sauces

Proverbs
Dichos

In doing, we learn.
Se aprende haciendo.

A merry heart goes a long way.
Corazón contento es gran talento.

You can't turn back the clock.
El diente miente, la cana engaña, pero la arruga no ofrece duda.

Advice most needed is least heeded.
El que no oye consejo, no llega a viejo.

Jack of all trades, master of none.
Aprendiz de todo y maestro de nada.

Basic Hot Salsa

Makes 1 cup

Wake up your taste buds by spreading this hot salsa over fried eggs for instant Huevos Rancheros (page 11). Hot is a relative term. Here on the Border, what we consider mild may be too hot for some who aren't used to spicy flavors. Add jalapeños bit by bit and try the sauce as you go.

3 medium tomatoes, diced and drained	**$^{1}/_{2}$ teaspoon dried oregano, crushed**
1 clove garlic, crushed	**2 tablespoons fresh or**
$^{1}/_{4}$ cup chopped onion	**canned jalapeños, diced**

Combine the tomatoes with all the other ingredients. (Cover and refrigerate for a day or more for best flavor.)

Blender Salsa

About 2$^{1}/_{2}$ cups

The addition of vinegar here adds a little kick to the chiles. The spiciness level of canned green chiles is indicated on the label.

2 medium tomatoes, cut into chunks	**4 teaspoons distilled white vinegar**
$^{1}/_{2}$ small onion	**1 tablespoon chopped fresh cilantro**
3 tablespoons canned diced green chiles	

Whirl all the ingredients in a blender or food processor until smooth. Season to taste with salt. The salsa keeps, covered, in the refrigerator for up to 2 days.

Salsa Cruda

This salsa has a nice bite to it. Spread some on your hamburgers or meat loaf for a Southwestern sensation.

2 (15-ounce) cans whole tomatoes, drained and chopped	1 teaspoon olive oil
1 teaspoon diced jalapeño	$^{1}/_{4}$ cup very thinly sliced onion
2 teaspoons fresh lime juice	

Combine all the ingredients and let stand for 1 hour. Refrigerate the salsa if you don't plan to serve it right away. The salsa will keep for about 1 week, stored in the refrigerator.

Salsa Fresca

Makes 2 cups

This is a fresh tasting salsa to be used as a dip or topping. Be sure to refrigerate it before serving. Chilling will enhance the flavor.

2 cloves garlic	1 pound firm ripe tomatoes,
$^1/_2$ medium size onion,	seeded and coarsely
quartered	chopped
1 jalapeño or other small	2 tablespoons vegetable oil
hot chile, stemmed and	Juice of 1 lime
seeded	Salt and pepper
$^1/_4$ cup minced fresh	
cilantro	

Blender method: Combine the garlic, onion, chiles, cilantro, and tomatoes in a blender and whirl briefly just until coarsely chopped. Add the oil and lime juice; whirl until the mixture is finely chopped. Season to taste with salt and pepper.

To make by hand: Using a sharp knife, mince the garlic, onion, and chiles. Finely chop the cilantro and dice the tomatoes. Combine in a non-reactive bowl; then add the oil and lime juice. Season to taste with salt and pepper.

If made ahead, cover and refrigerate for up to 2 days.

Salsa for a Crowd

▼ ▼ ▼ ▼ ▼ ▼   **Makes 6 cups**

Having a large gathering? Forget about those canned dips. Prepare this salsa recipe and have plenty of tostadas or chips on hand for your guests.

3 (28-ounce) cans, stewed tomatoes	2 cloves garlic, minced
1 (15-ounce) can tomato sauce	1 bunch fresh cilantro, chopped
3 medium tomatoes, diced	2 (4-ounce) cans chopped green chiles
3 bunches green onions, chopped	1 teaspoon sugar
1 tablespoon chopped canned jalapeños	

Using a food processor or your hands, as my mother taught me, mash the stewed tomatoes into small bits. Add all the remaining ingredients and mix well. Store in glass jars in the refrigerator for up to 1 week. The salsa can be prepared a day in advance.

Pico de Gallo

Here's your basic *pico* recipe. *Pico* goes great as a dip, as well as a topping on anything from tacos to hamburgers. *Pico de gallo* means a prick from the rooster's bill, which would feel like quite a "bite." The same goes for this salsa. There is a delicious bite to this combination of ingredients.

> 4 medium tomatoes, chopped
> 6 green onions, chopped with some of the tops
> 2 to 3 jalapeños, seeded and chopped
> 1^1/$_2$ tablespoons vegetable oil
> ^{1}/$_3$ cup chopped fresh cilantro

Blend all the ingredients and stir well. Chill before serving. The sauce keeps stored in the refrigerator for 3 to 4 days.

Ancho Sauce

Makes 2¹/₄ cups

The ancho chile is the dried form of the poblano chile. It has a mildly sweet flavor. You might want to run the sauce through a sieve to remove any unprocessed pieces of chile.

3 ancho chile peppers	**1 tablespoon dried**
4 ounces dried tomatoes	**oregano, crushed**
3 tablespoons minced	**1 tablespoon brown sugar**
garlic	**2 tablespoons**
¹/₂ cup chopped onion	**Worcestershire sauce**
4 beef bouillon cubes	**¹/₄ cup tomato paste**

Combine all the ingredients in a saucepan. Add 1¹/₂ cups water and bring to a boil over medium heat. Reduce the heat and simmer, stirring occasionally, for 10 minutes. Cool for 15 minutes.

Process the sauce until smooth, stopping often to scrape down the sides. The salsa will keep in the refrigerator for up to 1 week or in the freezer for 3 months.

Jalapeño Salsa

Makes 1 cup

This is certainly not for the faint of heart, but true chile-lovers won't eat any meal without a generous helping of this salsa. Put some on your next ear of corn. This is also delicious served with crackers or as a sauce for tacos. It's good with meat too.

---

4 small fresh jalapeño chiles, chopped

2 large tomatoes, peeled and chopped

1 onion, minced

$^{1}/_{2}$ teaspoon garlic powder

Dash salt

Mix all the ingredients thoroughly. The mixture keeps stored in the refrigerator for 3 to 4 days.

Serrano Salsa

Makes 1¹/₂ cups

This one is going to get hot, so have lots of *agua fresca* on hand to quench the fire. Or beer!

> **2 serrano chiles, seeded**   **¹/₄ teaspoon garlic salt**
>   **and diced**   **¹/₄ cup water**
> **2 tomatoes, diced**   **1 teaspoon dried oregano**
> **1 (8-ounce) can tomato**
>   **sauce**

Blend all the ingredients in a blender on medium speed. Let the salsa stand for at least 2 hours covered in a glass container in the refrigerator before serving. The salsa keeps for 3 to 4 days refrigerated.

Green Chile Sauce

Salsa de Chile Verde

Makes 1 cup

Most green chile is harvested when the veins running through the chile are at full piquancy so green chile dishes are spicier than those using red chile. Once a chile starts turning red, it takes on a slightly sweetened, smoky flavor. This sauce is good with tacos, tostadas, Huevos Rancheros (page 11), and as a dip. You might want to serve a pitcher of iced tea with this sauce.

1 (8-ounce) can tomato sauce	1 clove garlic, minced
1 (4-ounce) can chopped green chiles	$^1/_4$ teaspoon crushed red pepper
$^1/_2$ medium onion, chopped	Dash salt
	Pinch dried oregano

Mix all the ingredients together and store in the refrigerator for up to 10 days.

Red Chile Puree

Makes 2 cups

This recipe is more substantial and made to be thinned with broth or meat juices. If you would like a slightly hotter taste, mix in some dried *chile de arbol*. Please remember that when cooking with fresh chile, it is always best to wear gloves. If you handle the chiles without gloves and accidentally touch your eyes, it really stings.

9 dried New Mexico or California red chiles, hot or mild or a combination (about 3 ounces)	**1 small onion, chopped** **2 cloves garlic, chopped**

Preheat the oven to 350 degrees. Toast the chiles on a large baking sheet for approximately 4 minutes. Let cool slightly and then stem and remove the seeds.

Combine the chiles, onion, and garlic in a 4-quart pot and add 2 cups of water, or enough to cover the chiles. Cover and bring to a boil over high heat. Reduce the heat and simmer, covered, until the chiles are soft, about 30 minutes. Remove from the heat and cool slightly.

Whirl the chile mixture in a blender until smooth. Run through a sieve to remove any large pieces or unprocessed chile skins. The puree can be refrigerated, covered, up to 1 week.

Red Chile Sauce

The red sauce is great for *enchiladas rojas* or Menudo (page 30). It's not as spicy as green chile sauce.

12 whole dried ancho or pasilla chiles	**¹/₄ cup vegetable oil**
3 cups warm water	**¹/₂ teaspoon salt**
¹/₄ cup tomato sauce or tomato paste	**1 teaspoon dried oregano**
1 clove garlic, minced	**¹/₂ teaspoon ground cumin**

Preheat the oven to 400 degrees. Spread the chiles on a baking sheet and toast until fragrant, 3 to 4 minutes. Remove from the oven and let cool. Discard the stems and seeds. Place in a bowl with the water, and let stand for 1 hour.

Whirl the chiles in a blender with enough of the soaking liquid to moisten. Add the remaining liquid, tomato sauce, garlic, oil, salt, oregano, and cumin. Blend until smooth. Pour into a pot and simmer, uncovered, stirring occasionally, for 10 minutes. Keep warm. The sauce can also be made ahead and stored covered in the refrigerator for up to 1 week, or frozen for longer storage. Reheat before using.

Salsa Verde

No tomatoes, just tomatillos. This is what keeps the salsa green in color, and great tasting too. Use canned tomatillos for convenience, or go ahead and take the time to cook your own tomatillos for use in this recipe. Tomatillos are small green tomato-like vegetables covered in a husk.

---

1 (13-ounce) can tomatillos, liquid reserved	1 clove garlic
1 large onion, cut into chunks	1 (4-ounce) can diced green chiles

---

Combine all of the ingredients in a blender and whirl until smooth. The salsa keeps 3 to 4 days refrigerated.

Chile with Cheese and Beer

Chile con Queso y Cerveza

About 2 cups

The taste of beer with *queso* (cheese) is unbeatable. Experiment with different beers and cheeses until you find the combination you like. This recipe uses Monterey Jack. Perhaps a combination of Tecate Mexican Beer and asadero cheese could be an alternative. Lager beer tastes better in this dish than dark beer, which makes it a little too bitter. Use this as a dip or as a sauce over hamburgers, baked potatoes, or anything else you think might taste good with it.

1 cup Mexican beer	**2 tablespoons flour**
12 ounces Monterey jack	**$^1/_2$ cup bottled salsa**
cheese, cubed, 3 cups	**Tostada chips**

Add beer to the saucepan and bring to a simmer. Toss the cheese with the flour in a bowl. Add the cheese to the simmering beer and stir until melted and smooth. Add salsa and stir together. Serve warm with tostada chips.

Mexican-style Chile con Queso

Chile Con Queso Mejicano

▼ ▼ ▼ ▼ ▼

About 2 cups

So many chile con queso recipes and not enough chips to eat them with. You can always turn a simple hamburger into a Southwestern experience by topping it off with some *queso*. It also goes great on a baked potato.

6 fresh green chiles, roasted, peeled, and cut length-wise into slices	2 large fresh tomatoes, peeled and finely chopped
1 onion, chopped	10 ounces grated Jack or longhorn cheese, 2½ cups
2 tablespoons bacon grease	Salt
1 clove garlic, minced	

Sauté the chiles and onion in the bacon grease. Add the garlic and cook until soft. Add the tomatoes, cheese, and salt to taste. Heat until the cheese melts.

Pickled Chiles

Chile en Escabeche

This vinegar-based *chile en escabeche* is a must to have on hand with grilled meat or as a simple appetizer with tostadas.

1 large onion, thinly sliced	1 teaspoon dried oregano
5 large cloves garlic, minced	3 bay leaves
1/2 cup olive oil	12 green chiles, roasted, peeled, and seeded
1 cup white vinegar	
2 teaspoons salt	

Heat the oil in a skillet. When hot, sauté the onion and garlic until translucent. Add the vinegar, 1/2 cup water, salt, oregano, and bay leaves. Bring to a boil. Add the chiles and simmer for about 10 minutes. Store the chiles in jars and refrigerate.

Cilantro-Lime Salsa

Makes 2 1/2 cups

Cilantro and limes just seem to go well together in all Border foods. In this recipe, the combination adds to the jalapeños.

---

1 small onion, finely chopped

1 cup chopped fresh cilantro

1/2 cup chopped fresh parsley

1/2 cup vegetable oil

6 tablespoons fresh lime juice

3 tablespoons distilled white vinegar

2 cloves garlic, minced

1 jalapeño or other small hot chile, stemmed, seeded, and minced

---

Mix the onion, cilantro, parsley, oil, lime juice, vinegar, garlic, and chile in a non-reactive bowl. The salsa can be made ahead, and stored covered in the refrigerator for up to 1 day.

Homemade Guacamole

Makes about 2 cups

Warm up a few corn tortillas and spread with this guacamole recipe for a meal on the run. This can be enjoyed as a side dish or as a condiment.

---

3 ripe avocados, peeled and pitted	**2 teaspoons fresh lemon juice**
$^1/_2$ cup _Pico de Gallo_ (page 70)	**1 clove garlic, chopped**
$^1/_4$ cup chopped fresh cilantro	**$^1/_2$ teaspoon salt**
	$^1/_4$ teaspoon pepper
	1 tomato, chopped

Place the avocados, _Pico de Gallo_, cilantro, lemon juice, garlic, salt, and pepper in a medium bowl. Mash with a potato masher until chunky. Stir gently with a wooden spoon until well combined. Spoon the guacamole into a serving bowl and top with chopped tomato. Serve immediately or place plastic wrap directly on the surface of the guacamole (this helps prevent darkening) and refrigerate. Guacamole doesn't last long in the refrigerator, perhaps 2 to 3 days, so make only what you are going to use in the immediate future.

Avocado Salsa

Makes ¹/₂ cups

This avocado salsa has a very creamy texture because of the cream cheese. It works great as a dip.

2 large ripe avocados, peeled, pitted, and mashed	3 tablespoons fresh lime juice
1 (8-ounce) package cream cheese, softened	1 (4-ounce) can diced green chiles

Combine all the ingredients and blend. Serve as a topping for cooked vegetables.

Lemon Salsa
for Fish

Makes 1 1/2 cups

And you thought a good squeeze of lemon was all you needed on fish! Try this for a taste sensation. This salsa even makes fish sticks taste decent.

1 tablespoon cornstarch	3 tablespoons fresh lemon
1/2 cup sugar	juice
1/4 teaspoon salt	2 tablespoons butter
1 teaspoon grated lemon	1 (4-ounce) can diced
peel	green chiles, undrained

Mix the cornstarch, sugar, and salt in a medium saucepan. Blend with 1/4 cup water until smooth. Add another 3/4 cup water, stirring constantly. Bring the sauce to a boil, and then reduce the heat and simmer until the mixture thickens. Remove from the heat and stir in the remaining ingredients. Serve warm with fish.

Mango and Red Onion Salsa

Makes 1³/₄ cups

The mingling of sweet mangos, sharp red onion, and the heat of cayenne pepper is typical of Border tastes. The cayenne pepper gives it a nice kick. Try it, you'll like it.

---

2 small mangos, peeled, pitted, and diced
³/₄ cup chopped red onion
2 tablespoons chopped fresh cilantro
2 tablespoons fresh lime juice

1 teaspoon peeled and minced fresh ginger
¹/₂ teaspoon grated lime peel
¹/₈ teaspoon cayenne
Salt and pepper

Combine all the ingredients in a medium bowl and toss to blend. Let the salsa stand for 20 minutes. The salsa can be prepared 3 hours ahead, covered and kept in the refrigerator.

Pineapple-Orange Salsa

4 to 6 servings

The citrus flavors offset the heat of the fresh jalapeño. It's amazing how delicious the combination of hot and sweet can be. This salsa goes wonderfully with fish.

---

1 orange
2 cups chopped fresh
  pineapple
$^1/_2$ cup fresh orange juice
Juice of 1 lime
1 teaspoon grated lime
  peel

1 fresh jalapeño pepper,
  seeded and minced
2 tablespoons chopped
  fresh cilantro

Grate 1 tablespoon orange peel and set aside. Peel the orange, discard the peel and coarsely chop the fruit. Combine the grated orange peel, chopped orange, and remaining ingredients, except cilantro, in a medium bowl. Cover and refrigerate for 24 hours. Before serving, stir cilantro into salsa.

Mexican Mash

▼ ▼ ▼ ▼ ▼

6 (¹/₄ cup) servings

This salsa recipe is a wonderful party dip for guests who would like to experience Border cookery without the heat. Not everything has to be super-spicy to be enjoyed. Serve it with tortilla chips, corn chips, or taco shells.

¹/₂ cup sour cream	¹/₂ bottle mild red taco
¹/₂ cup mashed avocado	sauce
(from 1 large or 2 small	Chopped green olives
avocados)	Grated cheddar cheese
1 package taco seasoning	Chopped tomato
mix or Mexican Spice Mix	
(page 360)	

Layer all the ingredients in a shallow glass bowl in the order that they are listed.

Mole

Here it is, the chile-chocolate taste that gives chicken, and even enchiladas, that truly exotic Mexican flavor. Sure you can buy a bottle of mole paste, but making this recipe at least once is a must for any aspiring Border gourmet.

---

1 dried ancho chile
1 dried pasilla chile
1 dried New Mexico chile
20 blanched almonds
$^1/_4$ cup diced green-tipped banana
1 teaspoon ground cinnamon
1 clove garlic
2 corn tortillas, torn into pieces

2 tablespoons sesame seeds
1 tablespoon pine nuts
4 cups chicken broth
6 tablespoons ($^3/_4$ stick) butter
1 ounce semisweet chocolate
Salt (optional)

Preheat the oven to 350 degrees. Arrange each of the chiles on a large baking sheet. Bake until the chiles smell toasted, about 5 to 7 minutes. Discard the stems and seeds and grind the chiles to a powder in a blender. (Or substitute $^1/_4$ cup ground chile powder for roasted, ground chiles.) Add the almonds, banana, cinnamon, garlic, tortillas, sesame seeds, pine nuts, and 1 cup of the chicken broth. Whirl until pureed. The sauce will be grainy.

Pour into a pot, and the add butter, semisweet chocolate, and remaining 3 cups of chicken broth. Bring to a simmer, stirring constantly, then season to taste with salt, if desired.

Pumpkinseed Sauce

Pipián

Makes 3^1/$_2$ cups

Pepitas (fresh unsalted pumpkin seeds) are the basis for this paste. You might want to roast and salt a few extra seeds just for snacking while preparing the paste. They're tangier than sunflower seeds.

2^1/$_2$ cups hulled, unsalted pumpkin seeds	1 teaspoon each ground cumin
2 cups chicken broth	1 teaspoon white pepper
2 fresh (or canned) jalapeño chiles, stemmed and seeded	1 teaspoon salt ^{1}/$_4$ cup fresh cilantro

Preheat the oven to 350 degrees. Spread the pumpkin seeds on a large rimmed baking sheet. Toast the seeds in the oven until they begin to brown (about 12 to 15 minutes). Combine the seeds with the rest of the ingredients in a blender and whirl until smooth (the sauce will be grainy). The sauce can be made ahead and keeps in the refrigerator for up to 5 days. Freeze for longer storage.

Salsa for Chiles Rellenos

Salsa para Chiles Rellenos

This is my mother's recipe for chile relleno salsa. Again, it is the vinegar that adds that amazing flavor to the onion slices and brings out the taste in the relleno.

2 to 3 tomatoes, chopped
3 tablespoons minced fresh
   cilantro
1 teaspoon salt
1 medium onion, cut in long
   thin slivers

1 teaspoon olive oil
2 tablespoons white vinegar
2 teaspoons dried oregano

Mash the chopped tomatoes and combine with the remaining ingredients. Chill for 2 hours before serving. The salsa keeps 3 to 4 days refrigerated.

Tequila Salsa

Here's my kind of salsa. It's made with tequila. This can be used to marinade chicken and fish as well as served as a salsa.

$1/2$ cup olive oil	2 tablespoons Triple Sec
$1/2$ cup fresh lime juice	1 (4-ounce) can diced
$1/2$ cup tequila	green chiles, undrained

Combine all the ingredients. If using as a salsa, serve chilled with tostada chips.

Tomato Sauce

Makes 2 to 3 cups

---

2 tablespoons vegetable oil
1 large onion, chopped
2 cloves garlic, minced
2 to 3 fresh (or canned)
   jalapeño or serrano
   chiles, stemmed, seeded,
   and chopped

1 (28-ounce) can tomatoes
   and their liquid
Salt and pepper

Heat the oil in a 10- to 12-inch frying pan over medium-high heat. When the oil is hot, add the onion, garlic, and chiles. Add the tomatoes, breaking them up with a spoon. Cook, stirring until the sauce is thickened, about 10 to 15 minutes. Season to taste with salt and pepper. If you would like a smoother sauce, pour all ingredients into a blender or food processor and whirl until smooth. Run through a strainer to eliminate any unprocessed bits. The sauce will last about a week covered and refrigerated.

Did You Know?

▼ ▼ ▼ ▼ ▼ ▼ ▼

MUSIC ON THE BORDER

Music, like any other art, is always a matter of taste. You might like something I don't or I might listen to someone you can't stand. One thing we can all agree on though, is that music has always been a big part of Border life, from Brownsville to L.A. and San Diego. Like everything else, the styles and fads are always changing to meet the demands of a new audience, but for the traditionalists there will always be groups like Mariachi Vargas or Vicente Fernandez singing a *ranchera*.

I'm going to try to explain some of the various Latin musical styles that are most popular along the Border and make a suggestion or two of who you might listen to in order to get a good dose of each style. I can't include all musical styles but I'll do my best.

The music of the mariachis has changed little over the last hundred years. The musicians still wear their colorful *charro* outfits, and there have to be two trumpets, two violins, a *bajo sexto* (a six-string acoustic bass), and at least one guitar for a basic mariachi group. A really good mariachi group could have up to twenty musicians or more. What has changed for mariachis is the audience. These groups are not so popular in Mexico any more, yet you can find them in the Yellow Pages in El Paso. Times do change. I have to say though that the last mariachi group I saw in El Paso was at the opening of a new store and the three violinists did steps and the singer did some rap. It was different. Listen to Mariachi Vargas de Tecalitlán, Mariachi Real de Mexico, or, more recently, Laura Sobrino and Mariachi Mujer 2000.

Salsa music is a combination of African, Caribbean, and Latin rhythms. A carnival beat is driven by horn and percussion sections. It is music truly made for dancing and is real "world music." Check out Willie Colón, Mongo Santamaria, Willie Bobo, and some of Marc Anthony's music for good salsa.

Latin jazz is mostly jazz with that unique Latin percussion providing a back beat to which any instrument can float around and through. Some of the best musicians in this category include Gato Barbiaeri, Ray Barretto, Eddie Palmieri, Tito Puente, Pancho Sanchez, and Cal Tjader.

The *cumbia* is another form of Latin music that is really popular in dance clubs. Usually the band includes an accordion. It originally developed in the Andes, with African and European influences. It was (and still is) a staple in Colombia, where it is also called *vallenato*, and has made its way north, to the delight of dancers everywhere. Check out Carlos Vives, keeping the *cumbia* tradition alive from Colombia. For north of the border cumbia, give a listen to A.B. Quintanilla y Los Kumbia Kings.

Mambo and *conjunto* music both came out of Cuba and the Caribbean. Mambo began in the 1940s and has been called "Cuban Conjunto," but usually involves bigger bands than the smaller *conjunto* groups. Mambo bands normally have brass and rhythm sections and a singer fronts the band. One of the biggest mambo hits of all time was "Cherry Pink and Apple Blossom White" by Pérez Prado. His most famous lead singer, Benny More, also released some albums. *Conjunto* is basically a scaled down mambo. In Cuba, the bands use trumpets, while in Mexico it's an accordion. Classic examples are the Beto Villa Orchestra and Eddie con Los Shades. Eddie later became even more famous as Freddy Fender.

For me the Latin influence of pop music began with Carlos Santana. When Santana came out in the 1960s with "Evil Ways" and "Jingo" they had the unique beat that only congas and *timbales* could provide. Through "Oye Como Va" and on up to "Migra" (a sad and hilarious song) on his last album, Carlos Santana has pushed the boundaries of music while always staying true to his Latin roots.

Los Lobos is another band that rocks to the Latin beat. Whether they are performing a *corrida* or rocking the house down they always sound true, and that's not an easy thing to do after all the years they've been together. If you haven't heard Los Lobos, get their double CD "Just Another Band From East L.A." and enjoy.

Perhaps the first to play Tex-Mex music, and attract an American audience, was the late Doug Sahm from San Antonio. He had a couple of hits in the 1960s with "Medocino" and "She's About A Mover," both punctuated by an organ that could just as well have been an accordion. The last time I saw Doug Sahm he was playing with the Texas Tornadoes (Freddy Fender, Flaco Jimenez, and Augie Myers) at the Fiesta De Las Flores in El Paso a few years ago. They were great. RIP Doug, and long live all forms of Latin music.

Soups & Salads

Proverbs
Dichos

Eat to live, not live to eat.
Comer para vivir, y no vivir para comer.

The eyes are bigger than the belly.
Comer por los ojos.

Clothes do not make the man.
El habito no hace el monje.

A person is known by the company he keeps.
Dime con quien andas y te dire quien eres.

A good conscience makes a good pillow.
La mejor almohada es la conciencia sana.

Caesar-Margarita Salad

▼ ▼ ▼ ▼ ▼ ▼ ▼   **6 servings**

All recipes are adaptable. Taking the well-known Caesar salad and making it Border-style is no different. Cilantro gives the salad a very full, pungent taste.

Lime wedges	$^1/_4$ cup finely chopped
Coarse salt	fresh cilantro
1 large head romaine	1 red bell pepper, cut into
lettuce, torn into	thin strips
bite-size pieces	Margarita Dressing
4 ounces shredded	(recipe follows)
Monterey Jack cheese,	Tortilla chips
1 cup	6 lime wedges, for garnish

Rub the rims of 6 chilled salad plates with lime wedges. Place the salt in a saucer and roll each plate in the salt. Set aside.

Combine the lettuce, cheese, cilantro, and bell pepper in a large bowl, add Margarita Dressing, and toss gently. Arrange the salad on the plates and sprinkle with tortilla triangles. Garnish each plate with a lime wedge.

Margarita Dressing

▼ ▼ ▼ ▼ ▼ ▼ ▼   **Makes 1 cup**

$^1/_3$ cup vegetable oil	1 clove garlic, minced
$^1/_4$ cup fresh lime juice	1 serrano chile, seeded and
1 egg or 2 tablespoons	finely chopped
fat-free egg substitute	$^1/_4$ teaspoon salt
(optional)	$^1/_4$ teaspoons ground
1$^1/_2$ tablespoons tequila	cumin
1$^1/_2$ teaspoons Triple Sec	

Combine all the ingredients in a small bowl and stir well with a wire whisk. Cover and chill.

Avocado Salad with Jalapeño Dressing
Aguacate con Salsa de Jalapeño

▼　▼　▼　▼　▼　▼

4 servings

The jalapeño dressing is what makes this salad so special. But watch out, it can be hot. You'll figure out your own jalapeño tolerance the more you use it.

Jalapeño Dressing
(recipe follows)
2 large oranges
1 small cucumber
2 large ripe avocados

4 to 8 red leaf lettuce
leaves, washed and
crisped
Fresh cilantro sprigs
(optional)

Prepare the Jalapeño Dressing and set aside. Cut off the peel and white membrane from oranges. Cut crosswise into thin slices and set aside. Slice the cucumber and set aside.

Cut the avocados in half lengthwise. Pit and peel them. Fan each avocado half by slicing lengthwise at $1/2$-inch intervals, without cutting through tapered end of fruit; then push down gently on back of avocado with flat of knife.

Place the lettuce leaves on 4 dinner plates and place an avocado fan, pit side down, on the lettuce. For each serving, arrange the orange and cucumber slices around the avocado. Spoon 2 to 3 tablespoons of the dressing in a band over avocado. Garnish with cilantro, if desired.

Jalapeño Dressing

▼ ▼ ▼ ▼ ▼ ▼

Makes ³/₄ cup

---

¹/₂ cup plain yogurt
¹/₄ teaspoon cumin seeds, crushed
1 clove garlic, minced
2 tablespoons minced fresh (stemmed and seeded) or canned jalapeño peppers

2 tablespoons fresh orange juice
2 tablespoons chopped fresh cilantro
Salt

Stir together the yogurt, cumin seeds, garlic, jalapeños, orange juice, and cilantro. Season to taste with salt.

Christmas Eve Salad

Ensalada de Noche Buena

8 to 10 servings

Hispanic celebrations often center around food. This salad is named for Christmas Eve, *Noche Buena,* and is traditionally served on this night. It's beautiful to look at with all its colors and certainly a satisfying taste adventure.

---

2 pomegranates
1 head romaine lettuce
6 cooked beets, peeled and
  thinly sliced
4 oranges, peeled and
  thinly sliced crosswise
4 unpeeled red apples,
  cored and thinly sliced
4 bananas, peeled and
  thinly sliced

1 fresh pineapple, peeled,
  cored, and cut into chunks,
  or one (32-ounce) can
  pineapple chunks, drained
1 lime, thinly sliced
$^1/_4$ cup sugar
1 cup roasted peanuts,
  chopped
$^1/_2$ cup vegetable oil
$^1/_4$ cup red wine vinegar

Cut the crown end off the pomegranates and cut into quarters. Submerge in a bowl of cold water and break the sections apart, separating the seeds from the membranes with your fingers. (The seeds will sink to bottom, while membranes and peel float to top.) Discard the membranes and peel and drain the seeds in a fine strainer. Pat dry and set aside.

Remove 6 large outer leaves from romaine and shred the remaining lettuce. Line a large, shallow serving bowl with the whole leaves, and then add the shredded lettuce. Arrange the beets, oranges, apples, bananas, and pineapple in a decorative pattern over the lettuce and garnish with lime slices. Sprinkle with sugar, pomegranate seeds, and peanuts. Mix the oil and vinegar until blended and pour over the salad just before serving.

Cactus Salad

Ensalada de Nopalitos

Nopalitos are an exciting food to experience. Strips of *nopales* (cactus pads) are truly an authentic Mexican ingredient and definitely belong on the Southwest menu. It's fun to serve this salad and have your guests try to figure out what they're eating.

1 pound fresh *nopales* or 1 jar drained, rinsed *nopalitos*	**1 medium onion, thinly sliced and separated into rings**
1 jalapeño or serrano chile, stemmed and seeded (optional)	**Chopped fresh cilantro, for garnish**
2 medium ripe tomatoes, sliced	**2 limes, cut into 6 wedges**

If you are cooking fresh *nopalitos*, hold the pads with a towel to protect your hands and shave off the spines using a sharp knife. Trim around the pad to remove the thorny edge, then peel the pads with a vegetable peeler. Slice crosswise into ¼-inch strips.

Bring 1½ quarts of water to a boil in a 3- or 4-quart pan, add the cactus and jalapeño or serrano chile. Cook, uncovered, over high heat until the cactus is tender, 5 to 7 minutes. Drain and rinse with cold water. The cactus pads may be made ahead and refrigerated for up to 4 days.

On a platter, arrange the *nopalitos*, tomatoes, and onion. Garnish with cilantro. Offer lime to squeeze over individual servings.

Jicama and Fruit Salad

Ensalada de Jícama y Fruta

▼ ▼ ▼ ▼ ▼ ▼   **8 to 10 servings**

Here is a great way to serve jicama. The crunchy jicama combined with the sweet taste of papaya and mango gives your taste buds a Southwestern treat. The chili powder really brings out the cool crisp taste of the vegetable.

1 medium jicama	**$^2/_3$ cup fresh lime juice**
Fresh fruit (suggestions follow)	**1 teaspoon salt**
	1 tablespoon chili powder

With a small sharp knife, trim and discard the ends of the jicama, peel, and rinse. Cut the jicama in half, and then thinly slice each half. Mix the jícama and fruit with lime juice in separate bowls, then place each separately on a platter. Combine the salt and chili powder and sprinkle over the jicama and fruit.

Fruit
Choose from the following, using a total of 5 pounds of fruit: Honeydew, cantaloupe or watermelon, peeled and cut into chunks or slices; papaya, peeled, seeded, and sliced crosswise; mango, pitted, peeled, and cut in large cubes; orange, peeled and sectioned, white membrane discarded; kiwi, peeled and sliced crosswise; and green apple, cored and sliced.

Mexican Flag Salad

Makes 4 to 5 servings

I was inspired to create this salad after seeing an American flag dessert in a magazine a few years back. So, to all of you who enjoy Southwest Border cuisine, here's a salad to make and share on Cinco de Mayo and *16 de Septiembre*.

2 heads broccoli	**Pimientos**
1 large head cauliflower	**Jalapeño slivers**
2 (12-ounce) packages	**1 end-slice of bread**
cherry tomatoes	

Arrange the broccoli, cauliflower, and cherry tomatoes in three equal stripes on a rectangular serving platter, starting on the left side of the platter with the broccoli and ending on the right side with the cherry tomatoes.

With a shape knife, cut the bread into an eagle shape (or whatever shape you desire) and toast it in the toaster (or in the oven if you think the bread slice might break coming out of the toaster).

Position the bread in the center of the cauliflower. Beneath the eagle, form a half-circle with jalapeño slivers. Decorate with pimiento pieces. Position 1 jalapeño sliver by the eagle's beak to represent the snake. Chill in the refrigerator until serving time.

DIP	**$^1/_4$ cup chopped fresh**
$^1/_2$ cup sour cream	**cilantro**
$^1/_2$ cup mayonnaise	**1 teaspoon chili powder**
Minced onion or onion	**Salt and pepper to taste**
powder	**Pinch sugar**

Mix the sour cream and mayonnaise and chill in the refrigerator to allow flavors to mellow, 30 minutes. Add minced onion, cilantro, chili powder, salt, pepper, and a pinch of sugar. The seasonings can be adjusted to suit your tastes.

Layered Salad

Layering this salad keeps your guests coming back for more. Serve the salad in a deep clear bowl to allow them to see what the different layers contain. The food is the main thing, but presentation counts.

6 cups lettuce, torn into bite-size pieces	1 cup mayonnaise or salad dressing
1 package frozen peas, thawed	1 (8-ounce) container sour cream
1 cup garbanzo beans (chick peas)	2 teaspoons sugar
1 cup sliced celery	2 medium tomatoes, cut into thin wedges
$^3/_4$ cups green bell pepper or green chile, chopped	2 hard-cooked eggs, sliced
$^1/_2$ onion, chopped	$1^1/_2$ cups crumbled blue cheese

Layer half of the lettuce in a large clear salad bowl. Top with the peas, garbanzo beans, celery, green pepper, onion, and the remaining lettuce.

Stir together the mayonnaise, sour cream, and sugar. Spread over the lettuce. Arrange the tomatoes and eggs on top. Sprinkle with the blue cheese. Cover and chill for two hours. Serve cold.

Chicken and Fruit Salad
with Green Chile Dressing

▼ ▼ ▼ ▼ ▼ ▼ ▼ **4 servings**

This is an excellent chicken and fruit salad for brunch or, if you prefer, a light dinner. It's great to take for lunch, but keep the lettuce and cabbage in an airtight container and mix with the other ingredients when you're ready to eat.

---

3 cups mixed salad greens (in bite-size pieces) and shredded red cabbage
2 cups cubed cooked chicken or turkey
2 cups bite-size pieces of honeydew, cantaloupe, casaba, or Spanish melon (about 1^1/2 pounds unpeeled)

2 cups bite-size pieces of fresh pineapple
^{1}/2 small jicama, cut into julienne strips, or 2 stalks celery, sliced
Lime slices, for garnish (optional)
Cilantro springs, for garnish (optional)
Green Chile Dressing (recipe follows)

Arrange the salad greens and cabbage on a platter or 4 salad plates. Top with the chicken, melon, pineapple, and jícama. Garnish with the lime slices and cilantro, if desired. Serve with Green Chile Dressing.

Green Chile Dressing

Makes 1^1/4 cups

---

1 cup mayonnaise
2 tablespoons finely chopped green chiles
2 tablespoons fresh lime juice

1 green onion, thinly sliced
2 tablespoons minced fresh cilantro

Mix together all the ingredients.

Tex-Mex Flank Steak Salad

▼ ▼ ▼ ▼ ▼

4 servings

It's true: We do things bigger in Texas. This salad is no different. It's like a three-course meal in one concoction.

$1^1/4$ cups canned beef broth

3 dried ancho chiles

4 large cloves garlic

$1^1/2$ teaspoons ground cumin

1 pound flank steak, well trimmed

Salt

2 cups sliced onion, about 2 medium onions

2 fresh Anaheim chiles, quartered and thinly sliced

1 red bell pepper, quartered and thinly sliced

$1^2/3$ cups salsa (purchased fresh salsa or Salsa Fresca, page 68)

6 to 8 cups thinly sliced iceberg lettuce, about 1 large head

2 cups corn kernels, fresh or frozen and thawed

1 large tomato, chopped

$1/2$ cup fresh cilantro leaves

4 ounces grated mozzarella cheese, 1 cup

$1/4$ cup crumbled baked tortilla chips

Bring 1 cup of the broth and the dried chiles to a boil in small heavy saucepan. Cover and let stand for 20 minutes. Stem and seed the chiles. Rinse. Strain the cooking liquid. Transfer the chiles, garlic, and cumin to a blender and blend until smooth. Remove ⅓ cup of the puree and set aside. Spread the remaining puree over both sides of the steak. Season with salt and place in shallow baking dish. Cover and refrigerate overnight.

Simmer the remaining ¼ cup broth, onion, fresh chiles, and bell pepper in a medium heavy skillet until tender, about 5 minutes. Transfer to a bowl and cool.

Preheat the broiler. Transfer the beef to a baking sheet. Broil for 5 minutes, turn, and broil for another 3 minutes. Let the beef stand for 10 minutes. Cut into thin slices. Add any accumulated juices and ⅓ cup salsa to the reserved puree.

For each plate, layer in the following order: lettuce, salsa, pepper mixture, corn, beef, tomato, cilantro, cheese, and reserved puree. Garnish with tortilla chips and serve.

Mexican Shrimp Cocktail

Coctel de Camarón

 **4 servings**

Who says you can only serve fresh shrimp with cocktail sauce? Try this Mexican Shrimp Cocktail with salsa and enjoy the wonderful flavor.

12 large shrimp ($^1/_2$ pound)	1 tablespoon fresh lime juice
2 plum tomatoes, finely diced	1 teaspoon salt
1 green onion, thinly sliced	$^1/_2$ teaspoon black pepper
1 small clove garlic, minced	$^1/_2$ avocado
1 tablespoon fresh lemon juice	2 limes, sliced

Cook the shrimp in boiling salted water, stirring occasionally, until just cooked through, about 3 minutes. Drain, cool, and shell, leaving the tails attached if desired. Chill until cold, at least 15 minutes.

Stir together the tomatoes, green onion, garlic, lemon and lime juices, salt, and pepper.

Just before serving, finely dice the avocado and stir into the tomato salsa. Spoon the salsa into 4 serving dishes and arrange the shrimp and lime on top.

Ranchero Soup

Caldo Ranchero

6 to 8 servings

This roast soup contains enough meat and vegetables to make a complete meal. We like it with Jalapeño Cornbread (page 136) or a lightly toasted and buttered *Bolillos* (page 140).

---

2 pounds chuck roast or
   brisket
Salt
5 tablespoons olive or
   vegetable oil
5 tablespoons all-purpose
   flour
1 small onion, coarsely
   chopped

1 clove garlic
4 ears of corn, cooked and
   cut into 4 pieces
4 tomatoes, chopped
1 small cauliflower, divided
   into small sprigs
$^1/_4$ teaspoon pepper
1 bay leaf

Chop the meat into bite-size pieces. Place the meat in a saucepan with 3 quarts of lightly salted water and bring to a boil. Reduce the heat and simmer until the meat is tender and well cooked, about 1½ hours. Stir occasionally. Skim off the fat and take out 2 cups of soup stock and set aside.

Heat the oil and brown the flour. Sauté the onion, then add the reserved stock and mix thoroughly. Combine the meat and the gravy mixture. Blend well. Stir in the garlic, corn, tomatoes, cauliflower, 2 teaspoons salt, pepper, and bay leaf. Add up to 3 cups more water if needed, to keep the meat and vegetables covered. Cook, covered, over medium heat for 45 minutes, stirring occasionally. Remove the bay leaf before serving.

Chicken Soup with Avocado and Tortilla Chips

▼ ▼ ▼ ▼ ▼ ▼ ▼ **6 servings**

My grandmother always believed that chicken soup was good for *resfrios* (colds), even before it was a popular notion. The jalapeño chile added to this soup will clear up the sinuses too.

1 small onion	4 corn tortillas
2 cloves garlic	1/2 cup vegetable oil
1/2 fresh jalapeño pepper	2 firm, ripe avocados
1/2 cup fresh cilantro leaves	2 tablespoons fresh lime juice
2 chicken breast halves with bones and skin	Salt
3 1/2 cups chicken broth	Tortilla chips, for garnish

Coarsely chop the onion and garlic. Wearing rubber gloves, finely chop the jalapeño. Chop the cilantro. Remove and discard the skin from the chicken.

Cook the chicken in a 3-quart saucepan with the onion, garlic, jalapeño, 1 tablespoon of the cilantro, broth, and 3 cups of water at a bare simmer until just cooked through, about 15 minutes. Transfer the chicken to a cutting board with tongs and shred the meat, discarding bones. Pour the broth through a fine sieve into a bowl and return to a clean pan.

Halve the tortillas and cut crosswise into 1/8-inch-wide strips. Heat the oil in an 8-inch skillet over medium-high heat until hot but not smoking and, working in 3 batches, fry the tortilla strips, stirring gently, until golden brown. With tongs, transfer the fried strips to paper towels to drain.

Halve, pit, and peel the avocados and cut into 1/2-inch cubes. Add the chicken to the broth and heat over medium heat until hot. Add the remaining cilantro, avocado, lime juice, and salt to taste. Garnish the soup with tortilla chips.

Chile Cheese Soup

▼ ▼ ▼ ▼ ▼ ▼ **6 to 8 servings**

This soup lends itself to a touch of elegance. Serve it to start a meal, and guests will delight in the taste and prepare for a meal of Border goodies.

1 tablespoon vegetable oil	Salt
1 onion, chopped	1 potato, diced
1 (7-ounce) can green chiles, diced	2 cloves garlic, minced
1 (8-ounce) can tomato sauce	$1/2$ pound sharp cheddar cheese, shredded, 2 cups

Heat the oil and lightly fry the onion. Add the chiles and tomato sauce and cook for 10 minutes. Add 6 to 7 cups water, salt to taste, the potato, and garlic. Simmer until the potatoes are done. Add the cheese, stir, and serve.

Mexican Lime Soup

Caldo de Lima Mejicana

Limas (limes) are delicious in drinks, sauces, and now in soup. You can add a splash of tequila to this if you'd like.

2 tablespoons olive oil	1¹/₂ cups coarsely crushed
6 cloves garlic, sliced	tortilla chips
6 small skinless and	2 avocados, peeled, pitted,
boneless chicken breast	and diced
halves, cut crosswise into	3 tomatoes, chopped
¹/₂-inch strips	3 green onions, sliced
1¹/₂ teaspoons dried	¹/₄ cup chopped fresh
oregano	cilantro
Salt and pepper	¹/₂ cup minced jalapeño
9 cups chicken broth	chiles
¹/₃ cup fresh lime juice	6 lime slices, for garnish

Heat the oil in a large heavy pot over medium heat. Add the garlic and stir for 20 seconds. Add the chicken and oregano, and salt and pepper to taste. Sauté for 3 minutes. Add the broth and lime juice and bring to a simmer. Reduce the heat to medium-low and simmer gently until the chicken is cooked through, about 8 minutes. Season the soup to taste with salt and pepper.

Divide the crushed tortilla chips among 6 bowls. Ladle soup into bowls. Top the soup with avocados, tomatoes, green onions, cilantro, and jalapeños. Garnish with lime slices and serve.

Cilantro-Lime Soup

Caldo de Lima y Cilantro

▼ ▼ ▼ ▼ ▼ ▼ ▼   **4 servings**

Cilantro-lime soup is an invitation to the senses. The strong flavor and aroma of both ingredients express the finesse of Mexican cuisine.

1 large onion	5 cups chicken broth
2 cloves garlic	1 cup corn kernels, fresh or
2 fresh jalapeños,	frozen
stemmed and seeded	1 cup chopped, seeded
$^1/_4$ cup chopped fresh	tomatoes
cilantro	$^1/_2$ bunch cilantro, tied
2 tablespoons olive oil	together with kitchen
1 tablespoon chili powder	string
2 skinless and boneless	$^1/_4$ cup fresh lime juice
chicken breast halves,	Salt and pepper
cut into $^3/_4$-inch pieces	Sour cream, for garnish

Coarsely chop the onion and mince the garlic. Wearing rubber gloves, finely chop the jalapeños. Chop the cilantro. Remove and discard skin from chicken.

Heat the oil in large heavy saucepan over medium-high heat. Add the onion and garlic and sauté until softened, about 3 minutes. Add the chile powder and stir for 1 minute. Add the chicken and stir for 2 minutes. Add the broth, corn, tomatoes, and the bunch of cilantro. Bring to a boil. Reduce the heat and simmer until the chicken is cooked through, about 10 minutes. Discard the cilantro. The soup can be prepared ahead of time up to this point. Return to a simmer before continuing.

Add the chopped cilantro and lime juice to the soup. Season to taste with salt and pepper. Garnish with sour cream.

Tortilla Soup

Caldo de Tortilla y Gallina

Tortilla soup is the one dish everyone must try because it encompasses the rich flavors of chicken, tortillas, avocados, and chile all blended into one magnificent taste. There are many variations of this recipe; this is but one. Experiment and make up you own.

$^1/_4$ cup ($^1/_2$ stick) butter
$^1/_3$ cup olive oil
1 large onion, chopped
1 fresh jalapeño, chopped
   and seeded
4 cloves garlic, minced
2 carrots, diced
6 stalks celery, diced
1 pound skinless and boneless chicken breast, diced
1 teaspoon ground cumin
1 teaspoon salt
1 teaspoon chili powder
1 teaspoon lemon pepper

$^1/_2$ cup all-purpose flour
1 (14-ounce) can chopped
   tomatoes
4 ($10^1/_2$-ounce) cans
   chicken broth
6 to 7 stems cilantro
2 tablespoons fresh lime
   juice
Crushed tortilla chips
Sour cream
Diced avocados
Shredded Monterey Jack
   cheese

Heat the butter and oil in a large pot. Sauté the onion, jalapeño, garlic, carrots, celery, and chicken for 5 minutes. Add the cumin, salt, chile powder, lemon pepper, and flour. Stir to blend. Add the tomatoes and chicken broth. Simmer for 1 hour. Add the cilantro and lime juice. Place the tortilla chips, sour cream, avocados, and cheese in bowls in that order, and add the soup.

Zucchini Soup

Sopa de Calabacitas

4 servings

Calabacitas means little squash. This soup contains all the fixings for a generous meal, including the tequila.

3 tablespoons olive oil	3 cups chicken stock
1 medium onion, chopped	$^1/_2$ teaspoon salt
4 medium zucchini, chopped	$^1/_2$ teaspoon ground black pepper
3 tablespoons butter	2 tablespoons tequila
3 tablespoons all-purpose flour	1 cup diced cooked chicken
$^1/_2$ cup milk	Cilantro sprigs, to garnish

Heat the oil in a large pan. Sauté the onion and zucchini until the onion is soft. Remove the vegetables and set aside. Melt the butter in the same pan and stir in the flour to make a roux. Add the milk and cook over medium heat for 3 to 4 minutes, stirring occasionally. Stir in the chicken stock. Add the salt, pepper, and vegetables and cook for 15 to 20 minutes. Stir in the tequila and chicken and cook for 5 to 10 minutes, or until the chicken is warmed through. Serve garnished with cilantro.

Pinto Bean Soup

▼ ▼ ▼ ▼ ▼ ▼   **6 to 8 servings**

There is absolutely no Mexican meal along the border that you would want to serve without pinto beans. Black beans are served in many parts of Mexico and certainly in areas like Santa Fe, New Mexico, but in and around El Paso and other border areas, pinto beans are the bean of choice. This recipe offers the beans in a soup. The chorizo seems to intensify the flavors of this Border recipe.

1 pound dried pinto beans, picked over and rinsed	1 (32-ounce) can diced or pureed tomatoes, drained
1/4 cup vegetable oil	
3 medium onions, finely chopped	2 cups chicken broth
5 cloves garlic, minced	1/2 cup canned mild enchilada sauce (not salsa), or to taste
2 red bell peppers, chopped	
1 tablespoon chili powder	Salt
2 teaspoons ground cumin	3 tablespoons fresh lime juice, or to taste
1/2 pound cured chorizo, sliced 1/4 inch thick (optional)	1/3 to 1/2 cup chopped fresh cilantro

Soak the beans in water to cover by 2 inches in a bowl overnight or quick-soak* and drain.

Heat the oil over medium-high heat in a heavy kettle and sauté the onions and garlic, stirring, until pale golden. Add the bell peppers and cook over medium heat, stirring, until softened. Add the chili powder and cumin and cook, stirring, 30 seconds. Add the drained beans and 6 cups water and simmer, partially covered, until tender, about 1 to 1¼ hours.

While the soup is simmering, brown the chorizo in a skillet over medium-high heat, in batches if necessary, and drain on paper towels. Add the chorizo to the soup with the tomatoes, broth, enchilada sauce, and salt to taste and simmer, partially covered, stirring occasionally, for 30 minutes. The soup may be made up to 4 days ahead. Cool, uncovered, before chilling. Store covered.

Just before serving, stir in the lime juice and cilantro.

*To Quick-Soak Dried Beans:
Place the dried beans in a large saucepan with triple their volume of cold water. Bring the water to a boil and cook the beans, uncovered, over medium heat for 2 minutes. Remove the pan from the heat and let the beans soak for 1 hour.

Oxtail and Bean Soup

Sopa de Carne y Frijol

▼ ▼ ▼ ▼ ▼ ▼ ▼   **6 servings**

This combination of oxtails and beans makes a satisfying one-dish meal. Warm flour or corn tortillas would go great on the side.

---

¹/₂ pound dried pinto beans, picked through and rinsed

4 to 5 pounds oxtails, cut into 2-inch pieces

2 large onions, chopped

4 large cloves garlic, minced

4 cups beef broth

Salt and pepper

Chopped fresh cilantro

8 ounces shredded Monterey Jack cheese, 2 cups

Salsa Fresca (see page 68)

Place the beans in a large bowl. Cover with cold water and soak at room temperature for at least 12 hours. Drain. Or use the quick soak method (see page 117).

Arrange the oxtails on a rack on a broiler pan. Broil 4 inches from the heat, turning, until well browned on all sides, about 20 minutes.

Combine the beans, onions, garlic, broth, 4 cups of water, and oxtails in an 8- to 10-quart pan and bring to a boil over high heat. Reduce the heat, cover, and simmer until the beans mash easily and the meat pulls away from the bone, about 4 hours. The soup can be prepared ahead and stored, covered in the refrigerator.

Skim and discard the fat from the soup. Season to taste with salt and pepper. Offer cilantro, cheese, and Salsa Fresca in separate bowls to add to individual servings.

Meatball Soup

Sopa de Albóndigas

Albóndigas (meatballs) are a versatile food. In this recipe, they are the basis for a great tasting soup, very much Southwestern in style. This is a great dish to bring to a potluck.

SOUP	MEATBALLS
2 quarts chicken broth (defatted)	1 pound ground turkey or ground beef
1 medium onion, diced	3 tablespoons uncooked instant rice
3 stalks celery, sliced	$^1/_2$ cup finely minced onion
3 carrots, sliced	$^1/_4$ cup chopped fresh cilantro
1 cup chopped fresh cilantro	$^1/_2$ teaspoon garlic salt
$^1/_2$ cup mild salsa	$^1/_2$ teaspoon dried oregano

For the soup, combine all the ingredients in a soup pot and simmer for 10 minutes.

For the meatballs, mix all the ingredients together and form into small (1-inch) balls. Bring the soup to a boil and carefully place the meatballs into the soup. Cover, reduce the heat, and simmer for 30 minutes.

Pozole Stew

8 servings

This pozole dish is made with green chile sauce and is a little spicy. Experiment with the amount of green chile sauce to find your own level of taste and heat preference. Instead of starting out with 2 cups, gradually add ½ a cup at a time while you taste test.

Two (³/₄-pound) packages dried pozole or fresh frozen pozole
10 ounces pork shoulder, trimmed of fat and cut into 1-inch cubes
2 cups Green Chile Sauce (page 74)
6 cloves garlic, minced, or more to taste
1 white onion, finely diced

4 dried New Mexico chiles, rinsed, stemmed, seeded, and coarsely chopped
2 tablespoons chili powder
2 teaspoons ground cumin
1 tablespoon dried oregano
1 tablespoon hot red pepper flakes, or more to taste
2 teaspoons salt, or more to taste

If using fresh-frozen pozole, rinse it well under cold running water.

Place all of the ingredients in a large pot with 6 quarts water and bring to a boil. Reduce the heat to low and simmer, uncovered, stirring occasionally, until the kernels have opened up and are tender, 2½ to 5 hours, depending upon the type of pozole you are using. Add water as needed to keep the pozole just covered with liquid.

When the stew is ready, the consistency should be that of a thick soup. Adjust to taste with more garlic, dried red chile, and salt before serving.

Green Chile Stew

Guiso de Chile Verde

4 servings

Everyone enjoys a bowl of green chile stew. The savory taste of the green chile salsa makes the meat enjoyable alone or wrapped up in a warm flour tortilla, burrito style.

1 pound beef stew meat	1/2 cup Green Chile Sauce
1/2 yellow onion, chopped	(page 74)
2 tomatoes, chopped	3 carrots, peeled and cut
3 stalks celery, cut into	into 1/2-inch pieces
1/4-inch pieces	5 medium potatoes, peeled
2 teaspoons Meat	and diced
Seasoning (recipe follows)	Salt and pepper

Add the meat to a large casserole and cover with water. Bring to a boil and remove any film or residue from the surface. Turn down to a simmer and cook for 10 minutes. Add the onion, tomatoes, celery, Meat Seasoning, and Green Chile Sauce and continue cooking over low heat, just above a simmer. When the meat begins to become fork tender, after about 1 hour, add the carrots and continue cooking for 15 minutes. Just before serving, add the potatoes, adjust the seasoning, and serve when potatoes are cooked through.

Meat Seasoning

Makes 2 teaspoons

1/4 teaspoon paprika	1 teaspoon celery seed,
1/4 teaspoon cayenne	ground
1/2 teaspoon salt	

Mix together all the ingredients.

Mexican Chicken and Vegetable Stew

Guiso de Pollo y Verduras

4 to 8 servings

This could be considered either a stew or a soup, depending on how thick you like it. It's a great dish because it can be prepared ahead of time and reheated when you are ready to eat. Serve with *Bolillos* (page 140) or tortillas and *Agua Fresca* (page 285) and you have a complete meal.

---

1 teaspoon ground cumin
1 teaspoon chili powder
1/2 teaspoon ground cinnamon
2 teaspoons white wine vinegar
1 clove garlic, minced and mashed to a paste with a pinch of salt
3 tablespoons vegetable oil
Salt and pepper
8 chicken thighs
1 large onion, thinly sliced
2 cloves garlic, minced
2 tomatoes, coarsely chopped

4 zucchini, scrubbed, quartered lengthwise, and cut crosswise into 3/4-inch pieces
1/4 cup chicken broth
1 to 2 tablespoons minced pickled jalapeño peppers
1 red bell pepper, cut into 1/2-inch pieces
1 cup corn kernels, fresh or frozen and thawed
1/4 teaspoon dried oregano, crushed
2 ounces coarsely grated Monterey Jack cheese, 1/2 cup

Whisk together the cumin, chili powder, cinnamon, vinegar, mashed garlic, 1 tablespoon oil, and salt and pepper to taste in a small bowl. Coat the chicken pieces with the spice paste and grill on an oiled grill set 6 inches over glowing coals or in an oiled ridged grill pan over medium-high heat, turning once, 12 to 15 minutes on each side, until cooked through.

While the chicken is cooking, heat the remaining oil in a skillet and cook the onion, stirring occasionally, until lightly golden. Add the garlic cloves and the tomatoes and cook over medium-low heat, stirring occasionally, for 5 minutes. Add the zucchini, broth, jalapeño, bell pepper, corn, oregano, and salt and pepper to taste and simmer, stirring occasionally, for 20 minutes, or until the zucchini and bell pepper are tender.

Preheat the broiler. Combine the vegetable mixture and the chicken in a large (6-quart) flameproof shallow casserole, sprinkle the cheese over the top, and broil the mixture about 6 inches from the heat for 1 minute, or until the cheese is bubbling.

Old Clothes

Ropa Vieja

Ropa Vieja means old clothes. The name of this dish is quite appropriate because shredded flank steak resembles old clothes in some way. So when your family asks, "What's for dinner?" just say, "old clothes."

2 tablespoons olive oil	2 pounds flank steak
1 large onion, chopped	2 (15-ounce) cans tomato
1 large green bell pepper,	sauce
seeded and cut into thin	2 cups dry white wine
strips	$^1/_2$ teaspoon salt
1 garlic bulb, separated	$^1/_2$ teaspoon black pepper
into cloves, peeled and	
minced	

Heat the oil in a soup pot over medium heat. Add the onion, bell pepper, and garlic. Cook for 6 to 7 minutes or until the vegetables are tender, stirring occasionally. Add the steak, tomato sauce, wine, salt, and black pepper; mix well. Bring to a boil. Reduce the heat to low, cover, and simmer for 2 to 2½ hours, or until the steak is very tender, stirring occasionally.

Using 2 forks, finely shred the steak. Cover and simmer for 10 more minutes. Serve immediately.

Did You Know?

▼ ▼ ▼ ▼ ▼ ▼ ▼

LEGEND OF THE CHUPACABRA

The *chupacabra* is either a deadly menace or just a great story. Take your pick. *Chupacabra* translates into goatsucker and has been described as anything from half-alien to a vampire, or a big cat with a snake-like tongue. It does not harm humans, but has been known to suck the last drop of blood from cows, goats, and other animals.

The "X-Files" once did a program about two brothers who were exposed to some kind of alien goop and became *chupacabras*, and many people believe that this creature came from somewhere other than this planet, perhaps even as an escaped pet of some alien race. Some think that the entrance of the *chupacabra* to our world coincided with cattle and other animal mutilations back in the 1960s that took place in the United States, Mexico, and Puerto Rico. These animal killings were also blamed on aliens. Another theory attempting to explain this creature states that the *chupacabra* is some kind of genetic mutation, a mix of two different species that went terribly wrong.

It has also been rumored that American and possibly Puerto Rican authorities have captured at least one *chupacabra* but will not admit this or the results of an autopsy because even our best scientists do not know what to make of this being or where it might have come from.

There are differing opinions as to where the *chupacabra* first appeared to humans, but it is generally agreed that the creature has mainly been sighted in Puerto Rico, Florida, Texas, and Mexico. Some people claim to have actually seen a *chupacabra*; however the descriptions vary so much that it is difficult to know who might have really caught a glimpse of this mysterious creature.

Whether you believe it or not, the story of the *chupacabra* is sure to keep your children up at night.

Breads

Proverbs
Dichos

After the feast, comes the reckoning.
A un guztazo, un trancazo.

Easier said than done.
Del dicho al hecho hay largo trecho.

God helps those who help themselves.
Ayudate y el cielo te aydara.

Better to have than to wish.
Mas vale tener que desear.

Too much of a good thing is bad for you.
A la larga, lo mas dulce amarga.

Flour Tortillas

Tortillas de Harina

      Makes 1 dozen 9-inch tortillas

Making tortillas can be fun. Teach your kids how to make them. They will enjoy how creative they can be rolling out the dough. You can use tortillas as a substitute for bread for sandwiches or just about anything else. Roll up a tortilla with anything you want inside for breakfast, lunch, or dinner.

3 cups all-purpose flour	**¹/₄ teaspoon salt**
2 teaspoons baking powder	**1 cup warm water**

Mix the flour, baking powder, and salt together. Gradually stir in enough of the warm water to form a crumbly dough. Work the dough with your hands until it holds together. Turn the out onto a board and knead until smooth. Divide into 12 equal pieces and shape each piece into a smooth ball. Cover the dough lightly with plastic wrap and let rest for 15 minutes.

Flatten each ball into a 4- to 5-inch patty. Roll into about a 9-inch circle, working from the center to edges. Turn the tortilla often, stretching the dough as you carefully peel it off the board.

As each tortilla is shaped, place it in a ungreased heavy frying pan or griddle over medium-high heat. Tiny, dark blisters should appear on the dough almost immediately. Turn the tortilla and immediately press a wide spatula gently but firmly over the top. Blisters will form over most of surface as you press. Turn the tortilla again and press until the blisters turn golden brown. The tortilla should remain soft. If the tortilla sticks or scorches, reduce heat.

Stack the tortillas as they cook in a folded cloth towel inside a plastic bag. Close the bag and let the tortillas steam.

Serve the tortillas as soon as they are soft. If made ahead, let cool, remove from bag, wrap airtight and refrigerate or freeze. Reheat as directed for Corn Tortillas (page 130).

Corn Tortillas

Tortillas de Maíz

**Makes 1 dozen 6-inch or
2 dozen 4-inch tortillas**

Corn tortillas can be rolled out much the same as flour tortillas (page 129), or you can use a tortilla press lined with 2 sheets of wax paper. My grandmother made them just by patting the masa between her hands and they always came out perfectly round.

2 cups masa harina (corn tortilla flour)	**1^1/4 to 1^1/3 cups warm water**

Mix the masa flour with enough of the warm water to make a dough that holds together. Shape the dough into a smooth ball. Divide the dough into 12 equal pieces for 6-inch tortillas or into 24 equal pieces for 4-inch tortillas, and roll each piece into a ball. Cover with a damp paper towel.

To shape with a tortilla press, cover the bottom half of the press with wax paper and place a ball of dough on the paper, slightly off center, toward the hinge end of press. Lay another piece of wax paper on top and close the press tightly. Open the press and peel off the top paper. Repeat with the remaining dough, stacking the tortillas between pieces of wax paper.

To shape with a rolling pin, place a ball of dough between 2 pieces of wax paper and flatten the dough slightly with your hand. Lightly run a rolling pin over the dough several times. Flip the dough and the paper over and roll into a 4- to 6-inch circle. Carefully peel off the top paper. Repeat with the remaining dough, stacking the tortillas between pieces of wax paper.

To make a perfectly shaped tortilla, use a knife to trim edges. Or cut dough into a circle with the end of a 2 pound coffee can.

To cook, place a heavy ungreased 10- to 12-inch frying pan or griddle over medium-high heat. When the pan is hot, lift a tortilla, supporting it with the wax paper, and turn into the pan. Immediately peel off the paper. Cook the tortilla until the bottom is flecked with brown, about 30 seconds. With a wide spatula, flip the tortilla over and cook for 1 more minute. Remove from the pan and cover with foil. Repeat for remaining tortillas.

Serve immediately. If made ahead, let tortillas cool, wrap airtight and refrigerate or freeze. Tortillas may be wrapped in foil and reheated (thawed, if frozen) in a 350-degree oven for about 15 minutes. To reheat in the microwave, wrap in plastic and microwave on high for 6 to 7 seconds per tortilla.

Tortilla Tips

Here are a few tips on buying, serving and storing tortillas.

Buying and Storing Tortillas

If you are not making your own tortillas, buy packaged tortillas at your local supermarket in the ethnic foods section. Be sure to check the expiration date on the package to ensure the freshest tortillas possible. Gently bend the package to make sure they are flexible and that the tortilla edges are not dry or cracked.

Tortillas freeze well. They will keep for a few months without losing flavor in the freezer. In the refrigerator, they fare well for several days but tend to lose flavor and moisture. After opening a new package, rewrap unused tortillas in plastic or foil for storing in freezer. To thaw, gently separate, brush off ice crystals, and lay flat at room temperature for 5 minutes.

Heating and Serving Tortillas

To heat or reheat, remove tortillas from the package (thaw if frozen). If tortillas are dry and a little hard, dip your hand in water and rub tortillas lightly. Stack tortillas, wrap in foil, and heat in a 350 degree oven until hot, about 15 minutes. Or place tortillas, one at a time, on an ungreased frying pan or griddle over medium-high heat and cook, turning frequently with tongs, until soft and hot, about 30 seconds per tortilla.

To microwave, seal stacked tortillas in plastic wrap or puncture several holes in plastic packaging and microwave on high for 6 to 7 seconds per tortilla.

To toast, place tortillas on a grill 3 to 4 inches above medium-hot coals or on an ungreased frying pan or griddle over medium-high heat. Cook, turning once or twice, until very hot and slightly blistered, about 1 minute per tortilla.

To fry, pour $\frac{1}{2}$ an inch of vegetable oil into a wide frying pan and heat to 350 degrees. Cook tortillas, one at a time, turning once with tongs, until crisp and golden brown, about 1 minute. Drain on paper towels.

To serve warm, wrap warm tortillas in a cloth napkin and serve in a basket or covered dish. If desired, spread with butter or margarine, before serving, then fold or roll to keep melted butter inside.

To keep hot for several hours, seal warm tortillas in foil, wrap in a cloth and several layers of newspaper.

Tortilla-Lime Crackers

▼ ▼ ▼ ▼ ▼ ▼ **Makes 32 crackers**

These crackers are really tortilla chips flavored with butter and lime. They are so much better and more flavorful than any store-bought flavored crackers or chips you can buy. Serve with Pico de Gallo (page 70) for a great appetizer.

---

4 (8-inch) flour tortillas **1 tablespoon lime juice**
2 tablespoons butter or
  margarine, melted

Preheat the oven to 375 degrees. Brush the tortillas evenly with butter, then cut each tortilla into 8 wedges. Sprinkle the wedges evenly with lime juice and place on a baking sheet. Bake for 7 minutes.

Low-fat Flour Tortilla Chips

Makes 40 chips

▼ ▼ ▼ ▼ ▼ ▼

No one said all tortilla chips had to be made with corn tortillas. Some people prefer corn tortillas, and some people prefer flour tortillas made with wheat flour. Try these made out of flour. They too are good. They make a great bed for nachos or just to dip in some guacamole.

> **10 (7-inch) flour tortillas**

Heat the oven to 400 degrees. Stack the tortillas, 5 at a time, and cut into 8 wedge shapes. Arrange in a single layer on a baking sheet. Bake on the top rack of the oven for about 2 minutes, or until crisp. To avoid over baking, check frequently and remove from oven as soon as the chips brown.

Variation

For spicy Mexican-flavored chips, slightly moisten the tortillas by misting them with water before baking and season with garlic salt and chile powder.

Low-fat Corn Tortilla Chips

▼ ▼ ▼ ▼ ▼ ▼

Makes 48 chips

For those of you concerned with calories, here's a simple way to make tortilla chips without the frying.

> **12 (6-inch) corn tortillas**

Heat the oven to 400 degrees. Stack the tortillas, three at a time, and cut into 8 wedge shapes. Arrange in a single layer on a baking sheet. Bake on the top rack of the oven for about 3 minutes, or until crisp. To avoid over baking, check frequently and remove from the oven at the first signs of browning.

Variation: For spicy Mexican-flavored chips, slightly moisten the tortillas by misting them with water before baking and season with garlic salt, chile powder, and cayenne.

Jalapeño Cornbread

▼ ▼ ▼ ▼ ▼ ▼ **About 6 servings**

This is my kind of cornbread, made with jalapeños. It is commonly served in many places in El Paso, and we always miss it when traveling elsewhere. It's great with chili.

$^1/_2$ cup milk
$^1/_2$ cup buttermilk
1 egg
2 tablespoons vegetable oil
1 tablespoon sugar
2 teaspoons baking powder
$^1/_2$ teaspoon salt
1 cup cornmeal

$^1/_2$ cup all-purpose flour
2 tablespoons diced red
  bell pepper or pimiento
2 tablespoons minced
  jalapeños
2 tablespoons whole
  kernel corn

Heat the oven to 425 degrees. Generously grease an 8-inch cast-iron skillet or round pan. Whisk together the milk, buttermilk, egg, oil, sugar, baking powder, and salt in a medium bowl until well blended. Add the cornmeal and flour. Mix just until the dry ingredients are moistened. Fold in the red pepper, jalapeños, and corn. Pour the batter into the skillet.

Bake 20 to 25 minutes, or until light golden brown and a toothpick inserted in center comes out clean.

Mexican Cornbread

▼ ▼ ▼ ▼ ▼ ▼

12 servings

This recipe is similar to the Jalapeño Cornbread (page 136), but it's made with cream-style corn and green chiles instead of jalapeños. The result is a slightly milder taste but still different enough to get you some compliments from your guests.

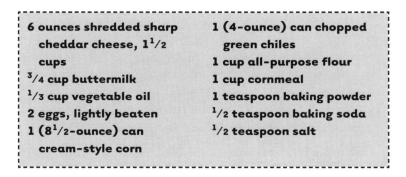

6 ounces shredded sharp
  cheddar cheese, 1¹/₂
  cups
³/₄ cup buttermilk
¹/₃ cup vegetable oil
2 eggs, lightly beaten
1 (8¹/₂-ounce) can
  cream-style corn

1 (4-ounce) can chopped
  green chiles
1 cup all-purpose flour
1 cup cornmeal
1 teaspoon baking powder
¹/₂ teaspoon baking soda
¹/₂ teaspoon salt

Heat the oven to 375 degrees. Generously grease a 1¹/₂-quart casserole. Combine the cheese, buttermilk, oil, eggs, corn, and chiles in a large bowl and mix well. Combine the flour, cornmeal, baking powder, baking soda, and salt in a small bowl and mix well. Add to the liquid ingredients and stir just until the dry ingredients are moistened. Pour into greased casserole.

Bake for 40 to 50 minutes or until deep golden brown and a toothpick inserted in center comes out clean. Cool for 10 minutes before removing from the casserole. Serve warm.

Corn Muffins with Chile Butter

▼ ▼ ▼ ▼ ▼ ▼   **Makes 8 muffins**

This is a great corn bread muffin recipe; it's good with Southwestern chili or picadillo. It is a good example of combining something Mexican and something American and coming up with Border food.

MUFFINS	CHILE BUTTER
1 (8^1/$_2$-ounce) package corn muffin mix	^{1}/$_2$ cup butter (1 stick), softened
^{1}/$_3$ cup milk	2 tablespoons chopped fresh cilantro
1 egg	1 fresh jalapeño chile, seeded and chopped
2 ounces shredded cheddar cheese, ^{1}/$_2$ cup	
3 tablespoons chopped red bell pepper	

Preheat the oven to 400 degrees. Line 8 muffin cups with paper baking cups. Prepare the corn muffin mix as directed on the package, using the milk and egg. Stir in the cheese and bell pepper. Divide the batter evenly into the paper-lined muffin cups. Bake for 18 to 22 minutes, or until the tops are light golden brown and a toothpick inserted in the center comes out clean. Remove from the pan immediately and cool on a wire rack.

Meanwhile, mix all the Chile Butter ingredients together, blending well. Serve with warm cornbread muffins.

Tequila Muffins

▼ ▼ ▼ ▼ ▼

Makes 12 muffins

These muffins are so good! Even if you opt not to use the tequila, they're still welcome at every table. Tequila doesn't leave a strong a taste in the muffins, just enough to let you know that it's there.

2 cups all-purpose flour	$^1/_2$ cup gold tequila
$^1/_2$ teaspoon salt	$^1/_4$ cup milk
2 teaspoons baking powder	$^1/_2$ teaspoon grated orange
2 tablespoons brown sugar	peel
1 egg, lightly beaten	$^1/_2$ cup pecans, chopped
2 tablespoons melted butter	

Preheat the oven to 400 degrees. Mix all the ingredients together, except the pecans. The batter will be lumpy. Then stir in the pecans and fill lightly greased muffin tins half full. Bake for 20 minutes.

Bolillos

Bolillos are similar to small loaves of French bread, but with a slightly sweet taste. They are also referred to as *francesitos* in many bakeries around the Southwest and are a staple in many Hispanic and Southwestern homes. They're delicious and can be served as a roll or used to make sandwiches. We really like them for brisket sandwiches.

$1^1/_2$ **tablespoons sugar**

1 tablespoon salt

2 tablespoons butter or
margarine

1 ($^1/_4$-ounce) package

active dry yeast

6 cups all-purpose flour

1 teaspoon cornstarch
dissolved in $^1/_2$ cup water

In a small pan, combine 2 cups of water, the sugar, salt, and butter and heat over low heat to 110 degrees. Pour into a large bowl and stir in the yeast. Let stand about 5 minutes.

Beat 5 cups of the flour into the liquid until incorporated. Knead the dough on a floured board until the dough is smooth and elastic, about 10 minutes, adding more flour as needed. Place in a greased bowl, turning to grease the top. Cover and let the dough rise in a warm place until doubled in size, about 1½ hours.

Punch the dough down and knead briefly on a lightly floured board. Divide into 16 equal pieces. Form each piece into a smooth ball. Then, by rolling and gently pulling, shape into an oblong form about 4 inches long (the center should be thicker than ends). Place the rolls 2 inches apart on greased baking sheets. Cover with a kitchen towel and let rise until almost doubled, about 35 minutes.

Preheat oven to 375 degrees. Bring the cornstarch mixture to a boil in a small pan, then cool slightly. Brush each roll with the mixture. With a sharp knife or razor blade, cut a lengthwise slash, about ¾ inch deep and 2 inches long, into the top of each roll.

Bake until the rolls are golden brown and sound hollow when tapped on the bottom, 35 to 40 minutes. Let cool on a rack. Wrap airtight to store. Bolillos will last in the refrigerator for about a week and 2 to 3 months in the freezer.

Mexican Pull-Apart Bread

▼ ▼ ▼ ▼ ▼ ▼   **Makes 2 loaves**

I love this bread; it pulls apart easily. For a little added touch, brush with additional melted butter after baking and sprinkle with chile powder and/or garlic salt.

1 cup evaporated milk	6 ounces shredded
1^1/$_2$ cups lukewarm water	Monterey Jack cheese,
1 (^{1}/$_4$-ounce) package	1^1/$_2$ cups
active dry yeast	^{1}/$_4$ cup diced green chiles
2 tablespoons sugar	1 tablespoon chile powder
1^1/$_2$ teaspoons salt	melted butter
3 to 3^1/$_2$ cups all-purpose	
flour	

Combine the evaporated milk and water in a large bowl. Dissolve the yeast in the mixture. Add the sugar, salt, and 2^1/$_2$ cups of the flour. Stir vigorously for about 1 minute. Stir in enough additional flour to make a stiff dough. Knead the dough on a floured surface, working in additional flour, until smooth and elastic, about 8 minutes. Place the dough in a buttered bowl, turning to butter the top. Cover the dough and let rise in a warm place until doubled in bulk.

Punch the dough down. Roll out to a 14 x 12-inch rectangle on a lightly floured surface. Combine the cheese, chiles, and chile powder and sprinkle over the dough. Roll up, starting at the long end. Cut into 1-inch pieces, then cut each piece into quarters. Divide the pieces of dough between 2 well-greased 8 x 4 x 2-inch loaf pans, with the cut sides turned in, not touching the sides or bottom of the Cover and let rise in a warm place until doubled in bulk, about 30 minutes.

Preheat the oven to 350 degrees. Bake for 20 to 25 minutes. Cool in the pans for 10 minutes.

Chorizo Bread

Pan de Chorizo

This *pan* (bread) is excellent for breakfast. Serve with scrambled eggs and a Sangria for Kids (page 302) and watch your family enjoy. It doesn't really need anything spread on it—the flavor speaks for itself.

5^1/$_2$ ounces chorizo

3 cups all-purpose flour

3 tablespoons grated
  Parmesan cheese

2 tablespoons brown sugar

4^1/$_2$ teaspoons baking
  powder

1 teaspoon fennel or
  caraway seeds

^{1}/$_2$ teaspoon salt

^{1}/$_4$ teaspoon baking soda

1 (8-ounce) package and
  1 (3-ounce) package
  cream cheese, softened

1 cup milk

2 eggs

^{1}/$_4$ cup butter or
  margarine, melted

Preheat the oven to 375 degrees. If necessary, remove the sausage casings. Coarsely chop the sausage and set aside. Combine the flour, Parmesan cheese, brown sugar, baking powder, fennel seeds, salt, and baking soda in a large bowl. In another bowl, beat the cream cheese until light and stir in the milk. Beat in the eggs, 1 at a time. Stir in the butter and sausages. Add to flour mixture, stirring just to moisten. Spoon the batter into a greased 9 x 5-inch loaf pan. Bake until well browned, about 55 minutes. Cool on a rack for 5 minutes. The bread can be made ahead, allowed to cool completely and stored tightly wrapped at room temperature for a day or frozen for longer storage, thawing wrapped. Reheat uncovered, in a 350 degree oven until warm, about 15 minutes.

Chocolate Bread
with **Walnuts**

Pan de Chocolate y Nuez

Enjoy the taste of Mexican chocolate in this quick bread. Slice it and lay it out on a platter with a small bowl of whipped butter for a special brunch. It's also good with a cream cheese spread.

4 tablespoons ($^1/_2$ stick) butter, softened	**$^1/_4$ cup cocoa**
$^2/_3$ cup sugar	**1 teaspoon baking soda**
1 egg	**$^1/_4$ teaspoon salt**
$1^1/_2$ cups all-purpose flour	**1 cup buttermilk**
$^1/_4$ cup pulverized Ibarra chocolate	**$^1/_2$ cup sour cream**
	$^1/_2$ cup chopped walnuts

Preheat the oven to 350 degrees. Grease and flour an 8 x 4 x 2-inch loaf pan. Cream the butter in a large mixing bowl. Gradually add the sugar, mixing well until blended. Add the egg and beat well. In a separate bowl, mix together the flour, Ibarra chocolate, cocoa, baking soda, and salt. Alternately mix the buttermilk and the flour mixture into the butter mixture. Stir in the sour cream and add the walnuts. Pour the batter into the prepared pan. Bake for 1 hour and 15 minutes or until a toothpick inserted in the center comes out clean. Cool for 15 minutes, then remove from pan. Allow to cool completely on a rack.

Bread for the
Day of the Dead

Pan de Muertos

This is a special recipe prepared for *Día de Los Muertos* (the Day of the Dead) or All-Souls Day. Some folks even make this bread for a Halloween buffet. As you celebrate life by remembering those that have gone before, enjoy a feast accompanied with *Pan de Muertos* on November 1.

$^1/_4$ cup milk	$^1/_4$ cup warm water
$^1/_4$ cup plus 2 teaspoons sugar	(about 110 degrees)
$^1/_4$ cup ($^1/_2$ stick) butter or margarine, cut into small pieces	2 eggs
	3 cups all-purpose flour
$^1/_2$ teaspoon salt	$^1/_4$ teaspoon ground cinnamon
1 ($^1/_4$-ounce) package active dry yeast	

Scald the milk in a small pan over medium-high heat. Remove from the heat and stir in $^1/_4$ cup of the sugar, butter, and salt. Let cool.

Stir the yeast into the warm water in the large bowl of an electric mixer and let stand until softened, about 5 minutes. Add the milk mixture. Separate 1 egg and add the yolk to the yeast mixture, reserving the white. Add the remaining egg and $2^1/_3$ cups of the flour. Beat until well blended.

Knead on a well-floured surface until the dough is smooth, about 10 minutes, adding more flour as needed. Place in a greased bowl and turn to grease the top. Cover and let rise in a warm place until doubled, about $1^1/_2$ hours. Punch down the dough and knead briefly.

Cut off ½ cup of the dough, wrap in plastic, and set aside. Divide the remaining dough into 3 equal pieces; shape each piece into a rope about 12 inches long. Braid the ropes, pressing the ends together to hold securely. Place the dough on a greased baking sheet and join the ends to make a small wreath. Divide the reserved dough in half and shape each portion into a bone. Cross the bones and place across wreath.

Preheat the oven to 350 degrees. Cover and let rise in a warm place until puffy, about 30 minutes. Lightly beat the reserved egg white and brush over the bread. Mix the cinnamon and remaining sugar and sprinkle over the loaf, avoiding the bones. Bake until richly browned, about 35 minutes. Cut into wedges and serve warm.

Sweet Bread

Pan Dulce

Makes 14 buns

This Mexican pastry is beautiful and good to eat, and not difficult to make either. In some parts of the Southwest, they call this *pan de huevo* (egg bread) or *molletes*. No matter what you call it, have a piece with some Mexican Coffee (page 283) or a tall glass of milk and you'll leave the table with a big smile on your face.

---

6 tablespoons ($^3/_4$ stick) butter or margarine, cut into chunks	**STREUSEL**
	1 cup sugar
1 cup milk	$1^1/_3$ cup all-purpose flour
1 ($^1/_4$-ounce) package active dry yeast	7 tablespoons butter or margarine, cold
1 teaspoon salt	4 egg yolks
$^1/_3$ cup sugar	2 tablespoons cocoa or ground baking chocolate
5 cups all-purpose flour	
2 eggs	1 egg beaten with 2 tablespoons milk

Combine the butter and milk in a small pan and heat over low heat to 110 degrees (the butter need not melt completely). Meanwhile, in the large bowl of an electric mixer, combine the yeast, salt, sugar, and 2 cups of the flour. Pour in the warmed milk mixture and beat, scraping the sides frequently, on medium speed for 2 minutes. Blend in the 2 eggs and 1 more cup of flour and beat on high speed for 2 more minutes. With a spoon, gradually beat in enough of the remaining flour to form a stiff dough.

Knead the dough on a floured board until smooth and elastic, about 5 minutes. Place in a greased bowl and turn to grease the top. Cover and let rise in a warm place until doubled, about 1½ hours.

Meanwhile, prepare the streusel. Stir together the sugar and flour. With a pastry blender or your fingers, mix in the butter until fine crumbs form. With a fork, blend in the egg yolks. Divide the streusel in half. Stir the cocoa into one of the halves.

Punch the dough down and turn out onto a floured board. Divide into 14 equal pieces and shape seven of the balls into seashells by patting dough into 3-inch rounds. Squeeze 1/4 cup of plain or chocolate streusel into a firm ball, then press it over the top of each round. Score in a crosshatch pattern or with slightly curved parallel lines to resemble a scallop shell.

Roll the remaining dough into 4 x 8-inch ovals. Top each piece of dough with 3 tablespoons of plain or chocolate streusel. To make horns, roll the oval from the short end; stop halfway and fold in the sides, and finish rolling. Curl the ends to form a crescent. To make ears of corn, completely roll up ovals from short end. Slash the tops crosswise with a knife, cutting halfway through dough.

Place the buns about 2 inches apart on greased baking sheets. Cover lightly and let rise until doubled, about 45 minutes. Brush with the egg mixture and bake in a 375 degree oven until lightly browned, 15 to 17 minutes.

Piloncillo Bread

Pan de Piloncillo

I first came across *Pan de Piloncillo* at the famous Bowie Bakery, here in El Paso. Although this recipe isn't by any means the same as Mr. Marquez's (owner of the Bowie Bakery), it gives you an idea of what *piloncillo* (brown sugar) bread should taste like, and it's delicious. Piloncillo can be found in most supermarkets in the Mexican or international food aisle. If for some reason you cannot find it, dry-out some dark brown sugar by leaving it on a baking sheet and then break into semi-large pieces to use in the recipe.

> **2 cups *piloncillo*,**   **1 recipe Pan Dulce**
> **in ¹/₄- to ¹/₂-inch chunks**   **(page 146), without**
> **the streusel topping**

Add the piloncillo to the dough after kneading. Bake in the same manner as Pan Dulce (page 146).

Orange Bread

Pan de Naranja

Another good morning breakfast bread, this one made with orange peel. Serve with orange marmalade and a sprinkling of cinnamon and enjoy. It also makes for a good snack with a mid-afternoon cup of coffee.

4 cups all-purpose flour	1 cup (2 sticks) butter,
$^3/_4$ cup sugar	at room temperature
1 ($^1/_4$-ounce) package	1 cup ground almonds
active dry yeast	$^1/_2$ cup finely chopped
1 cup warm milk	candied orange peel
4 eggs	

Sift the flour and sugar in a large mixing bowl. In a separate bowl, stir the yeast into the warm milk and let it stand for 5 minutes to dissolve. Add the dissolved yeast to the flour and sugar. Add the eggs and beat vigorously with a large wooden spoon. Add the softened butter and mix well. Turn the dough onto a lightly-floured board. Knead for several minutes until it is smooth and elastic. Place the dough in a greased bowl, cover, and let rise in a warm place until double in bulk.

Preheat the oven to 350 degrees and grease two 5 x 9-inch loaf pans. Add the almonds and candied orange peel and knead again until well blended. Shape into 2 loaves and place in the greased loaf pans. Cover and let rise until almost doubled in bulk, about 30 minutes. Bake for 50 to 60 minutes.

Mexican Fruitcake

Pastel de Posadas

10 servings

This Mexican fruitcake is quite delicious, though heavy.

2 cups all-purpose flour	**2 eggs**
1 teaspoon baking soda	**1 cup sugar**
1 teaspoon ground cinnamon	**$^1/_2$ cup (1 stick) butter, melted**
$^1/_2$ teaspoon ground nutmeg	**1 cup applesauce**
1 cup raisins	**1 tablespoon maple syrup**
1 cup chopped nuts	**Jarabe (recipe follows)**
1 cup chopped candied fruits	

Preheat the oven to 375 degrees. Grease and flour a 10-inch tube pan. Sift together 1 cup of the flour, the baking soda, cinnamon, and nutmeg and set aside. In another bowl, sift the remaining 1 cup flour over the raisins, nuts, and candied fruit. Toss to mix well.

Cream the eggs and sugar in a large mixing bowl until light. Add the butter, applesauce, and maple syrup. Stir the flour and spices into the egg mixture. Turn the floured fruit and nut mixture into the batter and stir with a wooden spoon. Pour the batter into the prepared pan and smooth the surface with a rubber spatula. Bake for 1 hour, or until a cake tester inserted in the center comes out clean. Cool in the pan on wire rack for 30 minutes. Invert and cool completely.

Soak the cheesecloth with *jarabe* and wrap the fruitcake in the cheesecloth covering all sides. Wrap well in foil. Moisten the cheesecloth with additional syrup every few days for a week. The rum will flavor the cake and help preserve it. The cake keeps 4 to 5 days at room temperature.

Jarabe

---

¹/₂ **cup sugar**	**1 cup hot water**
2 tablespoons instant	¹/₂ **cup rum**
coffee	

Combine the sugar, coffee, and water in a small saucepan. Bring to a boil and continue cooking until the syrup is thickened. Remove from the heat and add the rum.

Kings' Cake

Rosca de los Reyes

Makes 2 ring-shaped loaves

King's Cake is made and served during Epiphany or Carnival, Mexico's equivalent to Mardi Gras. It's a wonderful dessert or a great snack. Feel free to melt a little Mexican chocolate and drizzle it on top.

2 (^{1}/4-ounce) packages active dry yeast
^{1}/2 cup warm water
4 cups all-purpose flour
2 eggs
^{1}/2 cup sugar
^{1}/4 teaspoon salt
6 egg yolks
1 teaspoon grated lemon peel
1 teaspoon grated orange peel

1 cup (2 sticks) butter, at room temperature
2 cups finely chopped candied fruits
^{1}/2 cup chopped pecans
^{1}/2 cup raisins
2 tiny plastic baby dolls
Candied Fruits and nuts, for garnish
Sherry Glaze (recipe follows)

Preheat the oven to 375 degrees and grease two baking sheets. Dissolve the yeast in the warm water. Add enough of the flour to form a dough. Shape the dough into a ball and place in a warm spot until it has doubled in size, about 30 minutes.

Sift the rest of the flour into a mound. Form a well in the center and break 2 whole eggs into it. Add sugar and salt. Mix together and then add the egg yolks, 2 tablespoons water, grated lemon and orange peel, the butter, and the risen dough. Knead until smooth and elastic. Place in a greased bowl and allow to rise in a warm place until nearly doubled, about 20 to 30 minutes.

Combine the candied fruits, nuts, and raisins. Knead the fruits and nuts into the dough until evenly distributed. Divide the dough in half and form each half into a long roll. Join the ends of each roll to form rings. Hide 2 tiny baby dolls in dough and place on the prepared baking sheets. Let rise in a warm place until doubled in size, about 1 hour.

Bake for 30 minutes, or until nicely browned. Drizzle Sherry Glaze over the bread while still hot. Decorate with candied fruits and nuts.

Sherry Glaze

2 cups confectioners' sugar, sifted

$^1/_3$ cup sherry

Mix the sugar with sherry until icing is smooth.

Did You Know?

▼ ▼ ▼ ▼ ▼ ▼ ▼

MATACHINES

I've watched the *matachines* dance in front of our neighborhood church since I was very little (a long time now!), but not until I started researching *matachines* did I understand the significance of the individual dancers.

As with the Mariachis, the origins of the *matachines* are a little fuzzy. There is some opinion that the ritual dance began in the age of Montezuma. Yet others believe that it originated in Spain and like a lot of things, made its way across the waters to be enjoyed and adapted by yet another culture. Whatever its true history, the *matachin* dance and dancers have been with us for at least hundreds of years.

The dance itself is a portrayal of good versus evil, Christianity versus paganism. In Pueblo communities and tribes, the leader, *El Monarca* is said to have been Montezuma himself. There is *La Malinche*, representing innocence; she is usually danced by a young girl in a pastel dress or white First Communion dress. To balance out goodness, innocence, and virginity, we have *El Toro*, the bull, portraying evil. To round off the atmosphere of the dance, you have *El Abuelo*, (the Grandfather) who used to scare young children into behaving and *La Perejundia* a man dressed as an old woman. In more recent times, *El Abuelo* and *La Perejundia* act more like comic figures than dancers to offset the solemnity of the dance. The *Abuelo*, while joking around, keeps order and directs the different dances. The *Perejundia*, or *La Vieja* (old woman), plays around with the *Abuelo* and attempts to kill *El Toro*.

Costumes vary from town to town and region to region. In El Segundo Barrio where I'm from, the *matachines'* main color scheme is red with a picture of La Virgen de Guadalupe on the shirt-front or back. Most costumes are made by the dancers themselves. Some dancers start at a very early age. I've seen four- and five-year-old kids out there. Patience is required as the elders instruct them in the art of creating their costumes. This is an extraordinarily beautiful piece of work.

In the Segundo Barrio, a drummer keeps the beat during the lengthy dances. In other communities, a violinist and a guitarist accompany the dancers. Each dancer carries a *guaje* (rattle) in one hand and a three-pronged trident in the other.

Whatever traditions, beliefs, or customs have shaped the individual group of *matachine* dancers in your own community, it is important to note that we each take pride in another aspect of our cultural heritage through the wonderful *danza de los matachines* (dance of the *matachines*).

Main Dishes

Proverbs
Dichos

Home is where the heart is.
A donde el corazón se inclina, el pie camina.

Grin and bear it.
A lo hecho, pecho.

Too many cooks spoil the broth.
Obra de común, obra de ningún.

Diligence is the mother of good luck.
La diligencia es la madre de la buena ventura.

Do as I say, not as I do.
Haz lo que bien digo, no lo que mal hago.

Chile Relleno Pie

Chile Relleno Torta

▼　▼　▼　▼　▼　▼　　　**8 to 10 servings**

Here's another time saver. Chile Relleno Torta cuts out dipping and frying individual filled chiles by combining all the ingredients in a casserole-type dish. Same great taste, lots of time saved.

8 ounces grated cheddar cheese, 2 cups	**1²/₃ cups half-and-half**
8 ounces grated Monterey jack cheese, 2 cups	**1 (4-ounce) can diced green chiles or roasted, peeled, and seeded green chiles**
5 eggs	
¹/₃ cup all-purpose flour	**¹/₂ cup salsa**

Preheat the oven to 375 degrees. Grease a 10-inch pie plate. Mix the grated cheeses and spread evenly in the prepared pie plate. Beat the eggs, add the flour slowly, and then beat in the half-and-half. Strain the mixture if it is lumpy. Pour over the cheeses in the pie plate. Carefully spoon the chiles over the surface, and then spread the salsa over the top. Bake for about 45 minutes, or until the center is set.

Chicken and Rice

Arroz con Pollo

6 servings

Arroz con Pollo (Chicken and Rice)—there is no better comfort food than this. The combination of the chicken and rice with all the tasty seasonings, creates a meal in itself. Though not listed in this recipe, you might experiment by adding a can of Mexican beer to the broth for a unique change of taste.

CHICKEN BROTH
2¹/₂ to 3 pounds chicken
  parts
1 clove garlic, minced
1 teaspoon salt
1 bay leaf

CHICKEN AND RICE
3 tablespoons vegetable oil
2 cups long-grain white rice

2 tablespoons chopped
  onion
3 tablespoons diced green
  pepper
¹/₂ teaspoon salt
¹/₂ teaspoon pepper
Dash garlic salt
1 (8-ounce) can tomato
  sauce
1 cup hot water

To make the chicken broth, place the chicken in a soup pot with 1¾ quarts water and bring to a quick boil, covered. Add the garlic, salt, and bay leaf and cook the chicken over medium heat, covered, until the chicken is tender. Add hot water in small amounts if needed during cooking. When the chicken is cooked, remove it from the liquid. Bone and dice 2 cups of chicken and reserve the rest for another use. Reserve 4 to 5 cups chicken broth and save the rest for another use.

To make the chicken and rice, heat the oil in a skillet, add the rice, and brown over medium heat. Sauté the onion and green pepper until tender. Add the chicken stock, salt, pepper, and garlic salt and mix well. Add the tomato sauce. Cook the rice over medium heat for 45 to 50 minutes, covered and stirring occasionally. Add hot water if the rice becomes dry. When the rice is tender, add the chicken and mix well. Cover until ready to serve.

Asadero Chicken Bundles

▼ ▼ ▼ ▼ ▼ ▼   **6 servings**

This is the Tex-Mex version of Chicken Cordon Bleu. Instead of ham and Swiss cheese, we use green chile and asadero cheese. The taste is absolutely delicious. Make extras for lunches.

6 skinless and boneless chicken breasts	**1 tablespoon McCormick's Mexican Seasoning**
6 slices asadero cheese	**2 tablespoons butter**
12 strips green chile	**1 recipe Chile con Queso**
1 cup dried bread crumbs	**(page 79)**

Preheat the oven to 350 degrees. Flatten the chicken breasts by placing them between 2 sheets of wax paper and pounding with a mallet. Place 1 slice of asadero cheese on the chicken and 2 strips of green chile on top of the asadero. Roll up each chicken breast and fasten with a toothpick.

Mix the bread crumbs with the Mexican seasoning. Coat the chicken bundles in the bread crumbs. Melt the butter in a large skillet. Brown the chicken on both sides. Place on a greased baking sheet and bake the chicken for 30 to 40 minutes.

Remove the chicken from the oven and place on a warmed platter. Pour hot Chile con Queso over the chicken. Serve hot.

Chicken Chile Verde

▼ ▼ ▼ ▼ ▼ ▼ ▼ **12 servings**

This Chicken Chile Verde is delicious served as the recipe describes. It is also excellent as a filling in burritos or *gorditas* (fried masa pockets). You will soon discover your own spice threshold, but remember, you can always add spice, but you can't take it out. Go slow.

3 pounds skinless and boneless chicken thighs, cut into $1/2$-inch pieces	**5 cups frozen corn kernels, thawed**
Salt and pepper	**6 cups low-salt chicken broth**
5 tablespoons all-purpose flour	**12 tomatillos, husked and coarsely chopped**
7 tablespoons olive oil	**2 tablespoons chopped fresh oregano or 1 tablespoon dried oregano**
3 cups chopped onion	
3 tablespoons chopped garlic	**2 tablespoons chili powder**
$1^1/2$ cups chopped fresh Anaheim chiles (about 4 chiles)	**1 tablespoon ground cumin**
	1 teaspoon paprika
	2 cinnamon sticks
2 green bell peppers cut lengthwise into $1/4$-inch strips	**1 cup chopped fresh cilantro**
	Tortilla chips

Season the chicken with salt and pepper and coat with the flour. Heat 1 tablespoon of the oil in a large heavy skillet over medium-high heat. Add the chicken to skillet and sauté until golden brown, about 10 minutes. You will probably have to do this in batches, but do not crowd the skillet. Transfer the chicken to a large pot. Heat 2 tablespoons of oil in the same skillet over medium-high heat. Add the onion and garlic and sauté until tender, about 5 minutes. Transfer to the pot with the chicken. Heat 1 tablespoon of oil in the skillet over medium-high heat. Add the Anaheim chile and bell pepper. Sauté until tender, about 4 minutes. Transfer to the pot with the chicken.

Heat 1 tablespoon of oil in the skillet. Sauté half of the corn until tender, about 2 minutes. Transfer to the pot with chicken. Repeat with remaining 1 tablespoon oil and remaining corn. Add the chicken broth, tomatillos, oregano, chili powder, cumin, paprika, and cinnamon sticks to pot. Bring liquid to a boil. Reduce the heat and simmer, stirring occasionally, until the mixture thickens and the flavors blend, about 30 minutes. This dish can be prepared 1 day ahead. Refrigerate until cool, cover, and keep refrigerated. Reheat over medium heat.

Just before serving, mix the cilantro into Chile Verde. Transfer to a large serving bowl. Garnish with tortilla chips and serve.

Chicken Enchiladas in **Green Sauce**

Enchiladas de Gallina en Salsa Verde

4 servings

There are many ways to prepare this most traditional Mexican border dish. This is one of them. For an extra touch, spoon a dollop of sour cream on top of each serving.

3 skinless and boneless chicken breasts	**12 ounces grated Colby or 1 cup Monterey Jack cheese, plus additional for topping**
Vegetable oil	
¹/₄ medium onion, diced	
¹/₂ teaspoon chili powder	**8 (6-inch) corn tortillas**
¹/₂ teaspoon ground cumin	**Salsa Verde (page 77)**
¹/₂ teaspoon garlic powder	

Boil the chicken breasts until cooked and cut in cubes. Heat the oil in a large pan and sauté the chicken, onion, chili powder, cumin, and garlic powder until the onions are translucent. Allow the chicken to cool, then add the cheese. Heat the remaining oil in a skillet and sauté the tortillas on medium-high heat on each side until soft, about 3 to 4 seconds per side. Set the tortillas aside, until cool enough to touch, stacking to prevent drying. Place the chicken mixture in the center of each tortilla and roll. Place the enchiladas in a 9-inch square dish and cover with the Salsa Verde. Sprinkle the additional grated cheese on top and bake in a 350 degree oven for 15 to 20 minutes until the cheese is hot and bubbly.

Chicken Mole

Pollo en Mole

8 to 10 servings

Our family wedding and quinceañera receptions and dinners would never be complete without a piping bowl of chicken mole. Some people call it choco-late chicken. Even though there is some Mexican chocolate in the sauce, the chile is what you really taste.

Two (3-pound) chickens, cut into pieces	Dash ground cumin
Salt	Dash garlic powder
2 tablespoons bacon grease or olive oil	Dash ground cinnamon
2 cups Mole (page 88)	1 rounded teaspoon peanut butter
1$^{1}/_{2}$ cups chicken broth	$^{1}/_{8}$ round Mexican chocolate
$^{1}/_{2}$ teaspoon salt	2 teaspoons sugar
Dash ground coriander	1 heaping teaspoon raisins
	Hot buttered tortillas.

Simmer the chicken in water to cover until tender, adding salt to taste. Cook until the chicken is tender. When cool enough to handle, skin and bone the chicken. Heat bacon grease and add the Mole. Fry for a few minutes, add the remaining ingredients (except for the buttered tortillas), and simmer for 30 min-utes. Add a little left over chicken broth (or water if no chicken broth is left) if the mixture gets too thick. Place the chicken in the sauce and heat thoroughly. Serve with hot buttered tortillas.

Turkey Enchiladas with Green Chile Sour Cream

Enchiladas de Pavo con Crema de Chile Verde

 **2 dozen enchiladas**

Out of ways to use left-over Thanksgiving turkey? Not to worry. Your family will enjoy these so much you'll need to prepare them several times. Needless to say, we get a very large turkey every year.

FILLING
- ¹/₄ cup plus 1 tablespoon vegetable oil
- 4 cups shredded cooked turkey
- ¹/₂ medium onion, minced
- ³/₄ teaspoon ground cumin
- ¹/₂ teaspoon garlic powder
- Salt
- 8 ounces shredded cheese, 2 cups (your preference)

SAUCE
- 1 (10-ounce) can cream of chicken or cream of mushroom soup
- 1 (8-ounce) container sour cream
- 1 (4¹/₂-ounce) can chopped green chiles
- 2 tablespoons green chile salsa, canned or homemade
- 2 tablespoons chopped fresh cilantro
- ¹/₄ teaspoon ground cumin
- 24 corn tortillas

Heat 1 tablespoon of oil in a skillet. Add the turkey, onion, ¹/₂ teaspoon cumin, garlic powder, and salt to taste and heat thoroughly. Remove from the stove and cool slightly. Add 1 cup of the cheese. Set aside.

Preheat the oven to 350 degrees. Whisk together the soup, sour cream, chiles, salsa, cilantro, and ¹/₄ teaspoon cumin. Heat thoroughly. Heat the remaining oil in a deep skillet and cook the tortillas until soft, about 4 seconds per side. Remove the tortillas from the skillet. Place 2 heaping tablespoons of the turkey mixture in the center of each tortilla and roll up. Place each filled tortilla in 9 x 13-inch baking dish Continue until all the tortillas are filled and rolled. Pour the sauce over the tortillas. Sprinkle with the remaining cheese. Bake for 10 to 15 minutes.

Chicken or Beef Fajitas
▼ ▼ ▼ ▼

5 to 6 servings

Now we're getting true Southwest! Grilled chicken or beef fajitas with a ton of grilled onions on top and fresh hot salsa on the side. Also, make sure you have some guacamole on hand. *Una comida maravillosa!* (An excellent meal!)

FOR BEEF
3 cups orange juice
$1/2$ cup chopped onion
2 tablespoons dried oregano
2 tablespoons pepper
1 tablespoon minced garlic
1 teaspoon meat tenderizer
1 teaspoon salt
$2^1/2$ pounds skirt steak, cut crosswise into 4 to 6 pieces

FOR CHICKEN
1 cup dry red wine
$1/2$ cup chopped onion

2 teaspoons dried oregano
2 teaspoons ground cumin
1 teaspoon pepper
1 tablespoon Worcestershire sauce
2 teaspoons soy sauce
6 skinless and boneless chicken breasts, cut into strips

Grilled onions
Flour tortillas
Pico de Gallo (page 70)
Avocado Salsa (page 83)

Combine all the ingredients for either beef or chicken. Marinate the beef or chicken in the refrigerator, a minimum of 2 hours for chicken and overnight for beef. Remove the meat from the liquid and discard the marinade. To barbecue, grill 4 to 6 inches from coals. Or cook on the stove in a large nonstick skillet over medium-high heat, 5 minutes for steak, 4 to 6 minutes for chicken. Serve warm with flour tortillas, grilled onions, and Pico de Gallo or Avocado Salsa.

Baked Burritos

Chimichangas

8 chimichangas

Some Chimichangas (baked burritos) are deep-fried and some are baked. It all depends on your own taste. Both are quite good. Your kids will love saying Chimichangas.

1¹/2 pounds beef chuck roast	2 medium tomatoes, seeded and chopped
1 cup chopped onion	3 tablespoons butter, melted
1 to 2 teaspoons crushed red pepper flakes	¹/2 cup salsa
1 teaspoon coarsely ground black pepper	¹/2 cup sour cream
8 (9- to 10-inch) flour tortillas	¹/2 cup Guacamole (page 82)
1 (14-ounce) can refried beans	

Combine the beef, ¹/2 cup onion, and red pepper flakes with 6 cups of water in a large saucepan. Cover and cook over medium-high heat until the mixture comes to a boil. Reduce the heat to medium and cook 1 to 1¹/2 hours, or until the beef is fork tender, stirring occasionally and adding water if necessary. Remove the beef from the water. When it is cool enough to handle, shred the beef, using 2 forks to pull the meat apart along the grain.

Preheat the oven to 350 degrees. Spread ¹/4 cup refried beans, ¹/2 cup shredded beef, 1 tablespoon onion, and 2 tablespoons tomato in center of each tortilla. Fold the sides toward center and fold the ends up. Place, seam side down, on an ungreased baking sheet. Brush each burrito with melted butter.

Bake for 30 to 40 minutes or until golden brown and thoroughly heated. Serve with salsa, sour cream, and Guacamole.

Rolled Tacos

Flautas

Makes 6 flautas

You can vary the type of filling used in Flautas to suit your own taste. Some suggestions are: cheese, beans, shredded beef, chicken, turkey, pork, or *Barbacoa* (page 171). Whatever filling you decide to use, Flautas, with a few garnishes like sour cream, salsa, and guacamole, will be a big hit at any meal.

> **Half recipe *Barbacoa***   **Chopped onion (optional)**
>   **(page 171)**   **Salsa Fresca (page 68)**
> **6 (6-inch) corn tortillas**   **(optional)**
> **Vegetable oil**   **Sour cream (optional)**

Prepare the *Barbacoa* and keep warm. Heat the tortillas, one at a time, in an ungreased frying pan or griddle over medium-high heat, turning once, until flexible, about 10 seconds per side. Remove from the pan and spoon 2 to 3 tablespoons of filling down the center of the tortilla (you may have extra filling). Roll up tightly and secure with wooden toothpicks or skewers.

Pour oil to a depth of ½ inch into a wide frying pan and heat to 350 degrees on a deep-frying thermometer. Using tongs, cook each roll, turning once, until golden brown, about 30 seconds. Drain the flautas on paper towels. If desired, offer chopped onion, salsa, and sour cream to add to individual servings.

Fried Masa Pockets

Gorditas

4 servings

It's time to try your imagination again. These Gorditas have a ground beef filling, but just as with burritos, tacos, or enchiladas, you can come up with your own filling. Everyone is still sure to enjoy.

FILLING

1 pound ground beef
1 small onion, chopped
2 teaspoons salt
$1/4$ teaspoon pepper
1 teaspoon garlic salt
$1/4$ teaspoon chili powder

SHELL

2 cups masa harina
1 teaspoon baking powder
2 teaspoons salt

2 pieces fried bacon, crumbled
2 tablespoons shredded longhorn cheese
Vegetable oil for frying

GARNISHES

Shredded lettuce
Sliced or diced tomatoes
Grated cheese
Chile sauce
Salsa

Sauté the beef and onion together. Add the salt, pepper, garlic salt, and chili powder and cook until the meat is browned through.

While the meat is cooking, make the dough for the shells. Combine the masa harina, baking powder, and salt. Add water (about 1 cup total), a little at a time to ensure that the masa will hold together. Mix with your hands. Add the crumbled bacon and shredded cheese and combine well. Pinch off a small portion of dough and roll into a 2-inch ball. With a quick patting motion, flatten the ball to $1/2$ inch thickness about 3 inches in diameter. Fry in hot oil until golden brown, turning once. Drain. Make a pocket in the middle of the gordita, open slightly (like a taco shell), and stuff with the meat mixture, lettuce, tomatoes, and cheese. Serve with your favorite chile sauce or salsa.

Barbecue

Barbacoa

Barbacoa is wonderful for weekend fiestas. A five-pound roast goes a long way if the meat is shredded. Serve with warm tortillas and let everyone make their own tacos. Using lamb makes it a bit fancier.

Chile Seasoning	**Salt**
(recipe follows)	**3 tablespoons white wine**
5-pound bone-in beef	**vinegar**
chuck roast or 6- to	**Warm Tomato Salsa**
6½-pound leg of lamb,	**(recipe follows)**
boned and cut into	
chunks	

Prepare the Chile Seasoning and set aside. Season the meat to taste with salt and sprinkle with vinegar. Cover and refrigerate for 2 to 3 hours.

Preheat the oven to 350 degrees. Drain the meat and place in a 5- to 6-quart pan. Spread the seasoning over the meat. Cover and bake until tender when pierced, 2½ to 3 hours. About 20 minutes before serving, prepare the Tomato Salsa. Keep warm.

To serve, lift the meat from the pan and cut or shred into bite-size pieces. Offer Warm Tomato Salsa (page 173) to spoon over meat.

Chile Seasoning

4 dried New Mexico or
California chiles
2 dried ancho chiles
4 dried red hot chiles
$^1/_2$ cup hot water
10 cloves garlic
1 tablespoon dried oregano
2 tablespoons whole cloves

2 tablespoons cumin seeds
1 tablespoon cracked black
pepper
$^1/_2$ teaspoon ground
cinnamon
$^1/_2$ cup canned tomatillos,
drained.

Discard the stems and seeds from the chiles. Tear or break into pieces. Cover with the water and let stand until soft, about 20 minutes. Drain. In a blender, combine the drained chiles, garlic, oregano, cloves, cumin seeds, black pepper, cinnamon, and tomatillos. Whirl until the chiles are finely chopped. Makes approximately 5 cups.

Warm Tomato Salsa

Makes about 2 cups

2 tablespoons butter or margarine	4 large tomatoes, peeled, seeded, and cut into chunks
1 large onion, finely chopped	Salt and pepper
1 green bell pepper, seeded and chopped	

Melt the butter in an 8- to 10-inch frying pan over medium-high heat. Add the onion and bell pepper. Cook, stirring, until the vegetables are soft, about 10 minutes. Add the tomatoes and cook until heated through, about 2 more minutes. Season to taste with salt and pepper.

Brisket

I can't remember any celebration in our house where we haven't made brisket. Even if there are other meats or main dishes, we still cook brisket. If there is any left over, it makes great sandwiches or burritos for school and work lunches. Hint: You can put it in the oven before you go to bed and it'll be done when you get up in the morning.

8- to 10-pound beef brisket, trimmed and washed	1 package prepared onion soup mix
2 cups tequila	Our Best Barbecue Sauce (recipe follows)

Preheat the oven to 275 degrees. Place the brisket in a large roasting pan. Mix together the tequila, onion soup mix, and 4 cups of water. Pour over the meat, cover with aluminum foil, and bake for 8 to 10 hours, or until the brisket is tender.

Let the brisket cool to room temperature, take it out of the pan, wrap it in foil, and refrigerate for at least 6 hours.

Preheat the oven to 350 degrees. Slice the brisket across the grain while cold, layer in a large pan, cover with Our Best Barbecue Sauce, and heat for 30 to 45 minutes, or until warmed through.

Barbecue Sauce

2 cups catsup
$^1/_4$ cup maple syrup
$^1/_4$ cup orange marmalade
$^1/_4$ cup prepared mustard
2 cloves garlic, minced
$^1/_2$ onion, finely chopped
2 teaspoons
   Worcestershire sauce

$^1/_2$ teaspoon salt
1 teaspoon ground black
   pepper
2 jalapeño chiles, diced
$^1/_4$ cup lemon juice
$^1/_2$ cup tequila

Put all the ingredients in a saucepan and cook over medium heat until the mixture comes to a boil. Makes about 3 cups.

Roast Meat

Carne Asada

8 to 10 servings

Barbecue is an all-time favorite at our house. Kick up the flavor of this dish by placing pickled jalapeño slices over the meat right before serving. You can use leftovers to make a sandwich using *Bolillos* (page 140) and Chile con Queso (page 79).

> **3 pounds top round steak,**   **Freshly ground pepper**
>   **2 inches thick**   **1 large orange, halved**

Trim off all the fat from the steak and make diagonal cuts about $3/8$-inch deep and 1-inch apart. Rub lightly with pepper. Grill 4 or 5 inches above a solid bed of medium-hot coals until the meat is done to your liking, about 10 minutes on each side for rare. Transfer the meat to carving board. Squeeze orange juice evenly over the meat. Slice the meat thinly on the diagonal and moisten with accumulated juices.

Short Ribs in Chipotle Sauce

Costilla de Res en Salsa Chipotle

▼ ▼ ▼ ▼ ▼ ▼ **4 servings**

Short ribs over rice, a hearty dish for winter months. You can see here that you can take a basic American meal and turn it into a Border delight just by adding a few spices.

---

4 lean beef short ribs, cracked and trimmed of visible fat (about 4 pounds)
1 large onion, chopped
2 canned chipotle chiles in adobo sauce or 2 dried chipotle chiles

2^1/$_2$ cups chicken broth
Salt (optional)
About 3 cups hot cooked rice

Preheat the oven to 400 degrees. Arrange the ribs and onion in a deep 4- to 5-quart pan, tucking the chiles among ribs. Add 1 cup of the broth and cover tightly. Bake until the meat easily pulls away from bones, about 3½ hours. Uncover and bake until the meat is browned, about 15 minutes. With a slotted spoon, transfer the ribs and onion to a platter and keep warm.

Add the remaining 1½ cups broth to pan, scraping up the browned bits and mashing the chiles with the back of a spoon. Skim and discard the fat. Bring the juices to a boil. If desired, season to taste with salt. Serve the ribs with the onion, juices, and hot rice.

Steak Tampiqueña

Carne Tampiqueña

There is a restaurant in El Paso called La Hacienda that makes the best Steak Tampiqueña we've ever tasted. The restaurant is located by the Rio Grande and holds great historical significance. It was built in 1850 by Simeon Hart, whose son, Juan Hart went on to found the El Paso Times newspaper. Two hundred years earlier, Conquistador Juan de Oñate held what El Paso now calls the original First Thanksgiving dinner with the Native Americans on the very same piece of land the restaurant stands on. If you are in El Paso, try this place, you'll really enjoy it.

2 dried ancho chiles	**6 limes**
1 small tomato	**6 pieces asadero cheese**
1 clove garlic	**6 tortillas**
$^1/_2$ large onion	**Guacamole (see page 82)**
Salt	
1 tablespoon vegetable oil	**Warm flour tortillas**
1 small onion, sliced	**Beans**
6 thin strips sirloin steak	

Toast the chiles in a skillet over medium heat for 30 seconds to 1 minute on each side, but do not allow them to scorch. Tear the chiles into pieces, place them in a bowl, cover them with boiling water, and allow them to rehydrate and soften for 15 minutes. Place the chiles in a blender with the tomato, garlic, onion, and salt to taste and whirl until smooth. Heat the oil, grill the onions and keep warm.

Season the meat with salt and the juice from 3 limes. Grill or barbecue it, preferably over a high flame. Grill the cheese very quickly, taking care that it doesn't burn. On each plate, stack a strip of meat, a piece of grilled cheese, a tortilla dipped in the ancho chile salsa and folded in half, half a lime, guacamole, and a few slices of grilled onion. Serve with additional hot tortillas and beans.

T-Bone Steak with Tequila and Jalapeño Jelly

▼ ▼ ▼ ▼ ▼ ▼ ▼ **2 servings**

No matter how you slice it, steak and tequila go great together. Plus, the jalapeño jelly gives an extra kick by combining the hot and the sweet. If you give the bones to your dog, give the pooch a little extra water.

$^1/_4$ cup tequila

2 tablespoons sugar

1 tablespoon chopped fresh cilantro

1 teaspoon grated lime peel

$^1/_2$ teaspoon salt

2 tablespoons fresh lime juice

2 tablespoons jalapeño pepper jelly (page 44)

2 (10-ounce) T-bone steaks, about $^3/_4$ inch thick

Combine all the ingredients except the steaks in a shallow glass baking dish and mix well. Add the steaks and turn to coat. Cover and refrigerate for at least 4 hours. Turn the steaks at least once.

Heat the grill. When the grill is ready (the coals should be white), remove the steaks from marinade, reserving marinade. Place the steaks 4 to 6 inches from coals. Cook for 10 to 15 minutes, or until the steaks are of the desired doneness, turning once and brushing occasionally with reserved marinade. (Or you can broil the steaks. Place the broiler pan 4 to 6 inches from the heat and proceed as described above.)

Roast Beef with Chipotle Rub

▼ ▼ ▼ ▼ ▼

This chipotle rub is quite tasty, though hot. It's great on the roast, but try using it on chicken or pork for a change. This is not the chipotle you get in those fast food places; this is the real thing.

One (4- to 6-pound) rump roast	2 tablespoons shortening or vegetable oil
3 large cloves garlic, sliced into long slivers	Chipotle Rub (recipe follows)

Preheat the oven to 325 degrees. With a very sharp paring knife, make small slits into the roast. Insert the slivers of garlic. Rub the Chipotle Rub into the roast with your (gloved) hands. Melt the shortening or heat the oil in a large kettle over medium heat. Brown the roast on all sides over medium heat, about 15 minutes.

Place the roast, fat side up, on a rack in a shallow roasting pan. Place a loose tent of foil over the roast to keep it from browning too quickly. Roast for approximately 2½ to 3 hours, checking periodically. Remove the foil for last 20 minutes of roasting time to brown the rub. The roast is done when the internal temperature reaches 140 degrees. Allow the roast to stand for 20 minutes after removing from oven.

Chipotle Rub

Makes about $^1/_2$ cup

---

3 dried chipotle chiles
2 tablespoons black
  peppercorns
1 tablespoon pink
  peppercorns

1 tablespoon coarse salt
1 tablespoon ground cumin

Heat the chipotles in a microwave oven on high until they puff and smell slightly toasted, about 15 to 30 seconds. Trim and discard the stems. Slit the chiles open and remove the seeds and veins (remember to wear gloves). Coarsely chop the chiles. In a food processor or spice grinder, combine the chiles, black and pink peppercorns, salt, and cumin. Whirl until finely ground.

Mexican Shredded Beef

Salpicón

About 16 servings

The visual effect of this layered dish is outdone only by the flavorful mingling of the Salpicon with the beans, chiles, and avocados. We make this one when we have a few friends for dinner. Using the bottled Italian dressing is a convenient substitute. If you prefer, substitute oil, vinegar, oregano, and minced onion.

8 pounds beef top round or rib-eye roast	1 cup cooked garbanzo beans
2 cloves garlic	8 ounces Monterey Jack cheese, cut into
1 bay leaf	$^{1}/_{2}$-inch cubes
1 (15-ounce) can of tomatoes	1 cup chopped green chiles, fresh or canned
$^{1}/_{4}$ cup chopped fresh cilantro	2 avocados, peeled, pitted, and cut in strips
Salt and pepper	Chopped parsley, plus
1 (16-ounce) bottle Italian salad dressing	whole sprigs to garnish

Place the beef in a heavy pot, cover with water, and add garlic, bay leaf, tomatoes, cilantro, and salt and pepper to taste. Cook over medium heat for about 5 hours. Remove the meat from the broth and allow to cool, then shred the meat into bite-size pieces and place it in a 9 X 11-inch glass baking dish. Cover the beef with salad dressing and allow to marinate overnight in the refrigerator.

Before serving, layer the beans, cheese, chiles, and avocado over the beef. Decorate with parsley.

Mexican Stew

Caldillo

6 to 8 servings

Caldillo (Mexican stew) is great for any meal, weeknight or weekend. Serve it with rice and *Bolillos* (page 140), maybe a little salsa, and everyone is sure to enjoy.

3 pounds beef stew meat, cut into bite size pieces	**$^1/_2$ cup chicken stock**
1$^1/_2$ cups diced onion	**2 teaspoons salt**
Bacon fat or olive oil	**2 teaspoons pepper**
3 cups diced tomatoes	**2 teaspoons garlic salt**
1$^1/_2$ cups green chile strips	**2 teaspoons ground cumin**
$^1/_2$ cup beef stock	**2 pounds potatoes, cubed**

Sauté the beef and onions in the bacon fat. Add the tomatoes, chile, beef and chicken stock, salt, pepper, garlic salt, and cumin. Cook over low heat until the meat is tender, about 2 hours. Add the cubed potatoes during the last 30 minutes. (Caldillo may be frozen after preparation.)

Chile Colorado

About 12 servings

Chile Colorado is good served on its own or as a burrito filling. The taste is wonderful. If you're going to use it as a burrito stuffer, you might want to use a little less broth so that it doesn't leak through the tortilla.

4 ounces dried New Mexico chiles	**2 teaspoons dried rosemary**
¹/₂ cup olive or vegetable oil	**2 teaspoons dried tarragon**
2 large onions, chopped	**2 (28-ounce) cans tomatoes**
3 cloves garlic, minced	**1 (14¹/₂-ounce) can beef broth**
5 pounds boneless beef chuck, cut into 1¹/₂ inch-cubes	
¹/₂ cup all-purpose flour	**GARNISHES**
¹/₄ cup chopped fresh cilantro	**8 ounces shredded cheddar cheese, 2 cups**
2 teaspoons ground cumin	**2 cups diced tomatoes**
2 teaspoons ground cloves	**1 large onion, finely chopped.**
2 teaspoons dried oregano	

Rinse the chiles and discard the stems and seeds. Break the chiles into pieces. Combine the chiles and 3 cups of water in a 2¹/₂- to 3-quart saucepan and bring to a boil over high heat. Reduce the heat, cover, and simmer until the chiles are soft, about 30 minutes. Whirl the chiles and their liquid in a blender until pureed. Force the puree through a fine strainer and discard the residue. Set the puree aside.

Heat the oil in a 6- to 8-quart saucepan over medium heat. When the oil is hot, add the onions and garlic and cook, stirring often, until the onions are soft, about 10 minutes. Sprinkle the meat with flour. Add the meat and the chile puree to the pan and cook, stirring for 5 minutes. Add the cilantro, cumin, cloves, oregano, rosemary, tarragon, tomatoes and their liquid (breaking them up with a spoon), and broth. Bring to a boil over high heat. Reduce the heat and simmer, uncovered, stirring often, until the meat is very tender when pierced, 3 to 4 hours.

Arrange the cheese, tomatoes, and onion in separate bowls and offer as garnishes to add to individual servings.

Ribs with Bob's Barbecue Sauce

▼ ▼ ▼ ▼

Servings depend on how many ribs you want to make

After trying all sorts of barbecue sauces off the shelf, Bob came up with his own. To add a bit more of a Southwestern taste to the ribs, he's been known to add some minced jalapeño and a jigger of tequila to the mix. Delicious!

Ribs, ribs, ribs, as many as you want, beef or pork	**Bob's Barbecue Sauce (recipe follows)**

Place the ribs in a large pot of water and bring to a boil over medium-low heat. Continue cooking for 1 hour. Prepare the grill 15 minutes before the ribs are done boiling. Place the ribs over medium heat on the grill for 5 minutes on each side. Then, turn the heat to low and generously mop barbecue sauce over tops. Turn frequently and each time, add more barbecue sauce. Cook until the desired doneness of meat is achieved and the barbecue sauce is moist. Serve with lots of napkins!

Bob's Barbecue Sauce

1 tablespoon unsalted butter
1 medium onion, finely
  chopped
$^3/_4$ cup tomato sauce
$^1/_4$ cup ketchup
3 tablespoons brown sugar
3 tablespoons
  Worcestershire sauce
$1^1/_2$ teaspoons white
  vinegar

$1^1/_2$ teaspoons apple cider
Dash pepper
3 tablespoons pineapple
  juice
1 tablespoon pineapple bits
Juice of $^1/_2$ lemon
2 teaspoons mustard
1 tablespoon honey

Heat the butter and sauté the onion on medium-low heat until soft but not browned, about 5 minutes. Add the remaining ingredients and $^1/_4$ cup water, mixing well. Simmer over low heat for 20 minutes. Prepare the sauce the night before the barbecue so it has time thicken in the refrigerator. Makes about $2^1/_2$ to 3 cups.

Pork Loin Roast with Sangrita

4 to 6 servings

The aroma of the pork and tequila sauce baking in the oven will keep you in the kitchen waiting for the dish to be done. *Sangrita* means little blood, but that's just the color of the sauce.

---

3 medium dried ancho chiles, stems, seeds, and veins removed

2 cups fresh orange juice

3 tablespoons fresh lime juice

¹/₄ cup grenadine

¹/₂ cup tequila

1 teaspoon salt

1 teaspoon dried thyme

1 cup sliced white onion

One 3-pound lean boneless pork loin roast, or 2 smaller loins tied together

Salt and pepper

2 tablespoons lard or olive oil

Preheat the oven to 350 degrees. Toast the chiles on a skillet over medium heat for 30 seconds to 1 minute on each side, but do not allow them to scorch. Tear the chiles into pieces, place them in a bowl, cover them with boiling water, and allow them to rehydrate and soften for 15 minutes. Drain the chiles and place them in a blender. Add the orange juice and lime juice and blend for 1 minute. Strain the mixture through a fine sieve, then add the grenadine, tequila, salt, thyme, and onion and set aside.

Salt and pepper the pork. Heat the oil in a Dutch oven over medium-high heat until it is very hot but not smoking. Add the pork and sear it, turning as necessary, until it is golden brown on all sides, about 4 minutes. Remove the pork and set aside to cool.

Add the chile mixture to the Dutch oven, stirring well to incorporate any caramelized pieces of pork and juices from the bottom of the pot. Put the pork back into the Dutch oven, fat-side up and continue cooking until the sauce begins to boil gently, but do not bring to a full boil. Place the Dutch oven in the oven and bake, uncovered, until the pork reaches an internal temperature of 145 to 150 degrees, about 20 minutes per pound, spooning some of the sauce over the pork every 15 minutes. Remove the pork from the Dutch oven and allow it to rest for 5 minutes, then slice it into servings. Spoon sauce on each of 4 serving plates and top with sliced pork.

Pork Tenderloin with Lime Sauce

▼　▼　▼　▼　▼　▼　▼　**4 servings**

Limes (*limas* in Spanish) are used frequently in Mexican and Border cooking. Slices of lime are often served with beer as well. The lime sauce with white wine in this dish is excellent.

1¼ pounds pork tenderloin, cut into thin strips
Salt and pepper
1 tablespoon olive oil
1½ cups chopped onion
2 bacon slices, chopped
1 tablespoon seeded and chopped jalapeño chile
½ cup dry white wine

1 cup chicken stock or canned low-salt chicken broth
¾ cup whipping cream
¼ cup fresh lime juice
2 large tomatoes, seeded and diced
1 cup chopped green onions

Season the pork with salt and pepper. Heat the oil in large nonstick skillet over high heat. Add the pork and sauté until almost cooked through, about 1 minute. Transfer to a plate.

Add the onion, bacon, and jalapeño to same skillet and sauté until the onion is tender, about 5 minutes. Add the wine and cook for 1 minute. Add the stock and cream and simmer until the mixture is reduced to 1 cup, about 7 minutes. Return the pork to the skillet. Stir in the lime juice. Add the tomatoes and sauté until the pork is cooked through, about 1 minute longer. Transfer to a serving dish. Sprinkle green onions over the meat and serve.

Mango and Pork Picadillo

Picadillo de Mango y Puerco

4 servings

The taste of pork mingling with the sweet tanginess of mango is an authentic journey into Mexican cuisine. We suggest serving this dish over rice, but it also goes well with pasta.

---

1 pound lean ground pork
$^1/_3$ cup thinly sliced green
  onions
2 cloves garlic, minced
1 teaspoon ground
  cinnamon
1 teaspoon ground
  coriander
1 teaspoon ground cumin
1 teaspoon dried oregano,
  crushed

1 teaspoon dried thyme,
  crushed
1 cup thick and chunky
  salsa
1 mango, peeled, pitted,
  and cubed
2 tablespoons chopped
  almonds
2 tablespoons chopped
  fresh cilantro
Cooked rice, for serving

Cook the ground pork in a 10-inch skillet until no longer pink. Drain off the fat. Stir in the green onions, garlic, cinnamon, coriander, cumin, oregano, and thyme. Cook for 2 minutes, stirring. Gently stir in the salsa and mango. Cover and heat through, about 1 to 2 minutes. Spoon into a serving dish and sprinkle with chopped almonds and cilantro. Serve over cooked rice.

Crisped Pork Bits

Carnitas

6 to 8 servings

Carnitas are absolutely wonderful. Keep warm in a large serving bowl next to the garnishes for every guest to serve themselves. We use left over Carnitas for a homemade salad the following night. It's always a hit.

1 bone-in pork shoulder or butt (4 to 5 pounds)	**GARNISHES**
4 cups chicken broth	Sour cream
1 large onion, quartered	Salsa
1 tablespoon coriander seeds	Chile con Queso (page 79)
1 tablespoon cumin seeds	Guacamole (page 39)
1 teaspoon dried oregano	Hot corn tortillas
3 canned chipotle chiles in adobo sauce	
2 bay leaves	

Place the pork, broth, onion, coriander, cumin, oregano, chiles, and bay leaves in a 5- to 6- quart pan. Add enough water just to cover the meat. Cover the pan and bring to a boil. Reduce the heat and simmer until the meat pulls apart easily with a fork, 3 to 4 hours. Remove the meat from the liquid.

Preheat the oven to 450 degrees. Place the pork in a large roasting pan and bake, uncovered, until sizzling and browned, about 20 minutes. Pull off chunks of meat and shred with 2 forks, discarding any fat. Serve with sour cream, salsa, Chile con Queso, Guacamole, and hot corn tortillas.

Pork Skins in Chile Verde

Chicharrones en Chile Verde

▼　▼　▼　▼　▼　▼　　　**5 to 6 servings**

Here's a recipe that's inexpensive to prepare because you use pork skins instead of pork meat. It's quite an authentic dish in the Southwest United States and Mexico. Serve with warm corn tortillas and watch it disappear. Pour a little hot sauce on the chicharrones to spice them up.

$1^1/_2$ **pounds tomatillos**

4 to 5 serrano chiles, or to taste

1 clove garlic, roughly chopped

$^1/_4$ **cup (loosely packed) roughly chopped cilantro**

2 tablespoons lard or vegetable oil

3 tablespoons finely chopped white onion

Salt

6 ounces chicharrones, broken into squares about $1^1/_2$ **inches**

Remove the husks from the tomatillos and rinse well. Put the tomatillos and chiles into a saucepan, cover with water, and bring to a simmer. Continue simmering until soft, but not falling apart, about 10 minutes. Drain the tomatillo mixture and transfer to a blender with ¼ cup of the cooking water. Add the garlic and cilantro and whirl until smooth.

Heat the lard or oil in a frying pan, add the onion, and fry gently, without browning, for 1 minute. Add the tomatillo sauce and cook over high heat, stirring from time to time, until reduced and thickened, about 7 minutes. Add salt to taste and the chicharrones and continue cooking over medium heat until the chicharrones are just soft, about 5 minutes, depending on thickness and quality.

Shrimp Stew

Camarón Cocido

The *chiltecpins* (tiny chiles, also called *piquíns* or bird peppers) can make this shrimp dish very hot. You have been warned! Start with a small amount and add to achieve your liking. We really like shrimp, and this is one of our favorite ways to prepare it.

2 pounds fresh shrimp	$^1/_2$ teaspoon dried thyme
2 tablespoons olive oil	$^1/_4$ teaspoon pepper
$^1/_2$ cup chopped celery	$^3/_4$ teaspoon salt
1 small green bell pepper, chopped	1 teaspoon dried oregano
	1 teaspoon dried parsley
6 green onions, chopped	$^1/_2$ teaspoon garlic powder
$^2/_3$ cup sliced small fresh mushrooms	2 large cooked squash, such as zucchini, sliced
6 tablespoons chili powder	$^1/_2$ cup black olives, sliced
1 to 2 *chiltecpins*, minced	6 to 8 pickled yellow peppers

Wash the shrimp and cook, covered, in salted water until the shells turn pink. When the shrimp is cooked, drain, reserving the stock (about 4 cups). Shell, devein and chop the shrimp into bite-size pieces.

Heat the olive oil and sauté the celery, pepper, green onions, and mushrooms until fairly tender. Add the shrimp stock, chili powder, and chiltecpins to a Dutch oven or large pot. Dissolve the chili powder and bring to a slow boil. Add the thyme, pepper, salt, oregano, parsley, and garlic powder and blend well. Add the sautéed vegetables and simmer, covered, for 15 minutes. Stir in the chopped shrimp and cook for 20 to 25 minutes over low heat, stirring occasionally. Add the cooked squash and black olives during the last 10 to 15 minutes of cooking time. Garnish with pickled yellow peppers.

Shrimp with Tequila Sauce

Camarón con Salsa de Tequila

▼　▼　▼　▼　▼　▼　▼　**4 servings**

One more shrimp and tequila recipe adds to the variety you can offer your family and guests. They'll definitely be asking for more. If you've never barbecued shrimp, give it a try.

---

1 recipe Bob's Barbecue Sauce (page 187)

1/4 cup tequila

2 tablespoons fresh lime juice

2 fresh jalapeños, stemmed, seeded, and minced

4 dozen jumbo or 40 to 50 medium shrimp, cooked, peeled, and deveined

Metal or wooden skewers, soaked in water (optional)

Combine the barbecue sauce, tequila, lime juice, and minced jalapeños. Mix well. Cover and chill for at least 1 hour.

Heat the grill. You can use a gas grill, but charcoal is recommended. If using jumbo shrimp, you can probably grill them without using skewers. If using medium shrimp, use skewers.

Cook the shrimp over medium heat for about 3 minutes on each side, until slightly browned. Over low heat, mop the barbecue sauce on each side for about 5 minutes. (I only mop the shrimp with sauce once on each side, but you might like more.) Check the shrimp frequently so that they do not overcook and become tough. I like them warm through, but not hot. You can always pluck one right off the grill and bite into it to see if it's the way you like it.

Lobster and Tequila

Langosta y Tequila

▼ ▼ ▼ ▼ ▼ ▼ ▼   **4 servings**

Now we're talking an elegant dinner. This lobster and tequila is great for a small dinner party or even a candlelit dinner for two. Adding the tequila and the *chile de arbol* gives it an exotic taste.

---

1 lemon, cut in half
$^1/_4$ cup chopped celery
   leaves
4 (6- to 8-ounce) lobster
   tails, thawed if frozen

1 cup (2 sticks) butter
$^1/_4$ cup tequila
1 teaspoon crushed *chile*
   de arbol

Put the lemon halves and celery leaves in a large pot of water and bring to a boil. Plunge the lobster tails into the water and cook for 7 to 9 minutes, or until done. While they are cooking, melt the butter in a saucepan, stir in the tequila and chile, and keep warm.

When the lobster tails are done, drain, cut the shells with kitchen shears and remove the meat from the shells if desired. Arrange the lobster tails on a serving plate. Pour the butter into 4 small bowls and serve to dip the lobster in.

Did You Know?

▼ ▼ ▼ ▼ ▼ ▼ ▼

MEXICAN BEER

Viva La Cerveza! Does anything go better with a spicy Mexican dinner than a good Mexican beer? I didn't think so. Mexican beer is, as a rule, more full-bodied and a bit higher in alcohol content than American beer. Most good Mexican beers compare quite favorably to any premium European beer. Here in El Paso, where I can see both Mexico and New Mexico from my back yard, I can drive ten minutes, walk over the Santa Fe bridge downtown and pick up a case of my favorite beer. Life is good. These are some Mexican beers of that are imported in the United States. Try them for yourself.

Carta Blanca: This beer deserves your attention just for being the first mass-produced beer in Mexico. A fairly light beer for Mexico, a nice lager that goes with most any food.

Bohemia: One of my favorites, a bit heavy with a distinctive, strong taste. Dark and rich, great with or without a meal.

Tecate: One of the most readily available Mexican beers in U.S. markets. In El Paso it is normally served with a slice of lime. I say beware of any beer that has to have anything in it to improve the flavor. Call me a purist. I compare Tecate to Coors.

Sol: Also often served with lime. Watch out. I find it okay without the lime, though a little bit bitter.

Corona Extra: The number one selling beer in Mexico. That should tell you something. It has a fairly light taste that hits the spot on a hot summer day. Corona also makes a light beer just for the U.S. market. I say if you're counting calories, eat less food and drink a real beer.

XX (Dos Equis) Special Lager: This is the beer I order at any Mexican restaurant. It goes down easy and the flavor is both unique and absolutely delicious. If you haven't tried this one, do so.

XX (Dos Equis) Amber: The dark version of Dos Equis is also very good, but a little heavier and full-bodied. If you like a dark beer, try this one.

Pacifico Clara: Look for the yellow, beach motif label. A good lager beer with a light color and smooth taste. I've always thought that this would be the way American beer might taste if it grew up.

Superior: Another good lager. I find the taste a bit stronger than most but still quite refreshing. Good with or without food.

Modelo Especial: The best selling canned beer in Mexico, but buy it in the bottles. It's a good beer that also goes well with a meal. Not one I would normally get, but try it for yourself.

Negra Modelo: The dark cousin to Modelo Especial, richer and more flavorful than Especial and very good. If you like dark beer, I recommend that you skip the Modelo Especial and head right for the Negra Modelo.

Noche Buena: This is a holiday beer that Mexicans look forward to every year, and for good reason. It has a great taste and is good by itself or with any meal. If you can get some of this beer, by all means do so. *Aprovecho!*

Side Dishes

Proverbs
Dichos

Don't count your chickens before they're hatched.
No cantes victoria antes de la hora.

Every cook praises his own broth.
Cada ollero alaba su olla.

An apple never falls far from the tree.
De tal palo, tal estilla.

Business before pleasure.
Primero es la obligación que la devoción.

Never buy a pig in a poke.
Nunca compres a cierra ojos.

Rice with Peas and Ham

Arroz con Chicharos y Jamón

▼ ▼ ▼ ▼ ▼ ▼ ▼   **6 servings**

This delicious side dish with a kick of jalapeño, goes great with any main course. With ham in the ingredients though, this dish served with a side salad can also make a complete meal.

---

6 tablespoons ($^3/_4$ stick) butter

1 medium onion, finely chopped

1 clove garlic, minced

2 carrots, diced

2 jalapeño chiles, stemmed, seeded, and minced

$^3/_4$ pound baked ham, diced

2 cups long-grain rice

1 cup tomato puree

4 cups chicken broth

1 cup fresh or frozen and thawed peas

Melt the butter in a wide frying pan over medium-high heat. Add the onion, garlic, carrots, and jalapenos and cook, stirring, until the vegetables are soft about 5 minutes. Add the ham and rice and cook for 2 more minutes. Stir in the tomato puree and broth. Bring the mixture to a boil, reduce the heat, cover, and simmer until all the liquid is absorbed and rice is tender, 25 to 35 minutes. Stir in the peas. Let stand for 5 minutes.

Chile Cheese Rice

Arroz con Chile y Queso

8 to 10 servings

This dish is so good. For a change of pace from Spanish or Mexican rice, try this rice dish with sour cream and green chile. It's wonderful.

$^3/_4$ cup long-grain rice	2 (4-ounce) cans chopped
2 cups sour cream	green chile
Salt	$^1/_2$ cup grated Monterey
8 ounces Monterey Jack	Jack cheese
cheese, cut in $1^1/_4$-inch	Butter
cubes	

Preheat the oven to 350 degrees and grease a 2-quart casserole. Cook the rice. Combine with the sour cream and season with salt. Arrange half the mixture in the prepared casserole. Layer with the cubed cheese and the chile. Top with the remaining rice mixture and sprinkle with the grated cheese. Dot with butter and bake for 30 minutes.

Chile Rice

Arroz con Chile

Here is another fine way to prepare rice. Want to reduce calories? Use low-fat sour cream.

3 cups cooked rice	2 cups sour cream
2 (4-ounce) cans diced green chiles	4 ounces shredded cheddar cheese, 1 cup

Preheat the oven to 350 degrees and lightly grease a 4- to 5-quart baking dish. Combine the rice, chiles, sour cream, and cheese and pour into the prepared dish. Bake for 30 minutes.

Mexican Rice

Arroz Mejicano

6 to 8 servings

This dish of peas and rice is very Mexican in taste. Give it a slightly Cuban flavor by adding a can of beer.

2 cups long-grain rice	$^1/_2$ teaspoon salt
3 tablespoons shortening	1 small green pepper, diced
$^1/_2$ small onion, chopped	3 to 4 stewed tomatoes,
1 clove garlic, minced	chopped
4 to 5 cups chicken broth	$^1/_2$ cup frozen peas,
1 teaspoon chopped fresh	thawed
cilantro	

Soak the rice in hot water for 15 minutes. Work your fingers through the rice when the water is cool enough to handle. Rinse the rice in cold water and repeat until the water runs clear. Spread the rice on wax paper to dry for 10 to 15 minutes.

When the rice is dry, heat the shortening in a skillet and sauté over medium heat. Add the onion and cook until softened. Add the garlic and chicken broth. Bring to a boil, then reduce the heat, and simmer. Add the cilantro, salt, pepper and tomatoes. Cover and cook for 40 minutes, stirring frequently to prevent from sticking. Add the peas and cook for an additional 5 minutes.

Salsa Rice

Arroz con Salsa

This is simple and easy to prepare to serve with your favorite outdoor meal. Of course you can make fresh salsa and cook your own black beans. Remember fresh is always better, but time doesn't always allow us this luxury. This recipe is a time-saver.

$^1/_2$ **cup long-grain rice**
1 cup mild salsa
1 cup cooked black beans
3 tablespoons chopped
 fresh cilantro or parsley

1 tablespoon grated lime
 peel
$^1/_2$ **teaspoon salt**
$^1/_4$ **teaspoon cayenne**

Cook the rice. Stir in the salsa, beans, parsley, peel, salt and cayenne and cook, stirring occasionally, until heated through, about 2 minutes. Transfer to serving bowl.

Mexican Skillet Potatoes

Papas Doradas

4 servings

A very tasty way to serve potatoes. The green pepper and cilantro really give them a lift.

> **3 large baking potatoes, peeled and diced**
> **3 to 4 tablespoons bacon fat or vegetable oil**
> **1/2 small onion, sliced**
> **1 small green bell pepper, diced**
>
> **Salt**
> **1/4 teaspoon coarsely ground pepper**
> **4 cilantro sprigs, finely chopped**

Rinse the potatoes thoroughly. Heat the bacon fat in a skillet and cook the potatoes, covered, over medium heat until barely tender. Add the onion, green pepper, and salt to taste. Cover and cook until the green pepper is tender. Season with pepper and cilantro and simmer for 10 minutes. Serve hot.

Red Potatoes

Papas Coloradas

6 servings

These *papas coloradas* are made red by the salsa and crushed red pepper flakes. They are a delicious accompaniment to any meal.

2 pounds boiling potatoes, cut into 1-inch cubes	**1 teaspoon garlic salt**
	4 tablespoons salsa
3 tablespoons chopped fresh cilantro	**2 tablespoons crushed red pepper flakes**

Boil the potatoes and drain thoroughly. Return the potatoes to the pot and add the cilantro, garlic salt, salsa, and red pepper flakes. Gently stir to coat potatoes. Serve hot.

Potatoes with Asadero Cheese

Papas con Asadero

I love preparing these for my family. The taste of melting asadero cheese is very good. If you would prefer not to have melted cheese, try *queso fresco*.

---

1 cup whole milk

1 cup whipping cream

About 5 ounces crumbled
asadero cheese, 1 cup

1 clove garlic, minced

$1^1/2$ teaspoons salt

$^1/2$ teaspoon black pepper

Dash nutmeg

2 pounds baking potatoes,
thinly sliced

Preheat the oven to 325 degrees. Generously grease an 11 x 7 x 2-inch glass baking dish. Whisk the milk, cream, cheese, garlic, salt, pepper, and nutmeg together in a medium bowl to blend. Arrange a third of the potatoes slices in the bottom of the prepared baking dish, overlapping slightly and covering completely. Pour a third of the cream mixture over the potatoes. Repeat layers of potatoes and cream mixture 2 more times. Bake, uncovered, until golden brown in spots, about 1 hour and 15 minutes. Serve hot. (If potatoes start to brown too quickly, cover with aluminum foil.)

Stuffed Potatoes

Papas Rellenadas

6 servings

These stuffed potatoes can actually be a complete meal all by themselves. They are luscious—and filling as well.

---

3 large baking potatoes
1 (3-ounce) package
   cream cheese
$^1/_2$ cup (1 stick) butter
$^1/_2$ cup hot milk
Salt and pepper
1 tablespoon olive oil
1 small onion, minced
$^1/_4$ cup green chile, canned
   or fresh, roasted, peeled,
   seeded and stemmed

1 large tomato, seeded
   and chopped
1 teaspoon minced garlic
2 tablespoons chopped
   fresh cilantro
2 cups cooked and shredded
   chicken breast
8 ounces grated asadero
   cheese, 2 cups

Preheat the oven to 325 degrees. Scrub the potatoes. Bake until soft, about 1½ hours. When the potatoes are cool to the touch, cut in half lengthwise. Scoop out the potato flesh and set the shells aside. Mash the potatoes with the cream cheese and butter. Add the hot milk and whip with a handmixer. Season with salt and pepper to taste.

Heat the olive oil in a frying pan over medium heat. Sauté the onion until soft. Add the green chile, tomato, garlic, and cilantro and mix well. Add the chicken and allow to heat through for 15 minutes on low heat.

Raise the oven temperature to 350 degrees. Fill each potato shell with the chicken mixture and top with mashed potatoes. (You can get fancy and use a pastry bag and star tip to top the shells with the mashed potatoes if you like.) Carefully place the filled potato shells on a baking sheet. Top each shell with grated asadero. Bake for 10 minutes, or until the cheese is melted and slightly browned.

Chile Mashed Potatoes

Pure de Papas con Chile

4 servings

There are many ways to prepare the same foods. Here we take good old mashed potatoes and spice them up with chile, carrots, and sour cream.

---

6 large red potatoes,
   peeled and quartered
   (about 4 pounds)
2 carrots, finely chopped
2 (4-ounce) cans chopped
   green chiles, drained

$^1/_2$ cup sour cream
$^1/_4$ cup ($^1/_2$ stick) butter,
   softened
1 teaspoon salt
$^3/_4$ teaspoon pepper
$^1/_4$ teaspoon ground cumin

Cook the potatoes covered in boiling salted water for 25 minutes. Add the carrot and cook 5 minutes more, or until the potatoes are tender. Drain and stir in the chiles.

Beat the potato mixture, sour cream, butter, salt, pepper, and cumin with an electric mixer at medium speed until smooth.

Mashed Potatoes with Green Chile

Pure de Papas con Chile Verde

 **4 servings**

There are mashed potatoes with butter and sour cream. There are mashed potatoes with cream cheese. There are even mashed potatoes prepared with chicken broth, but these will certainly be a favorite with any border meal you prepare. The tartness of the red onion and the bite of the green chile will have your guests asking for more.

4 medium russet potatoes	**¹/₂ cup sour cream**
1 teaspoon olive oil	**¹/₄ cup chopped fresh**
2 cloves garlic, minced	**cilantro**
1 medium red onion,	**Salt and pepper**
chopped	
1 (4-ounce) can diced	
green chiles	

Wash and cut the potatoes into 2-inch pieces. Place in a pot and cover with cold water. Boil for 20 minutes, or until tender. While the potatoes are cooking, heat the oil in a nonstick skillet. Sauté the garlic and onion until tender and add the green chiles. Drain and mash the potatoes. Stir in the sour cream and add the onion, chiles, and cilantro. Season to taste with salt and pepper.

Border Pasta

4 servings

Make this with fewer calories by using low-fat cream cheese. It will make a great tasting and filling light lunch.

---

1 (8-ounce) package pasta
1 (8-ounce) package
  cream cheese
3 tablespoons diced green
  chiles

¹/₂ cup chopped fresh
  cilantro
¹/₂ teaspoon garlic salt

Cook the pasta according to the package instructions. Combine the cream cheese, green chiles, cilantro, and garlic salt in a large saucepan. Gently warm over low heat, stirring to blend. Pour the cooked pasta over the sauce and gently stir to mix thoroughly. Serve warm.

Pasta with Jalapeño Sauce

▼ ▼ ▼ ▼ ▼ ▼ ▼ **4 servings**

Here's a new way to prepare pasta. Need a light lunch with a kick? Try this dish.

6 large fresh jalapeño chiles	**$1/4$ teaspoon salt**
1 ounce freshly grated Parmesan or Romano cheese, $1/4$ cup	**6 ounces dry pasta, such as rigatoni**
2 tablespoons olive oil	**2 tablespoons chopped Italian parsley**

Preheat the oven to 425 degrees. Roast the jalapeños on a foil-lined baking sheet for 25 to 30 minutes, or until the skin is blackened. Place the peppers in a paper bag and seal. Let stand 20 to 30 minutes, or until the peppers are cool enough to handle. Wearing gloves, carefully peel and seed the jalapeños. Combine the jalapeños, Parmesan cheese, oil, and salt in a food processor or blender. Process or blend until almost smooth and set aside.

Meanwhile, cook the pasta according to package instructions. Drain and rinse with cold water. Toss the cooked pasta with the jalapeño sauce and parsley. Cover and chill in refrigerator.

Vermicelli

Sopa Seca de Fideo

Sopa was always a mainstay in our household. It just wouldn't be a meal without it.

8 ounces coiled vermicelli (fideo) or spaghetti	**3 large tomatoes, peeled, seeded, and chopped**
2 tablespoons butter	**1 teaspoon dried oregano**
3 tablespoons vegetable oil	**1 cup fresh or frozen and thawed peas**
1 medium onion, chopped	**2 cups chicken broth**
2 cloves garlic, minced	**Salt and pepper**
2 Anaheim chiles, stemmed, seeded, and chopped, or 1 (4-ounce) can diced green chiles	

Place the noodles in a plastic bag, arranging in one layer. With a rolling pin, break the noodles into small pieces. Heat the butter and oil in a 10-inch frying pan over medium-high heat. When the butter is melted, add the onion, garlic, and chiles and cook, stirring until soft, about 5 minutes. Add the noodles and stir well. Continue cooking, stirring constantly, for 2 more minutes. Add the tomatoes, oregano, peas, and broth and bring to a boil. Reduce the heat, cover, and simmer until the liquid is absorbed, about 15 minutes. Season to taste with salt and pepper.

Spicy Cornbread Stuffing

▼ ▼ ▼ ▼ ▼ ▼   **Makes 5 cups**

Cornbread stuffing has always been a favorite in our family. Whether we make it at Thanksgiving or with roast chicken, there are never any leftovers. Using a combination of regular sausage and chorizo cuts down on the spiciness and appeals to everyone. If you want to make it a notch more interesting, add chopped green chile or minced jalapeños.

1¼ cups (2½ sticks) butter	2 (6-ounce) bags packaged cornbread stuffing (or make one 9 x 13-inch pan of cornbread, crumble, and allow to dry overnight in refrigerator)
1 cup chopped onion	
2 cups chopped celery (including tops)	
2 cups gizzards, cooked and chopped	
2 cups spicy sausage	2 eggs, lightly beaten
1 to 1½ cups turkey or chicken broth (leftover from cooking the gizzards)	1 cup chopped pecans
	Salt and pepper

Preheat the oven to 325 degrees and grease a 9 x 13-inch pan.

Melt ¼ cup of the butter in a skillet over medium-low heat and sauté the onion and celery until soft, about 10 to 15 minutes. Set aside. In the same skillet, brown the sausage. Drain and add the gizzards to the skillet. Heat thoroughly and set aside.

In medium-size pot, heat the broth with the remaining butter until the butter melts. Simmer for 2 minutes.

In large bowl, combine the stuffing, sausage, gizzards, onion, celery, and pecans. Mix in the eggs. Slowly add the broth mixture until well moistened and blended, but not mushy. Season with salt and pepper. Spoon the stuffing into the prepared pan. Cover tightly with foil and bake for 45 minutes.

Easy Enchilada Casserole

Chilaquiles

This is an easy way to prepare an enchilada dinner for your family when time is a factor. *Chilaquiles*, called "chili-killers" by an old friend of ours, have the same great taste as rolled enchiladas, but are a little simpler to prepare.

$^1/_4$ **cup vegetable oil**
3 tablespoons flour
Salt and pepper
Dash garlic powder
6 tablespoons chili powder
$^1/_2$ **small onion, diced**

6 to 8 corn tortillas,
   cut into eighths
$^1/_2$ **cup sliced green olives**
4 ounces grated longhorn
   cheese, 1 cup

Make a basic chili sauce by heating 3 tablespoons of the oil over medium heat. Add the flour and cook, stirring to brown. Add the salt, pepper, and garlic powder to the browned flour and stir well. Dissolve the chili powder in 2 cups of water and add it to the flour mixture.

Heat the remaining oil in a skillet and sauté the onion. Add the tortilla pieces and cook to soften soften. Add the green olives and then the chili sauce, stirring thoroughly. Cook for 5 minutes over medium heat. Add the cheese, stir, and cook covered over low heat until the cheese is melted.

Summer Squash and Corn Tarts

▼ ▼ ▼ ▼ ▼ ▼ **Makes 8 tarts**

Zucchini had always been a vegetable that I just couldn't convince my kids to eat. Then, along came this recipe with the Asadero cheese baked in small tart shells. The kids gobbled them down. *Calabacitas* are now a family favorite. With all the fiestas held in our household, they go great on a buffet table and I know they will not go to waste.

$^1/_4$ cup ($^1/_2$ stick) butter
4 small to medium zucchini, diced
2 cups corn kernels
$^1/_2$ cup diced green chile
$^1/_4$ cup milk
5 green onions, finely sliced
Salt and pepper
8 frozen individual tart shells, baked according to package instructions
5 ounces shredded *asadero* cheese, 1 cup

Melt the butter in a sauté pan over medium heat. Add the zucchini, corn, and green chile and cook for 1 minute. Add the milk and cook for 4 to 5 minutes more, until the vegetables are just tender. Remove from the heat, add the green onions and season with salt and pepper to taste.

Preheat the oven to 350 degrees. Fill the tart shells three quarters full and sprinkle with asadero cheese. Bake for 8 to 10 minutes, or until the cheese melts.

Zucchini with Green Chile

Calabacitas con Chile Verde

5 servings

Green chile added to the squash gives this dish a little kick.

2 tablespoons vegetable oil	1 cup chopped green chile,
$^1/_2$ cup finely chopped	canned or fresh, roasted,
onion	peeled and seeded
2 medium zucchini, peeled	$^3/_4$ cup corn kernels
and diced	$^1/_8$ teaspoon salt
2 cloves garlic, minced	$^1/_8$ teaspoon pepper

Heat the oil in a nonstick skillet over low heat. Sauté the onion in the oil. Add the zucchini and cook over medium heat for 5 minutes, stirring occasionally. Add the garlic and chile to the zucchini mixture. Cook for 3 minutes, stirring occasionally. Add the corn, salt, and pepper. Cover and cook over low heat for 8 minutes, or until the squash is tender.

Summer Squash with Corn

Calabacitas con Elote

8 to 10 servings

This dish not only tastes good, but its green and yellow colors look pretty on a springtime table.

3 tablespoons butter or margarine	1 red bell pepper, seeded and diced
2^1/$_2$ pounds zucchini, thinly sliced	1 medium onion, chopped
1^1/$_2$ cups fresh or frozen and thawed corn kernels	2 cloves garlic, minced
	Salt and pepper

Melt the butter in a wide frying pan over high heat. Add the zucchini, corn, bell pepper, onion, and garlic. Cook, stirring, until the vegetables are barely tender, about 5 minutes. Season to taste with salt and pepper.

Summer Squash
with Ham

Calabacitas con Jamón

6 servings

Anyone who has ever cooked green beans with ham or a ham hock knows the flavor enhancement you get. Now you can try adding *jamón* (ham) to summer squash to get the same delectable effect.

---

2 pounds summer squash, diced
1 tablespoon butter
$^1/_2$ onion, diced
2 tomatoes, diced
1 (4-ounce can) diced green chiles

2 cups cubed cooked lean ham
$^1/_4$ teaspoon garlic powder
Salt and pepper

Cook the squash in water until tender and drain. Heat the butter in a large nonstick skillet and sauté the onion until tender. Add the squash, tomatoes, chiles, ham, garlic powder, salt and pepper to taste. Mix well, cover, and simmer for 5 minutes.

Zucchini and Corn a la Mejicana

Calabacitas y Elote Mejicana

This zucchini dish is made with corn. The combination of cheeses and chile almost makes it a chile con queso-type of dish, which isn't bad either.

1 medium onion, diced	1 cup milk
2 teaspoons butter	2 ounces Monterey Jack
2 teaspoons chopped fresh	cheese, $^1/_2$ cup
cilantro	2 ounces longhorn cheese,
2 teaspoons bacon bits	$^1/_2$ cup
4 medium zucchini, diced	$^1/_3$ cup green chile strips,
1 (16-ounce) can whole	fresh or canned
kernel corn	Salt

Preheat the oven to 350 degrees and lightly grease a 2-quart casserole dish. Heat the butter and sauté the onion. Add the cilantro, bacon bits, and zucchini. Simmer over low heat long enough to combine but, not cook. Remove from the heat and add the corn and milk. Taste and season with salt. Put into the casserole dish, alternating the zucchini mixture, Monterey Jack cheese, longhorn cheese, and chile strips. Bake the zucchini 15 to 20 minutes. Do not overcook.

Sweet Potatoes with Lime and Tequila

Camotes con Lima y Tequila

▼ ▼ ▼ ▼ ▼ ▼   **6 to 8 servings**

My favorite sweet potato dish when I was young was made with pineapple and marshmallows. Then I grew up and discovered the fascinating taste of tequila and lime.

2 pounds sweet potatoes, peeled and coarsely shredded	**2 tablespoons tequila**
	1 tablespoon fresh lime juice
³/4 cup (1¹/2 sticks) butter or margarine	**Salt and pepper**
	Lime wedges
2 tablespoons sugar	

Melt the butter in a 12- to 14-inch frying pan, over medium heat. Add the potatoes and sugar. Cook, turning occasionally, until the potatoes begin to caramelize and look slightly translucent, about 15 minutes. Stir in the tequila and lime juice and continue to cook for 3 more minutes. Season to taste with salt and pepper. Serve with lime wedges.

Red Chile-Orange Sweet Potatoes

Camotes en Chile Colorado con Naranja

▼　▼　▼　▼　▼　▼　　　**6 to 8 servings**

In our continued attempt to experiment with foods favored in the Southwest, we tried sweet potato with red chile. It was good, but it lacked something, so we added cinnamon, cloves, and a touch of orange to give it a festive appeal.

1 recipe Red Chile Puree (page 75)	**$^{1}/_{2}$ cup orange juice**
$^{1}/_{2}$ teaspoon ground cinnamon	**2 tablespoons honey**
$^{1}/_{8}$ teaspoon ground cloves	**Salt**
Pepper	**2 tablespoons butter, melted**
3 pounds sweet potatoes	**Chopped cilantro, for garnish**
1 tablespoon chopped orange peel	**Orange slices, for garnish**

Preheat the oven to 350 degrees. Lightly grease a 4-quart baking dish. Combine the chile puree, cinnamon, cloves, pepper to taste, and $^{1}/_{2}$ cup water in a small saucepan and heat thoroughly. Slice the sweet potatoes into $^{1}/_{4}$-inch slices. Combine the orange peel, orange juice, and honey. Add the chile mixture to the orange juice mixture to the desired piquancy and taste. Add salt to taste. Place the sweet potatoes in the prepared dish. Spoon the sauce over the sweet potato. Cover with foil.

Bake for 45 minutes, or until the sweet potatoes are tender. Uncover the baking dish and bake for an additional 10 minutes to thicken the sauce if needed. Arrange on a heated platter and garnish with chopped cilantro and orange slices.

Eggplant and Green Chile

Berenjenas con Chile Verde

▼ ▼ ▼ ▼ ▼ ▼ ▼ **4 servings**

This eggplant casserole shows that you can encourage people (especially the younger ones) to eat their vegetables, especially when they have a great southwesterny taste with chile and bacon.

1 large eggplant	**1 cup chopped green chile**
Salt and pepper	**2 cups soft bread crumbs**
1 small onion, diced	**6 strips bacon**
1 egg, well beaten	

Preheat the oven to 350 degrees and grease a 4- to 5-quart casserole dish. Peel the eggplant. Cut into cubes and cook in salted water until tender, about 20 minutes. Drain the eggplant and cool slightly. Mash eggplant.

Combine the onion, egg, chile, breadcrumbs, and salt and pepper to taste. Add to the eggplant and mix well. Spoon into the casserole dish, top with bacon strips, and bake for 45 minutes.

Grilled Corn

Elote Asado

6 servings

Elote asado (grilled corn) partners well with any barbecued meat you throw on the grill. Simple and easy, it's done when the meat is done.

---

6 ears corn
¹/₄ cup (¹/₂ stick) butter,
   at room temperature
¹/₂ cup (firmly packed)
   chopped cilantro
Salt and pepper
1 cup sour cream (optional)

6 ounces grated or crumbled
   ***cotija* (*queso añejo* or**
   ***queso seco*) or Parmesan**
   cheese, 1¹/₂ cups

Gently peel back, but do not tear off cornhusks. Remove the silk, rinse the corn and pat dry. Cut six 6 x 8-inch rectangles of aluminum foil. Rub butter over each ear of corn and sprinkle with cilantro. Season to taste with salt and pepper. Pull the husks back over the corn and wrap each ear in foil.

Place the corn on a grill 4 to 6 inches above a solid bed of medium-hot coals. Cook, turning 2 or 3 times, for 20 minutes. Remove the corn and carefully peel off the foil. Let cool slightly. Peel back the husks and spread each ear with sour cream, if desired. Sprinkle with cheese.

Mexican-style Corn

Elote Mejicano

6 servings

The chili powder gives this corn dish a little bite. If taking this to a potluck, keep it warm (although my kids swear it tastes just as good cold).

1 small onion, chopped	2 tablespoons butter
1 tablespoon olive oil	Salt and pepper
2 cups tomato puree	3 cups uncooked corn
2 tablespoons chili powder	kernels, cut from cob

Preheat the oven to 350 degrees and grease a 2-quart casserole dish. Heat the oil in a skillet until hot and sauté the onion until golden. Combine the tomato puree, chile powder, butter, salt and pepper to taste, and corn in a large bowl. Add the sautéed onions and mix well. Pour the corn into the casserole dish and bake for 1 hour.

Mexicorn

This is a great side dish to serve along with some BBQ'd burgers or hot dogs after a swim. Serve some Sangria for Kids (page 302) along with it and you'll have a mini-fiesta.

2 tablespoons butter	8 ounces cream cheese,
2 green onions, minced	cut into pieces
1/2 cup minced red or	2 (17-ounce) cans corn,
green bell pepper or a	well drained
combination	Salt and pepper
2/3 cup milk	

Melt the butter in a medium saucepan over medium-low heat. Sauté the green onions and bell pepper 1 to 2 minutes. Reduce the heat. Add the milk. Add the cream cheese and stir until the sauce is smooth. Stir in the corn. Add salt and pepper to taste. Serve when hot.

Asparagus with Tomatillos

Esparragos con Tomatillos

My mother loved *esparragos* (asparagus) with a dollop of mayonnaise on top. I made this dish for her one Mother's Day, and she never went back to the mayo.

---

1 pound asparagus
3 tablespoons olive oil
4 large tomatillos, husked, rinsed, and finely diced
1 small roma tomato, cored and finely diced

1 ounce *cotija* cheese (or *queso añejo* or *queso seco*) crumbled or finely shredded, $^1/_4$ cup
Lemon wedges
Salt and pepper

Snap off and discard the tough ends of the asparagus and rinse the spears. Pour 1 inch of water into a wide frying pan and bring to a boil over high heat. Add the asparagus and cook, uncovered, until barely tender when pierced, 3 to 5 minutes, and drain. Immerse in ice water. When cool, drain again. Arrange the asparagus on a platter or on 4 salad plates. Mix the oil, tomatillos, and tomato and spoon the mixture over the asparagus. Sprinkle with cheese and garnish with lemon wedges. Season to taste with salt and pepper.

Mexican Creamed Spinach

Espinacas

Here's another tasty vegetable dish. The green of the spinach and the red of the pimento make it not only delicious, but pretty to look at. This would certainly make an attractive dish on a Christmas buffet table.

4 tablespoons vegetable oil	$^1/_4$ teaspoon pepper
4 tablespoons flour	$^1/_4$ teaspoon salt
3 tablespoons diced onions	$^1/_8$ teaspoon garlic powder
4 tomatoes, diced	Diced pimientos (optional)
1 (16-ounce) can spinach, drained	

Heat the oil in a skillet. Add the flour and cook, stirring until browned. Add the onions and sauté until tender, then add the tomatoes. Cook 1 minute. Add the spinach, pepper, salt, and garlic powder and mix well. Cover and simmer over low heat for 15 minutes, stirring occasionally. Serve hot. Sprinkle with diced pimentos, if desired.

Green Beans
ala Mejicana

▼ ▼ ▼ ▼ ▼

6 to 8 servings

A wonderful side dish made with ordinary green beans. The mushrooms and the chiles go well together.

---

1 pound green beans, trimmed	1 (4-ounce) can chopped green chile
1 medium onion, chopped	1 teaspoon salt
4 fresh tomatoes, chopped	$^1/_2$ teaspoon pepper
2 tablespoons butter or margarine	$1^1/_2$ teaspoons sugar
1 (3-ounce) can sliced mushrooms	4 to 5 slices bacon, cooked and crumbled ($^1/_2$ cup)

Cook the green beans in a pot with a little water. Drain. Heat the butter in a skillet and sauté the onion and tomatoes. Add to the green beans along with the mushrooms and chile. Season with salt, pepper, and sugar and add the bacon. Simmer the beans over low heat for 30 minutes.

Kahlúa Carrots

▼ ▼ ▼ ▼ ▼

6 servings

These are my kind of carrots. The coffee flavor of the Kahlua adds just the right touch. This side dish blends well with any sit-down dinner main course.

3 cups diagonally sliced carrots	$^1/_4$ teaspoon salt
1 tablespoon butter	3 slices bacon, cooked and crumbled
1 tablespoon brown sugar	1 tablespoon chopped parsley
1 tablespoon honey	
3 tablespoons Kahlúa	
1 teaspoon cornstarch	

Place carrots in a vegetable steamer over a small amount of boiling water. Cook covered, 4 to 5 minutes, just until tender. Remove from the heat.

Melt the butter in a large skillet over medium heat. Stir in the brown sugar, honey, and 2 tablespoons of the Kahlúa and cook over medium heat until bubbly.

Combine the remaining Kahlúa and cornstarch and stir well. Add to the brown sugar mixture and stir in the salt. Continue cooking until thickened and bubbly. Add the carrots, tossing gently to coat. Cook just until the carrots are thoroughly heated. Spoon into a warmed serving dish. Sprinkle with crumbled bacon and chopped parsley.

Cactus Pads with Chile Sauce

Nopalitos con Chile

4 to 5 servings

Nopalitos (cactus pads), a common food along the Border, are very exotic to much of the rest of the country. If you don't want to bother making fresh *nopales*, buy the ready cooked *nopalitos* in a jar.

$1/2$ pound fresh *nopales* or 1 cup pre-cooked, diced	**3 tablespoons chili powder**
3 tablespoons all-purpose flour	**2 cups meat broth**
3 tablespoons olive or vegetable oil	**2 ounces grated longhorn cheese, $1/2$ cup**

If you are cooking fresh *nopalitos*, hold the pads with a towel to protect your hands and shave off the spines with a sharp knife. Trim around the pad to remove the thorny edge, then peel the pads with a vegetable peeler. Slice crosswise into ¼-inch strips. Bring 1½ quarts of water to a boil in a 3 to 4-quart pan and add the cactus. Cook, uncovered, over high heat until the cactus is tender, 5 to 7 minutes. Drain and rinse with cold water. (The *nopales* may be made ahead up to this point, covered and refrigerated for up to 4 days.) Makes 1 cup.

Heat the oil in a skillet. Add the flour and cook, stirring until browned. Dissolve the chile powder in the meat broth and blend into the browned flour. Bring to a boil, then reduce the heat to simmer. Simmer 5 minutes, then add *nopales* and cheese. Serve warm.

Special Mushrooms

Hongos Especiales

4 to 6 servings

Hongos (mushrooms) are prepared here with piquin chili flakes. They're quite good. Remember to start off with a small amount of chile and taste until you reach the amount of heat that's just right for you.

3 tablespoons olive oil	$^1/_2$ teaspoon ground white
1 pound mushrooms,	pepper
washed and sliced	$^1/_4$ cup tequila
1 tablespoon chopped	$^1/_2$ teaspoon piquin chile
fresh parsley	flakes
1 teaspoon chopped dill	1 cup low-fat sour cream
weed	

Heat the oil in a deep frying pan or Dutch oven. Sauté the mushrooms for 5 to 6 minutes, or until just tender. Add the parsley, dill, pepper, tequila, and chile and cook for 3 to 4 minutes. Stir in the sour cream and cook over medium heat until warmed through.

Mexican Vegetable Casserole

▼ ▼ ▼ ▼ ▼ ▼   **4 to 6 servings**

Here's a super delicious way to get all your veggies in at one shot. Even your kids won't refuse.

4 cups spinach leaves, washed and drained	1 teaspoon chili powder or $^1/_4$ teaspoon cayenne
2 yellow crookneck squash, diced	1 cup tomato juice
2 zucchini, diced	$^1/_4$ cup tequila
2 green bell peppers, diced	$^1/_4$ cup bread crumbs
1 onion, chopped	2 ounces grated Parmesan cheese, $^1/_2$ cup
2 tablespoons raisins	$^1/_2$ teaspoon paprika
$^1/_4$ teaspoon ground allspice	2 tablespoons butter
1 teaspoon ground cumin	

Preheat the oven to 350 degrees and grease a 6-quart casserole. Layer half the spinach leaves in the bottom of the baking dish. Combine the squash, zucchini, bell peppers, onion, raisins, allspice, cumin, and chili powder together and spread them over the spinach. Mix the tomato juice and tequila together and pour half over the vegetables. Layer the rest of spinach leaves on top of the vegetables and pour the remaining tomato-tequila mixture over the top. Mix together the bread crumbs, Parmesan cheese, and paprika and sprinkle over top of the casserole. Dot with butter and bake for 45 minutes, or until the casserole is hot and bubbly.

Beans

Frijoles

This is your basic pinto bean recipe. Delicious as is and even tastier when combined with other ingredients.

1¹/₂ cups dried pinto beans, picked over and rinsed	**¹/₂ cup diced onion**
2 teaspoons vegetable oil	**1 teaspoon salt**
2 teaspoons unbleached flour	

You can prepare the beans for cooking by soaking them in water overnight or use one of the following methods:

To quick-soak dried beans, combine the dried beans in a large saucepan with triple their volume of cold water. Bring the water to a boil and cook the beans, uncovered, over medium heat 2 minutes. Remove the pan from the heat and let the beans soak 1 hour. Drain.

Combine the beans with 6 cups water and simmer, partially covered, until tender, about 1 to 1¹/₄ hours.

To cook dried beans in a pressure cooker, place the beans in pressure cooker. Add 7¹/₂ cups of water. Secure the lid. Cook over medium-high heat for about 20 minutes, or until the cooker reaches a state of pressure. Continue cooking over medium-low heat for 45 minutes. Release the steam and uncover. (You may also cook the beans in a crockpot on high for approximately 6¹/₂ hours, or until the beans turn reddish brown.)

Heat the oil in a small skillet. Add the flour and cook, stirring until golden brown, making a roux. Add the roux, onion, and salt to the cooked beans. Cook, uncovered, over low heat for 15 minutes. Mash if desired.

Drunken Beans

Frijoles Borrachos

6 to 8 servings

Frijoles Borrachos means Drunken Beans. The reason they're called drunken beans is because the recipe calls for a full can of beer. My husband swears you can't get drunk on one can of beer, and you won't with these either, but the taste will be incredibly delicious.

1 pound dried pinto beans	**2 cloves garlic, minced**
1 medium onion, diced	**1 can beer**
3 fresh tomatoes	**Salt**
4 green chiles, diced	

Rinse and pick over the pinto beans. Add the onion and 5 to 6 cups of water to the beans and bring to a boil. Do not drain. Remove from the heat and leave covered for 2 hours.

Peel the tomatoes and chop into small chunks. Add the tomatoes, chile, garlic, and beer to the beans and bring to a second boil. Reduce the heat and simmer for 5 to 6 hours. Season with salt half an hour before serving.

Beans with Chorizo

Frijoles con Chorizo

5 servings

Beans with chorizo are very Border tasting. This recipe almost makes a Southwestern-type chili.

> **2 teaspoons vegetable oil**
> **2 cups cooked pinto beans**
> **1/8 teaspoon garlic salt**
> **Salt**
> **1 cup cooked and drained**
> **chorizo, store bought or**
> **homemade**
>
> **1/3 cup chopped onion**
> **1/4 cup dried cilantro**
> **Shredded cheddar cheese,**
> **to garnish**

Heat the oil in a skillet, add the beans, and mash them with a potato masher. Cook the beans for 2 minutes, then add the garlic salt and salt. Add the chorizo and blend well. Add onion and cilantro. Cover and let simmer over low heat for 10 to 15 minutes. Stir frequently. Garnish with shredded cheese.

Frontier Beans

6 servings

Here are some ingredients that can be added to your pinto beans: chorizo, green onions, chiles, tomatoes—all so good!

1 cup sliced green onions (about 10)	1 large tomato, chopped (about 1 cup)
$^1/_2$ pound chorizo	$^1/_4$ teaspoon salt
2 cups cooked pinto beans	
3 small poblano chiles, roasted, peeled, seeded, and chopped	

Preheat the oven to 350 degrees. Cook the green onion and chorizo in an 8-inch skillet over medium heat, stirring occasionally, until the chorizo is no longer pink. Drain. Mix the chorizo mixture with the beans, chiles, tomato, and salt in an ungreased 2-quart casserole. Bake, uncovered, about 30 minutes, or until hot and bubbly.

Garbanzos

6 servings

Garbanzos, also known as chick peas, have a great texture. Don't forget to remove the clear skin from the garbanzos before cooking them.

---

3 tablespoons vegetable oil
3 tablespoons flour
2 tablespoons diced onion
2 tablespoons diced
   pimiento
2 chopped stewed tomatoes
2 tablespoons chopped
   cooked green chiles

1 (15-ounce) can garbanzo
   beans, rinsed and
   drained
Salt and pepper
Pinch garlic salt

Heat the oil in a skillet. Add the flour and cook, stirring until browned. Add the onion and pimiento and sauté until the onion is tender. Add the tomatoes and chiles to make a thick gravy mixture. Add 1 cup of water and the garbanzos, blend well, then add salt, pepper, and garlic salt. Simmer for 10 minutes, covered, over low heat, stirring occasionally. Remove from the heat and let stand 5 minutes to let the flavors mix.

Refried Beans

▼ ▼ ▼ ▼ ▼

3 to 4 servings

Ever wonder how they get those refried beans in restaurants to taste so good? Well, here you go. The secret is in the bacon drippings. The name implies that these beans have been fried more than once. Well, in actuality they have. Every time you turn them over with the spatula, you are re-frying them.

$1/3$ cup bacon drippings or vegetable oil	3 cups cooked pinto beans
$1/2$ cup finely chopped onion	3 ounces shredded Monterey Jack, longhorn, or mozzarella cheese,
1 large clove garlic, minced	$3/4$ cup

Heat the drippings in a large, heavy skillet over medium heat. Cook the onion and garlic until soft. Reduce the heat, add 1 cup partially drained beans and mash until smooth. Gradually add 2 more cups, mashing to your desired consistency. Cook until crusty on the bottom. Turn the bean mixture with a large metal spatula and cook until another crusty layer forms. Top with cheese. Serve hot once the cheese has melted.

Tex-Mex Beans

▼ ▼ ▼ ▼ ▼

5 to 6 servings

This is a favorite type of Southwestern chili that my family likes to eat. Serve it with Jalapeño Cornbread (page 136) and a glass of Sangria (page 301) and you're eating the Texas way.

1 pound ground beef	**Salt and pepper**
2 large onions, thinly sliced	**8 to 10 fresh green chiles,**
1 clove garlic, minced	**roasted, peeled, seeded,**
2 (14^1/2-ounce) cans	**and stemmed.**
whole tomatoes	**1 pound meaty salt pork**
2 (7^1/2-ounce) cans hot	**4 to 5 cups cooked pinto**
tomato-jalapeño salsa	**beans**

Brown the meat in a large skillet, add the onions, garlic, tomatoes, salsa, salt and pepper to taste, and bring to a boil. Reduce the heat and simmer 15 to 20 minutes. Cut the chiles into 1/4-inch strips and set aside. Cut the salt pork into small pieces. Fry slowly in a small skillet until golden brown and crispy. Drain the salt pork and reserve the grease. Slowly add the beans and salt pork grease to the ground meat. Mix well. Cover and simmer for 5 to 10 minutes. Remove from heat and pour into a large serving dish. Top with green chiles and garnish with crispy salt pork pieces.

Did You Know?

▼ ▼ ▼ ▼ ▼ ▼ ▼

LA LLORONA

Many versions of "La Llorona" have been written. Songs and poems have been composed to add passion to the legend.

Some stories say that a woman named Maria was shunned by a promising beau because of her children. Terribly distraught at the thought of losing this man, she drowned her two children in the nearby river. Immediately realizing the tragedy that had just occurred, she committed suicide. Since then, her spirit can be seen and her cries and agonized wailing heard along riverbanks as she searches for her dead children.

For years and years this legend has been passed on from generation to generation. Parents warn their children to behave or La Llorona will come and snatch them away. (Sort of a Chicano version of the boogieman. You've heard of negative repercussions for unacceptable behavior! Perhaps a warning is in order for all those who frighten others with violence on schoolyards, playgrounds, and nice quiet neighborhoods.)

A myth or legend, some say based on true facts. The Candy Man, Bloody Mary, the Boogieman, La Llorona. Do you believe in them? I don't. But then ... I still won't call out the Candy Man's name five times in the mirror or walk along a river, canal, or ditch at night!

Check out www.lallorona.com for a different version of the legend. The web site is beautifully done and details the legend from its beginnings.

Desserts

Proverbs
Dichos

Work helps you stay out of trouble.
Oficio, quita vicio.

Honesty is the best policy.
Vale mas una verdad amargada, que muchas mentiras dulces.

The eyes are the windows to the soul.
Los ojos son las ventanas del corazón.

A stumble may prevent a fall.
No hay mal que por bien no venga.

Like father, like son.
De tal palo, tal estilla.

Annie's Polvorones

Makes about 5 to 6 dozen small _polvorones_.

This is my grandmother's recipe for _polvorones_. She never wrote it down, but rather showed me how to make them when I was twelve or thirteen. I in turn have taught my daughter how to make them. Everyone in my family expects dozens of these treats for holidays and special occasions.

6¹/₂ to 7 cups all-purpose flour	**¹/₂ cup warm milk**
2 tablespoons baking powder	**Powdered sugar for dipping cookie cutters**
2 tablespoons sugar	**2 teaspoons ground cinnamon, mixed with 1 cup of sugar for coating**
2 teaspoons ground cinnamon	
1 pound lard	

Preheat the oven to 350 degrees. Combine the flour, baking powder, sugar, and cinnamon in a large mixing bowl. Mix well. Cut the lard into flour mixture with a pastry blender (or do it the way my grandmother taught me; with your clean hands, scoop up flour and lard and gently rub between the palms of your hands). Continue until the flour-lard mixture is in pea-size pieces. Add the warm milk and mix until well blended. Do not over mix the dough, as it toughens the pastry, just like pie pastry. Roll out small portions of the dough between 2 pieces of wax paper. Remove the top layer of wax paper and cut the dough with 1 to 2 inch cookie cutters dipped in powdered sugar.

Bake on ungreased cookie sheets for 10 minutes. Allow the cookies to cool for 6 to 8 minutes. Immediately coat with the cinnamon sugar mixture.

Mexican Shortbread

Biscochos

   Makes about 5 to 6 dozen small cookies

Remember that these little melt-in-your-mouth cookies go fast, so make plenty. I know that not many people cook with lard, but it's really the only way to make these cookies the right way.

> 4 cups all-purpose flour
> 4 teaspoons baking powder
> $^{1}/_{2}$ teaspoon aniseed
> 1 cup sugar
> 1 pound lard
> 3 eggs
>
> $^{1}/_{2}$ cup wine, such as a
>   rosé, or brandy
> 2 teaspoons ground
>   cinnamon, mixed with
>   1 cup of sugar for coating

Preheat the oven to 350 degrees. Mix the flour, baking powder, and aniseed in a medium bowl and set aside. In a large bowl, cream the sugar and lard until light, then add the eggs and wine until well blended. Add the dry ingredients and mix well.

Roll out the dough on a lightly floured surface, ¼-inch thick. Cut the dough with a 1- to 2-inch cookie cutter. Place the cookies on ungreased cookie sheet. Bake until browned, about 10 to 12 minutes. While still warm, roll the cookies in the cinnamon-sugar to cover completely.

Wedding Cookies

Pasteles de Boda

 **Makes about 48 cookies**

This recipe is similar to pecan sandies. As with *biscochos*, *pasteles de boda* are traditional fare at weddings. If you don't like your cookies too sweet, don't cover them with the powdered sugar.

---

1 cup (2 sticks) butter or margarine
$^{1}/_{2}$ cup confectioners' sugar, sifted
1 teaspoon vanilla extract
2 cups all-purpose flour, sifted

$^{1}/_{4}$ teaspoon salt
1 cup pecans, finely chopped
Confectioners' sugar

Cream the butter, sugar, and vanilla until well blended. Gradually add the flour, salt, and nuts and mix thoroughly. Shape the dough into 2 long rolls about 1$^{1}/_{4}$ inches in diameter. Wrap in wax paper and refrigerate for several hours.

Preheat the oven to 350 degrees. Cut the dough into $^{1}/_{4}$-inch slices and place close together on ungreased baking sheet. Bake for 15 minutes to 20 minutes, or until lightly browned on top. Immediately remove from the baking sheet and roll in confectioners' sugar. Place on a rack to cool.

Variation
The cookies may also be rolled into small balls and baked in a 350 degree oven for 15 minutes. Remove from oven and roll in confectioners' sugar while still warm.

Butter Cookies

Galletas de Mantequilla

Makes about $1^1/2$ to 2 dozen,
depending on the size of the cookies

This is my mother's recipe. She was a "lunch lady" cook for the El Paso Independent School District for twenty-five years. During that time she collected and developed many recipes of her own. This is just one of them. It is so easy to make and the dough is so versatile, your kids can experiment with making their own creations for all the holidays.

1 cup (2 sticks) butter, softened	2 to $2^1/2$ cups all-purpose flour
$^1/2$ cup sugar	Colored sugar, for decorating (optional)
1 teaspoon vanilla extract	

Cream the butter and sugar together. Add the vanilla. Slowly add the flour and mix well. Chill the dough in the refrigerator for 30 minutes for easier handling.

Preheat the oven to 325 degrees. Roll out a small portion of the dough between 2 pieces of wax paper until ¼-inch thick. Dip the cookie cutters in flour and cut out desired shapes. Bake in the middle of the oven on an ungreased cookie sheet for 10 to 12 minutes. Sprinkle with colored decorating sugars, if desired.

(If desired, add food coloring to the dough during the mixing process.)

Mexican Chocolate Pralines

 **Makes about 2¹/₂ dozen**

My kids and I make these wonderful pralines at Christmas to ship out to relatives who live away from the Border and yet crave a taste of it. We always send recipe cards and a box of Chocolate Abuelita or Chocolate Ibarra too.

1¹/₂ cups sugar
³/₄ cup brown sugar
2 ounces unsweetened
   chocolate
1 round Mexican Chocolate
   disk, pulverized

6 tablespoons (³/₄ stick)
   butter
¹/₂ cup milk
1¹/₂ cups chopped pecans

Lightly coat a few sheets of wax paper with nonstick cooking spray. Combine the sugars, chocolates, butter, milk, and pecans in a heavy saucepan and bring to a boil, stirring constantly. Boil for 2 minutes, or until a candy thermometer reaches 220 degrees. Remove from the heat and beat with a wooden spoon for 5 minutes. Drop by the tablespoon onto the wax paper and let stand until firm, approximately 1 hour, unless it's hot and humid, then maybe a little longer. Store in an airtight container. Pralines keep for 7 to 10 days.

Mexican Fritters

Buñuelos

Makes 20 fritters

Buñuelos can be made any time of the year, but they are most often found around the holidays, Christmas and New Year's. You know, the time of the year when you forget about that diet.

3 cups all-purpose flour
   sifted twice
1 teaspoon baking powder
1 teaspoon salt
1 tablespoon sugar
2 eggs
$^1/_2$ cup butter or margarine,
   at room temperature
	$^3/_4$ cup milk
	Vegetable oil for frying
	Cinnamon-sugar,
	   for topping

Mix the flour, baking powder, and salt in a large bowl. In another bowl, beat the sugar, eggs, and butter. Stir in the milk and add to the flour. If the dough is too dry, add a few more drops of milk. Mix the dough until it is very smooth. Shape into twenty 2- to 3-inch balls. Cover and let stand for 30 minutes.

Heat the oil 1-inch deep in a large skillet to 360 degrees. Roll out each ball of dough on a lightly floured board into a very thin 6-inch circle. Fry the *buñuelos* until golden brown, turning once. Drain on paper towels. Sprinkle with cinnamon-sugar while still warm. (*Buñuelos* can be frozen by wrapping them individually in freezer bags. Defrost and place in a 350 degree oven for a few minutes to crisp.)

Fritters

Churros

Makes 1 to 1^1/$_2$ dozen

Whether you dust *churros* with confectioners' sugar or cinnamon-sugar (my personal favorite), the taste will transport you to somewhere along the Border. You've got to try one.

1 cup all-purpose flour	**1 slice bread**
^{1}/$_2$ teaspoon ground	**^{1}/$_2$-inch slice lemon**
cinnamon	**Oil, for frying**
^{1}/$_2$ teaspoon salt	**Confectioners' sugar**
1 egg	

Sift the flour and cinnamon 4 times into a medium bowl. Bring 1 cup water to a boil with the salt and add it to the flour mixture, stirring vigorously until the batter is fluffy. Add the egg and continue beating until the mixture is shiny. Place the bread and lemon slice in 1 inch of oil in a deep skillet. Heat the oil to 360 degrees, or until the bread is golden brown. Remove bread and lemon.*

Place the batter in a pastry tube with a large star tip and squeeze 4-inch lengths into the oil. Fry until golden brown. Remove the *churros* and drain on paper towels. Sift confectioners' sugar over the *churros* while warm.

* The lemon flavors the oil, and the bread is used as a thermometer. When the bread turns golden brown, the hot oil is just the right temperature to drop in the *churros*.

Puffed Pastry with Honey

Sopaipillas

Makes 50 to 60

One of the best things about eating at an El Paso Mexican restaurant is the *sopaipillas* for dessert. Warm and dripping with honey, they are so good.

4 cups all-purpose flour	**About $^1/_2$ cup milk**
1$^1/_4$ teaspoons salt	**Oil, for frying**
3 teaspoons baking powder	**Cinnamon-sugar,**
3 tablespoons sugar	**confectioners' sugar or**
2 tablespoons shortening	**honey, for serving**

Sift the flour, salt, baking powder, and sugar. Cut in the shortening and add just enough milk to make a soft dough, just firm enough to roll. Cover the bowl and let the dough rest 30 to 60 minutes. Roll the dough ¼-inch-thick on a lightly floured board and cut into 3- to 4-inch diamond-shaped pieces.

Heat 1 inch of oil in a deep frying pan to approximately 370 to 380 degrees. Add a few *sopaipillas* at a time. Turn immediately so they will puff evenly on both sides, then turn back to brown on both sides. Drain on paper towels. Sprinkle with cinnamon-sugar or confectioners' sugar, or serve with honey.

Flan Tips

1. Caramelizing When melting sugar, use a small skillet. Nonstick pans work best. Do not overcook the sugar or it will taste bitter. Remember to tilt and swirl the baking dish so that the caramel spreads to coat bottom and sides evenly.

2. Mixing Beat the ingredients using an electric mixer, hand mixer, or blender. This assures an smooth mixture. The eggs should be beaten for at least one minute.

3. Baking Always place the baking dish in a larger baking pan filled with hot water. During baking, do not let the water boil. If the water starts to simmer, add a little cold water. Flan is not set until a knife inserted in the center comes out clean. Check the baking times closely for each recipe so as not to over-cook the flan.

4. Unmolding Before unmolding, loosen outer edges of the flan with a thin knife. Place a rimmed serving plate over the flan and invert. Scrape additional caramel sauce from the dish and spoon over the flan.

5. Serving Flan tastes best when made several hours before serving. Flans may also be frozen for 7 to 10 days. Remove from the freezer and defrost in the refrigerator. If need be, place the baking dish in a large pan of hot water for a minute to loosen the flan before inverting it on a serving plate.

Mexican Chocolate Flan

Flan de Chocolate Abuelita

8 servings

This is definitely my favorite flan. Using a Mexican chocolate, like Abuelita, adds a real Southwestern taste to all your cooking and baking. The cinnamon and the ground almond blended into the chocolate give it a unique taste.

1$^{1}/_{2}$ cups milk

2 circular tablets (3 ounces) Chocolate Abuelita, Mexican-style sweet chocolate, coarsely chopped (about $^{3}/_{4}$ cup)

One 2-inch cinnamon stick

$^{2}/_{3}$ cup sugar

3 eggs

1 recipe Mexican Chocolate Sauce (recipe follows)

Sliced almonds

Preheat the oven to 325 degrees. Combine the milk, chocolate, and cinnamon stick in a heavy medium saucepan. Cook over medium heat until the mixture simmers. Remove from the heat and discard the cinnamon stick. Remove the saucepan from the heat and set aside.

Meanwhile, cook the ⅓ cup of the sugar in a heavy 8-inch skillet over medium-high heat until it begins to melt, shaking the skillet occasionally to melt the sugar evenly. Do not stir. Once the sugar starts to melt, reduce the heat to low and cook for about 5 minutes, or until all the sugar is melted and golden, stirring as needed with a wooden spoon. Immediately divide the caramelized sugar among four 6-ounce custard cups to evenly coat the bottoms. Let the cups stand 10 minutes.

Using a rotary beater or whisk, lightly beat the eggs in a large mixing bowl just until mixed. Pour the chocolate mixture and remaining sugar into the beaten eggs. Beat until well combined, but not foamy. Place the custard cups in a 2-quart square baking dish. Divide the chocolate mixture evenly among the custard cups. Pour boiling water into the baking dish around the custard cups to a depth of 1 inch. Bake for 30 to 35 minutes. Remove the cups from the water. Cool slightly on a wire rack. Cover and chill.

To unmold, loosen the edges by slipping the tip of a knife around the side of the custard cups. Invert a dessert plate over each cup, turn the cup and plate over at same time, and lift the cup off of the flan. Drizzle with Mexican Chocolate Sauce and sprinkle with sliced almonds.

Mexican Chocolate Sauce

> **1 ounce ($^1/_4$ cup) Mexican-style chocolate, grated**   **$^1/_3$ cup heavy cream**

Melt the chocolate in a small heavy saucepan over low heat just until melted. Gradually stir in the cream. Cook, stirring over medium heat about 3 minutes. Remove from the heat and cool slightly. Makes ½ cup.

Chocolate Flan

Flan de Chocolate

8 to 10 servings

Here's another Mexican chocolate flan recipe. You can never have too many, and it's just different enough from any American dessert that you'll always impress.

---

2 cups sugar

1 quart milk

2 circular tablets (3 ounces)
    Mexican chocolate, like
    Abuelita or Ibarra, grated,
    or 6 ounces semisweet
    chocolate squares plus
    2 teaspoons ground
    cinnamon

$^1/_4$ teaspoon salt

8 eggs

2 teaspoons vanilla extract

Whipped cream

Heat 1 cup sugar in a small skillet over medium-high heat. When the sugar begins to melt, reduce the heat to medium. Continue to cook the sugar, stirring occasionally. When the sugar is melted, immediately pour it into a 2-quart baking dish, tilting to coat the bottom and sides completely.

Combine the milk with the remaining sugar, chocolate, and salt in a large saucepan. Simmer until the chocolate and sugar are dissolved, about 10 to 15 minutes. Cool the milk mixture completely.

Preheat the oven to 325 degrees. Beat the eggs with the vanilla and add to the milk. Mix well. Pour the mixture through a strainer into the baking dish. Cover loosely with foil to prevent excess browning. Place the dish in a larger baking pan and pour hot water into pan halfway up the sides of baking dish. Bake for about 1$^1/_2$ hours, or until a knife inserted in the center comes out clean. Remove the baking dish from the water and place on a rack to cool. Refrigerate for several hours or overnight.

To serve, run a knife around edge to loosen flan. Place a rimmed serving plate over the flan and invert. Garnish with whipped cream.

Flan

This is the flan you will find in most Mexican food restaurants. It's absolutely delicious. It looks a bit like custard but the taste and texture is completely different. You need to try it.

---

4 cloves	**2 cups milk**
2 allspice berries	**1 teaspoon vanilla extract**
2 cardamom pods, crushed	**1 tablespoon cold water**
1 (3-inch) cinnamon stick,	**$^2/_3$ cup sugar**
broken in half	**6 eggs**

Preheat oven to 325 degrees. Place the cloves, allspice, cardamom, and cinnamon in a cheesecloth bag or tea ball. Place in a 2-quart saucepan with the milk and vanilla and set aside.

Mix the water and $^1/_3$ cup of the sugar in a small, heavy skillet. Stir gently until the sugar dissolves. Place the pan over high heat and cook the syrup, swirling the pan occasionally, until clear and medium amber in color. Immediately pour the syrup into a 1$^1/_2$-quart soufflé dish or 9-inch pie pan. Tilt and swirl the dish to evenly coat the bottom and halfway up the sides. Set on a wire rack to cool (caramel will harden quickly).

Bring the milk and spices to a simmer over medium heat. Remove from the heat and cool slightly. Discard the spices. Beat the eggs with the remaining sugar in a large bowl, then gradually add the milk, stirring quickly with a wire whisk or fork. Pour into the prepared dish. Place the dish in a larger baking pan. Pour hot water into the pan, halfway up the sides. Bake, uncovered, until a very shallow crevice forms when center of custard is pushed with back of a spoon, about 25 minutes if using soufflé dish, or 15 minutes if using pie pan. Remove the dish from hot water and place on a wire rack to cool. Cover and refrigerate for at least 6 hours.

To unmold, run a knife around the edge to loosen flan, then cover dish with a rimmed plate. Invert quickly. (If necessary, briefly dip the bottom of the dish into hot water to loosen.) To serve, cut into wedges and top with the caramel.

Peaches Olé

6 servings

I remember inventing this dessert with my husband a few years ago. We were asked to be judges on a radio food show called "Local Flavor." Different cooks and chefs were given a secret ingredient they had to prepare a dish with. We were also asked to bring in a new dish we could create literally overnight with the secret ingredient. The secret ingredient at this show was peaches. We had Peach Margaritas, Peach Salsa, Peach Sangria, even Peach-Lime-Cilantro Crab Cakes and of course our very own Peaches Olé.

1 cup heavy cream	6 Tortilla Bowls
2 tablespoons sugar	(recipe follows)
2 tablespoons brandy	Sliced peaches
2 large fresh peaches,	Chopped pecans
peeled, pitted, and	Brandy Sauce
cubed	(recipe follows)

Whip the cream until soft peaks form. Add the sugar and whip just until incorporated. Add the brandy and mix for 1 more minute. Fold in the cubed peaches. Cover and chill for 2 hours.

Spoon the whipped cream mixture into Tortilla Bowls. Garnish with a slice of fresh peach and chopped pecans. Drizzle Brandy Sauce on top.

Tortilla Bowls

These can be prepared a few days in advance and be kept refrigerated.

6 (6-inch) corn tortillas	Cinnamon-sugar
Melted butter	

Warm the tortillas on a griddle until soft. Brush both sides with melted butter. Sprinkle cinnamon-sugar on 1 side only. Drape the tortillas over balls of aluminum foil and place on cookie sheet, cinnamon side up. Bake for 6 to 7 minutes. Remove from the aluminum balls and allow to cool on cooling rack.

Brandy Sauce

Makes 1 cup

¹/₂ cup sugar	Dash ground cinnamon
¹/₄ cup brandy	2 tablespoons butter,
2 tablespoons cornstarch	softened
Dash grated nutmeg	1 teaspoon vanilla extract

Mix 1 cup water, sugar, brandy, cornstarch, nutmeg, and cinnamon in a small saucepan. Bring to a boil over medium heat and boil for 5 minutes. Remove from the heat and stir in the butter and vanilla.

Rice Pudding

Arroz con Leche

Arroz con leche reminds me of my mother's kitchen. When life was hard and she wanted to make me smile, she'd always make a pot of this recipe. I can still smell the aroma in the kitchen.

$1/2$ cup long-grain white rice	$1^1/4$ cup sugar
1 cinnamon stick	2 egg yolks, lightly beaten
2 strips lemon peel	$1/2$ cup raisins
2 cups milk	Ground cinnamon

Soak the rice in hot water for 15 minutes. Drain and rinse well with cold water. Combine the rice, 2 cups of water, cinnamon stick, and lemon peel in a large saucepan and bring to a boil. Lower the heat and simmer until the mixture has thickened and most of the water has been absorbed. Add the milk and sugar and continue to simmer until the rice is tender. Add the beaten egg yolks and bring to a boil.

Remove the pudding from the heat and pour into a serving dish. Remove the cinnamon stick and lemon peel. Stir in the raisins. Cool completely; then sprinkle cinnamon over the rice and refrigerate.

Drunken Pudding

Budín Borracho

This is a pretty dessert with lots of flavor. Serve with Café Mejicano to give your guests a special treat. The rum that we use for this is Bacardi Gold, but you can use your favorite.

10 ladyfingers	**2 cups hot milk**
$^1/_2$ cup rum (you can also use brandy or sherry)	**1 teaspoon vanilla extract**
	1 cup heavy cream
6 egg yolks	**1 cup almonds, chopped**
$^1/_4$ cup sugar	**Maraschino cherries, for**
Dash salt	**garnish**

Break the ladyfingers into 1-inch pieces and place in a medium bowl. Sprinkle with rum and set aside.

Beat the egg yolks with the sugar and salt in the top of a double boiler until well blended. Gradually add the hot milk. Cook over simmering water, stirring occasionally, until the custard coats the back of a spoon. Remove from the heat. Add the vanilla and cool.

Whip the cream. Fold the cream and custard into rum-soaked ladyfingers. Add the nuts and chill. Serve in individual dessert dishes and garnish with a cherry on top.

Bread Pudding

Capirotada

8 to 10 servings

Another traditional dish for the holiday season. This is the authentic recipe, but once again, feel free to experiment. As long as the recipe has cheese, bread, eggs, and milk and can be baked, there are all sorts of ingredients you can add. Bananas? Chocolate? *Piloncillo*?

**8 slices bread, toasted
(or day old pound cake)**
3 eggs, beaten
5 tablespoons milk
1 teaspoon ground cinnamon
2 tablespoons brown sugar
**¹/₂ cup toasted slivered
almonds**
¹/₂ cup unsalted peanuts

¹/₂ cup walnuts, chopped
¹/₂ cup raisins
**1 medium apple, peeled,
cored, and thinly sliced**
**1 cup cubed Monterrey Jack
cheese**
**Panocha Syrup
(recipe follows)**

Preheat the oven to 350 degrees. Grease a 9 x 9-inch baking dish. Place 4 bread slices in the dish. Mix the eggs, milk, cinnamon, and brown sugar. Pour half of the egg mixture over the bread. Sprinkle with half of the almonds, peanuts, walnuts, raisins, apple, and cheese. Add another layer of bread and repeat. Top the *Capirotada* with Panocha Syrup and bake for 25 minutes, or until the cheese is melted. Serve warm or reheat in a 350 degree oven, covered, for 15 minutes.

Panocha Syrup

Makes 2¹/₂ cups

---

2 cups brown sugar   **1 cinnamon stick**

Combine the brown sugar, 2 cups water, and the cinnamon stick in a medium saucepan. Bring the syrup to a boil. Lower the heat and simmer for about 15 minutes, or until the syrup is slightly thickened. Remove the cinnamon stick.

Kahlúa Cake

Makes 10 to 12 servings

This recipe is easy. The cake is a box mix and you just mix in the other ingredients. Is it cheating to use a mix? When the results are this good, who cares? Of course you can always use your favorite chocolate cake recipe, but when you're in a hurry to create a delicious dessert, by all means use a mix. Kahlúa Cake, because of its chocolate-coffee taste, makes an excellent finish to any Mexican fiesta.

---

1 box German chocolate cake mix
1 ($3^1/2$-ounce) box instant chocolate pudding
4 eggs
$^2/3$ cup vegetable oil

2 cups sour cream
$^1/2$ cup Kahlúa
1 (12-ounce) bag chocolate chips
Confectioners' sugar

Preheat the oven to 350 degrees. Grease and flour a bundt pan.

Mix the cake mix, pudding, eggs, oil, sour cream, and Kahlúa, then add chocolate chips and mix well. Pour the batter into the prepared pan and bake for 1 hour. Remove from the oven and allow to cool on a wire rack for 10 minutes. Then, invert the pan onto a cake plate and sift confectioners' sugar over the cake.

Mexican Chocolate Cake

Makes 8 to 10 servings

This cake tastes similar to one I had at the Shangri-La restaurant in Juárez, a great Chinese restaurant located a few miles over the Border. Their menu has an eclectic mix of Asian-Mexican fare. Wonderful cuisine.

---

1 tablespoon ground cinnamon	4 eggs, separated
Grated peel of 2 oranges	1/2 cup sugar
2 ounces grated bittersweet chocolate, 4 tablespoons	2 tablespoons fresh orange juice
1 1/2 cups (6 ounces) unblanched almonds, toasted and ground	2 tablespoons Grand Marnier
	Chocolate Glaze (recipe follows)

Preheat the oven to 325 degrees. Grease, flour, and paper an 8- or 9-inch cake pan. Combine the cinnamon, orange zest, grated chocolate, and ground almonds in a mixing bowl. Set aside.

Beat the egg yolks with 1/4 cup of the sugar and stir in the orange juice. Set aside. In another bowl, beat the egg whites to soft peaks while gradually adding the remaining 1/4 cup of sugar. Stir the egg yolks and orange juice into the chocolate-almond mixture, then fold in half the beaten egg whites. Blend well and gently fold in the remaining egg whites. Spread the mixture evenly in the prepared cake pan and bake for 35 to 40 minutes, or until the cake pulls away from the sides of the pan. Cool for 10 minutes and invert onto a wire rack. When cool, brush the Grand Marnier on the cake with a pastry brush and cover with the glaze.

Chocolate Glaze

5 ounces bittersweet chocolate	**1 tablespoon corn syrup**
$^{1}/_{2}$ ounce unsweetened chocolate	**$^{1}/_{4}$ cup chopped candied orange peel**
$^{3}/_{4}$ cup ($1^{1}/_{2}$ sticks) butter, softened	

Place the bittersweet chocolate, unsweetened chocolate, $^{1}/_{2}$ cup of the butter, corn syrup, and 1 tablespoon water in a double boiler over simmering water. Stir until melted. Remove from the heat and stir in the remaining $^{1}/_{4}$ cup of butter. The glaze is ready to pour when it reaches the consistency of maple syrup (between 86 and 96 degrees). Place the cake on a wire rack over wax paper and pour the glaze over the cake, tilting to coat evenly. Decorate with candied orange peel.

Three Milks Cake

Pastel de Tres Leches

 **Makes 10 to 12 servings**

This is a most authentic Mexican pastry. There's a restaurant in Canutillo, right outside El Paso, called the Little Diner. It's famous for its Pastel de Tres Leches.

CAKE
6 eggs, separated
1/4 teaspoon baking soda
1/4 teaspoon salt
1/4 cup sugar
1 teaspoon vanilla extract
1/2 cup (1 stick) butter, melted and cooled
1 cup all-purpose flour

MILK MIXTURE
1 (12-ounce) can evaporated milk
1 (14-ounce) can sweetened condensed milk

1 1/2 cups whole milk
2 tablespoons vanilla extract or amaretto

Whipped Cream:
2 cups heavy cream
2 tablespoons sugar
1/4 cup Amaretto

GARNISH (OPTIONAL)
Sliced fruit, such as strawberries, kiwi, star fruit, etc.

Preheat the oven to 350 degrees. Grease and flour a 9-inch round cake pan. Beat the egg whites, baking soda, and salt on medium speed until soft peaks form, 2 to 3 minutes. In a separate bowl, lightly whisk the egg yolks. With the mixer on low speed, combine the yolks with the egg whites. Slowly add the sugar and vanilla. With a rubber spatula, fold in the cooled melted butter. Sift 1/4 cup of the flour into mixture and fold with spatula to combine. Add the remaining flour in the same manner. Pour the batter into the prepared pan. Bake for 20 to 25 minutes. The cake is done when a toothpick inserted in the center of the cake comes out clean. Cool 5 minutes on wire rack.

For the milk mixture, about 5 minutes before cake is done baking, combine the 3 milks and vanilla. After the cake has cooled for 5 minutes, remove it from the pan and place on a rimmed cake plate, so that the milk mixture does not run off of the plate. Pierce the top of cake with a fork or toothpick. Pour the milk mixture onto the cake and allow 3 to 5 minutes for the milk to be absorbed. Once the cake has cooled completely, cover and refrigerate until serving time.

For the whipped cream, thoroughly chill a bowl and mixing beaters. Whip the cream with a mixer until it begins to thicken. Slowly add the sugar and amaretto. Beat until stiff peaks form. When ready to serve, cut the cake into portions and top with the whipped cream. Garnish with sliced fruit.

Chocolate Tequila Cheesecake

▼ ▼ ▼ ▼ ▼ ▼   **8 servings**

This has got to be one of the favorites in our house. Not only does it contain tequila, it also has a topping made with cocoa. Try grated Mexican chocolate if you like instead of the cocoa. One of our friends has asked us never to give her husband any more of this because he cannot stop eating it!

CRUST

1³/4 cups graham cracker crumbs, about 36 crackers

1/4 cup walnuts, chopped

1 teaspoon grated orange peel

1/2 cup melted butter

FILLING

3 eggs, lightly beaten

2 (8-ounce) packages cream cheese

1 cup granulated sugar

Juice of 1 lime

2 tablespoons tequila

1 tablespoon Triple Sec

3 cups sour cream

TOPPING

1/2 cup butter

1/2 cup milk

1 cup confectioners' sugar

1/4 cup cocoa

1 tablespoon tequila

Sliced kiwi

Raspberries

Mint leaves

Preheat the oven to 375 degrees. For the crust, mix together the graham cracker crumbs, walnuts, orange peel, and melted butter and press into the bottom and sides of a 9-inch springform pan.

For the filling, beat together the eggs, cream cheese, and granulated sugar until smooth. Stir in the lime juice, tequila, Triple Sec, and sour cream until well blended. Spoon the filling into the crust and bake for 1 hour. Turn off the oven and let the cheesecake sit 4 to 5 hours. Then refrigerate for at least 6 hours before serving.

For the topping, heat the butter and milk in a microwave until the butter has melted. Beat the sugar and cocoa into the milk mixture until smooth. Stir in the tequila and then spread on top of the cheesecake. Refrigerate for 2 hours. Place the kiwi slices around the edge of the cake, arrange the raspberries across the top, and add mint leaves to garnish.

Mother's Day Mango-Walnut Cake

▼　▼　▼　▼　▼　**Makes 10 to 12 servings**

We came up with this cake idea for Mother's Day a couple of years ago, when I was on a mango binge.

1 yellow cake mix	$^3/_4$ cup vegetable oil
1 (3.4 ounce) box instant vanilla pudding	$^3/_4$ cup mango nectar
2 cups sour cream	1 cup walnut pieces
4 eggs	Cream Cheese Frosting (recipe follows)

Preheat the oven to 350 degrees. Grease and flour a bundt pan. Mix the cake mix, pudding, sour cream, eggs, oil, and mango nectar together until smooth. Fold in the walnut pieces. Pour the batter into the prepared pan and bake for 1 hour. Cool for 10 minutes. Invert the cake onto a cake plate and cool completely. Decorate the cake with Cream Cheese Frosting.

Cream Cheese Frosting

1 (8-ounce) package cream cheese, at room temperature	4 cups confectioners' sugar
	1 teaspoon vanilla extract
$^1/_2$ cup (1 stick) butter, at room temperature	Slices of mango
	Whole walnuts

Blend the cream cheese and butter in a large bowl with an electric mixer on low speed for 1 minute. Gradually add the sugar. Add the vanilla and increase the mixing speed to medium, beat until frosting is fluffy.

Heat 1 cup of the cream cheese frosting in a medium saucepan over low heat until pourable. Pour over the bundt cake to cover. Decorate the bottom edge of the cake with the remaining frosting. Place mango slices and whole walnuts around the cake to decorate.

Mexican Chocolate Pie

Pastel de Chocolate Mejicano

▼ ▼ ▼ ▼ ▼ ▼ ▼   **6 servings**

This pie is very easy to make. To make it even easier, instead of making the crust, just buy a graham cracker crust ready to go.

---

2 cups graham crackers, crushed, about 38 crackers

1 cup pecans, finely chopped

$^1/_2$ cup (1 stick) butter, melted

2 cups milk

1 (3-ounce) tablet Mexican chocolate or 3 ounces semisweet chocolate plus 2 tablespoons sugar

1 (3.4-ounce) package chocolate pudding

1 (8-ounce) package cream cheese, at room temperature

Whole pecans, for garnish

Combine the graham cracker crumbs and pecans. Set 1 cup of the mixture aside. Add the melted butter to the remaining mixture, and press into a 9-inch pie pan.

Heat the milk and chocolate over low heat. Add the pudding and stir occasionally until thickened. Add the cream cheese and stir until melted. Pour the mixture into the pie pan. Cool.

Refrigerate for several hours before serving. Garnish with the reserved nuts and crumbs around the edge of the pie. Decorate with pecans.

Margarita Pie

A pie like this one is best reserved for the adults. Grownups are allowed to have their cake, or pie and eat it too, you know.

$^1/_2$ cup (1 stick) butter or margarine	$^1/_2$ teaspoon salt
$1^1/_2$ cups chocolate wafer crumbs	1 (12-ounce) can condensed milk
$^1/_2$ cup walnuts, ground	1 teaspoon grated lime peel
$^1/_4$ cup lemon juice	1 (8-ounce) container whipped topping
$^1/_3$ cup lime juice	Sweetened chocolate curls
1 tablespoon Triple Sec	
1 tablespoon tequila	

Melt the butter and combine it with the chocolate wafer crumbs and ground walnuts. Press the mixture into the bottom and sides of a 9-inch pie pan.

Mix the lemon juice, lime juice, Triple Sec, tequila, and salt with the condensed milk. Stir in the lime peel, fold in the whipped topping, and spoon into the prepared chocolate crust. Refrigerate for at least 2 hours before serving. Garnish with chocolate curls and serve.

Cinnamon Tortilla Shells with Ice Cream

▼ ▼ ▼ ▼ ▼ ▼   **4 servings**

This is the perfect cooling dessert to top off a special dinner of hot and spicy foods. Make the tortilla bowls in advance and refrigerate them until you are ready to serve the ice cream. It couldn't be easier.

---

2 tablespoons sugar
$^1/_2$ teaspoon ground cinnamon
4 (8-inch) flour tortillas, at room temperature
1 tablespoon butter or margarine, melted

1 quart of your favorite flavor of ice cream
Ice cream topping (optional)

Preheat the oven to 400 degrees. Lightly grease the outside of four 10-ounce custard cups. Place the cups upside-down on a baking pan.

Combine the sugar and cinnamon in a small bowl. Lightly brush 1 side of each tortilla with melted butter and sprinkle with the sugar-cinnamon mixture. Place the tortillas, sugared side up, over the inverted custard cups. (Tortillas will mold to cups during baking.) Bake for 5 to 8 minutes, or until crisp and lightly browned. Remove from the custard cups and cool. Refrigerate if desired.

To serve, place 2 scoops of ice cream in each cooled shell. If desired, top with your favorite ice cream topping.

Mango Ice Cream

Helado de Mango

6 servings

This *helado* (ice cream) is made with mangos. Mangos are becoming more common in the U.S. but, in past years, they were certainly the fruit of choice in the Southwest. They were considered quite exotic and delicious.

> 1 large fresh or canned
> mango, cut into small
> pieces
>
> $1^1/2$ cups nonfat milk
> 3 tablespoons sugar
> Juice of $^1/2$ lemon

Combine the mango and 1¼ cups of the milk in a small freezer dish. Freeze until firm. Just before serving, break the frozen mixture into small pieces and place in blender with remaining ¼ cup milk. Add the sugar and lemon juice and process until the mixture is smooth. Serve in sherbet cups.

Watermelon Sorbet

Sorbete de Sandia

OK, you've got your *helado de mango*, now try *sandia* (watermelon). Next you can try papaya or *membrillo* (quince). You can find unseeded watermelons at most grocery stores.

1 cup sugar	**4 pounds watermelon, seeded or seedless**

Combine 1 cup of water and the sugar in a medium saucepan and boil for 5 minutes. Remove from heat.

Puree the watermelon in a blender. (If you are using watermelon with seeds, be sure to remove the seeds first.) Strain the juice and add 3 cups to the sugar mixture. Pour into a freezer container, cover, and chill in the refrigerator for 2 hours. Cover and freeze. Break the mixture into pieces and slush in the blender. Serve in sorbet cups.

Mexican Chocolate Sauce

▼ ▼ ▼ ▼ ▼ ▼ ▼

This sauce goes great over Mexican chocolate ice cream, or any ice cream for that matter. You can also use it to make chocolate milk a little different.

¹/₂ cup heavy cream	**¹/₂ teaspoon ground**
1 round Mexican chocolate	**cinnamon**

Bring the cream, sugar, and chocolate to a boil over medium heat, stirring constantly. Boil, stirring 30 seconds, or until the chocolate is melted. Remove from the heat and stir in the cinnamon.

Did You Know?

▼ ▼ ▼ ▼ ▼ ▼ ▼

CHOCOLATE

One of the sweetest gifts anyone can give is chocolate, and that is what Mexico gave to the rest of the world. Columbus was the first European to encounter beans from the cacao tree back in 1502, on his last trip to the Americas. The Aztecs used the cocoa beans as a form of currency, which they kept quiet because of the value they placed on the bean. When cocoa beans were brought back to Europe, their potential value was overlooked by the King and Queen.

The Aztecs also used cocoa beans to prepare a bitter tasting drink called *chocolatl* (meaning warm liquid), a drink the Aztecs claimed as fit for the gods. An ancient Toltec legend recounts that the god Quetzalcoatl brought the seeds for the cacao tree down from heaven.

Montezuma served his Spanish guests the *chocolatl*. The Spanish did not care very much for this drink because of its bitter taste. During his conquest of Mexico, Cortez also found the Aztecs using the cocoa bean to prepare *chocolatl*. When he returned to Europe, he brought the cocoa beans back with him. On the voyage back, he and others on board the ship conceived of the idea of sweetening the bitter beverage with cane sugar to make it more agreeable to the aristocracy of Spain. Later, cinnamon and vanilla were also added and the new *chocolatl* drink quickly made cocoa a profitable business.

The Spaniards planted the cocoa bean and kept secret the art of making cocoa for close to a hundred years. Spanish monks were in charge of processing the cocoa bean. They eventually let the secret out. The beverage spread throughout Europe, and the rest is history.

The three best-known brands of Mexican chocolate are Chocolate Abuelita, Chocolate Ibarra, and El Popular. Park Kerr, famous author of cookbooks on Southwestern cuisine, says he prefers Chocolate Ibarra. Rick Bayless, author of *The Mexican Kitchen Cookbook*, prefers El Popular. If possible, get samplings of each brand and make your own choice. If acquiring authentic Mexican chocolate is not possible, cheat! Mix cinnamon and vanilla in your favorite cocoa drink and enjoy!

Beverages

Proverbs
Dichos

Better aught than naught.
Más vale algo que nada.

Thirty days has September, April, June, and November. All the rest have 31, except February, which has 28.
Treinta dias trae novembre, abril, junio y septiembre. Veintiocho trae uno, los demas treinta y uno.

Better late than never.
Más vale tarde que nunca.

Ask and you shall receive.
Quien tiene lengua, a Roma llega.

Money talks.
Con dinero baila el perro.

Hot Chocolate

Bebida de Chocolate

Being a chocoholic is one thing. Being a Mexican chocolate chocoholic is even better. Mexican chocolate has a wonderfully subtle, different taste. This warm libation is a staple at our house all year long.

3^1/$_2$ ounces sweet chocolate, preferably Mexican chocolate	^{1}/$_2$ teaspoon ground cinnamon
4 cups milk	^{1}/$_2$ teaspoon vanilla extract

Place the chocolate and milk in a large saucepan. Heat over medium heat until the chocolate has melted. Bring to a boil. Remove from the heat and add the cinnamon and vanilla. Pour into a blender and process for a few seconds at high speed until frothy. Serve hot.

Cocoa Kahlúa

Who said cocoa is just for kids? Try this grown-up version. It will keep you nice and warm.

> **2 round disks (6 to 7 ounces)**
> **Mexican chocolate,**
> **preferably Ibarra**
> **1 quart whole milk**
> **1 quart half-and-half**
>
> **2 teaspoons vanilla extract**
> **$^1/_2$ cup Kahlúa**
> **Whipped cream (optional)**
> **Ground cinnamon (optional)**

Break the chocolate disks into wedges. Heat the milk and half-and-half to steaming but not boiling. Pour into a blender and add the chocolate and vanilla. Blend until the chocolate is dissolved. Add the Kahlúa and pulse several times. Serve in mugs. You can top this off with whipped cream and cinnamon, if you like.

Mexican Coffee

Café Mejicano

4 to 6 servings

After Mexican hot chocolate, Café Mejicano has got to be my favorite drink. There are people who enjoy their gourmet coffees and their French roasts. Here in the Southwest, one of our favorites is this flavorful coffee made with *piloncillo* (Mexican brown sugar) and cinnamon.

---

¹/₂ cup ground coffee
1 (3-inch) cinnamon stick, broken in half

1 small (about 3-ounce) cone *piloncillo*, chopped, or 4 tablespoons (firmly packed) brown sugar (optional)

Place the coffee in a filter container of a drip-style pot; scatter the cinnamon and piloncillo over the coffee. Brew with 4 cups of water. Pour into cups.

Mexican After-dinner Coffee: Prepare as directed above or use plain coffee, sweetened if desired. Pour ¹/₂ to 1 ounce Kahlúa into each cup, add the hot coffee, and garnish with 2 tablespoons whipped cream, about 1 tablespoon grated semisweet chocolate, and 1 cinnamon stick.

Kahlúa Coffee

If you like coffee as much as I do, you'll love the combination of the Kahlúa and tequila in the coffee. Don't drink and drive after this one though!

---

4 cups freshly brewed coffee	**$^1/_3$ cup (3 ounces) tequila**
4$^1/_2$ cups Kahlúa	**$^1/_2$ pint whipping cream, whipped**

Mix the coffee, Kahlúa, and tequila. Divide evenly among 6 mugs. Top each with whipped cream and serve.

Agua Fresca

Makes about 1 quart

Have your kids set up an Agua Fresca stand instead of a lemonade stand for the summer, and they'll be the hit of the neighborhood. Cool the *agua* in the refrigerator or serve over ice. Add a sprig of mint for more cool flavor.

2²/₃ cups seeded, peeled, and chopped cantaloupe or watermelon	2 to 3 tablespoons lime juice
3 to 4 tablespoons sugar	Ice (optional)

Puree the fruit in a blender and season to taste with sugar and lime juice. Combine the fruit mixture and 2 cups of water in a large pitcher. If desired, pour through a strainer to eliminate pulp. Cover and refrigerate for up to 1 week. Serve over ice, if desired.

Kiwi Agua Fresca: Prepare as directed above, using 1²/₃ cups peeled and chopped kiwi fruit, 2 to 3 tablespoons sugar, 2 teaspoons lime juice, and 2 cups of water.

Strawberry Agua Fresca: Prepare as directed above, using 2¼ cups rinsed and hulled strawberries, 3 to 4 tablespoons sugar, 1½ tablespoons lime juice, and 2½ cups water.

El Chuco Smoothie

El Chuco, as *pachucos* (*zootsuiters*) called El Paso back in the 1940s and 1950s, has its own smoothie. It's as smooth and tasty as these *batos* (guys) considered the Border town. Hey baby, *qué pasó*?

¹/₂ cup sliced banana	**2 cups milk**
¹/₂ cup chopped mango, papaya, or guava	**1 tablespoon honey**

Place the fruit, milk, and honey in a food processor or blender. Cover and process on high speed until smooth. Strain if using mango to remove the fibers.

Atole de Leche

▼ ▼ ▼ ▼ ▼

8 to 10 servings

Here's a traditional holiday drink for the winter months that will warm you up and satisfy your sweet tooth. If the drink comes out too thick, thin it with additional cream. Try it instead of hot chocolate.

¹/₂ cup masa harina	**1 cup sugar, or to taste**
One 2-inch cinnamon stick	**3 cups whole milk**
or vanilla bean	**1 cup cream**

Pour the masa harina into a large saucepan and gradually stir in 2 cups of water. Add the cinnamon and bring to a simmer over low heat. Cook, stirring constantly, until the liquid has thickened. Remove from the heat and add the sugar, milk, and cream, stirring well. Return to low heat and cook until the sugar has dissolved. Remove the cinnamon stick and serve warm.

Chocolate Atole

Champurrado

6 to 8 servings

Here's another *atole*, this one made with chocolate. Again, if this mixture is a little too thick for your taste, add more milk. Sit in front of the fireplace and enjoy a cup, or two.

6 cups whole milk	**1 cup masa harina**
3 ounces unsweetened	**1 cinnamon stick**
chocolate, grated, 3 to 4	**1 cup brown sugar**
rounded tablespoons	

Heat the milk and chocolate in a saucepan, stirring to dissolve the chocolate. When the chocolate is completely dissolved, remove from the heat and set aside, covered to keep warm.

Mix the masa harina with 2 cups of water in another saucepan; place over low heat, add the cinnamon stick and cook until the mixture thickens and the masa becomes translucent. Add the chocolate milk and brown sugar. Stir to dissolve the sugar and simmer for a few minutes. Remove the cinnamon stick and serve the *champurrado*, hot, in cups or mugs.

Horchata

Makes 4 to 6 servings

Here's a delicious recipe for *horchata*, this one made with rice water. It always reminds me of the *kermezes* (bazaars) at our neighborhood church of San Ignacio. I can hear them calling out the characters for the *loteria*, a sort of Mexican bingo, every time I make it.

6 tablespoons rice	**1 cinnamon stick**
6 ounces blanched	**3 strips lime peel**
almonds, 1$^1/_4$ cup	**1 cup sugar, or to taste**

Pulverize the rice in a blender or spice grinder. Transfer to a medium bowl and add the almonds, cinnamon stick, and lime peel. Stir in 2$^1/_4$ cups hot water, cover, and let stand at least 6 hours or, preferably, overnight.

Place the mixture into a blender and blend for 3 to 4 minutes, or until no longer gritty. Add 2 cups of water, then blend for a few seconds more. Set a large sieve over a mixing bowl and line it with 3 layers of dampened cheese-cloth. Pour the almond-rice mixture into the sieve a little at a time, gently stirring to help the liquid pass through. When the liquid has been strained, gather up the corners of the cheesecloth and twist them together. Squeeze the cheesecloth firmly to expel all the remaining liquid.

Add 2 cups of water and stir in enough sugar to sweeten the drink to your taste. If the consistency is too thick, add additional water. Cover and refrigerate until very cold. Stir before pouring. Serve the Horchata without ice, which would dilute its delicate flavor.

Mango Horchata

▼ ▼ ▼ ▼ ▼ **Makes about 6 to 8 servings**

Here we go with another *horchata* drink, this one with the sweet taste of mango. If you've never tried mango, this is an excellent way to develop a taste for it.

---

1 quart milk	**1 tablespoon vanilla**
4 cinnamon sticks	**extract**
$^3/_4$ cup sugar	**1 large mango, peeled,**
$^1/_4$ cup rice flour or $^1/_3$ cup	**seeded, and cubed**
white rice crushed to a	
powder in the blender	

Bring the milk to a boil in a saucepan. Reduce to a simmer and cook, stirring frequently, until reduced by half, about 20 minutes. Strain into a large saucepan and add 2 quarts of water and the cinnamon sticks. Bring to a boil, reduce to a simmer, and cook 5 minutes. Remove from the heat and let sit 15 minutes. Remove the cinnamon sticks and discard. Combine the sugar, rice flour, vanilla, and mango in a bowl. Add milk mixture, whirl in blender, strain into a pitcher and refrigerate at least 4 hours. Serve cold over ice.

Margaritas

Here's your traditional margarita recipe. Turn to The Legend of The Margarita (page 307) to find out how this drink originated.

---

1 slice lime
Coarse salt
$^1/_2$ tablespoon fresh lime
  juice
$1^1/_2$ tablespoons tequila

$1^1/_2$ teaspoons
  orange-flavored liqueur,
  such as Triple Sec
2 to 4 ice cubes

Rub the inside rim of a chilled glass with the slice of lime. Pour the salt into a saucer and dip the glass into the salt so it adheres to the moistened rim. Combine the lime juice, tequila, orange-flavored liqueur, and ice cubes in a cocktail shaker. Shake well and strain into the salt-rimmed glass.

To make a pitcher: In a large pitcher, dilute a can of frozen limeade, according to package instructions. Add 1 cup of tequila and $^1/_2$ cup of orange-flavored liqueur. Mix well and chill. Serve over ice.

Jalapeño Margaritas

▼ ▼ ▼ ▼ ▼ ▼ ▼

I've always said that recipes are not carved in stone. They are ideas and suggestions that you can take and experiment with to reflect your personal likes and tastes. This one proves it. Without experimentation, who would have ever thought of a Jalapeño Margarita?

Jalapeño peppers
Sour mix (1 part sugar
 syrup and 1 part lemon
 juice)
Tequila

Triple Sec
Dash Tabasco
Whole jalapeños,
 for garnish
Lime slices, for garnish

Soak the jalapeños in the sour mix for 1 hour. In a blender, mix the tequila, Triple Sec, Tabasco, and sour mix. Garnish each drink with a whole jalapeño and a slice of lime.

Mock Margaritas

Makes about 3 quarts

Don't care for alcohol? No problem. You can still enjoy the fine taste of a margarita without the tequila. Some people say that's like a bullfight without the bull, but everyone to their own taste.

1 (12-ounce) can frozen lemonade concentrate, thawed	1 cup confectioners' sugar
	6 cups crushed ice
	Lime wedges
1 (12-ounce) can frozen limeade concentrate, thawed	Coarse salt
	1 liter bottle club soda, chilled

Process half of the lemonade, limeade, sugar, and ice in a blender until smooth. Pour into a 4-quart plastic container. Repeat procedure. Freeze until slushy.

Rub the lime around the rims of stemmed glasses. Place salt in a saucer and place the rim of glass in salt. Stir the soda into the frozen mixture until slushy and pour into glasses.

Mexican Bloody Mary

Vampiro

The name alone makes this drink perfect for any Halloween or *Día de los Muertos* celebration you might have.

1¹/₄ cups tomato juice	Salt
¹/₂ cup orange juice	Cayenne to taste
2 tablespoons lime juice	1 cup tequila
1¹/₂ tablespoons finely chopped onion	Ice cubes
¹/₂ teaspoon Worcestershire sauce	

Combine the tomato juice, orange juice, lime juice, onion, Worcestershire sauce, salt to taste, and cayenne in blender. Pour into a pitcher and chill in the refrigerator for at least 4 hours. Just before serving, blend in the tequila. Serve over ice.

Piña Colada

Try this beverage with tequila instead of rum. You get a slightly different flavor, but oh so good. Check out our section on tequila (page 305) to see which one you'd like to try.

$1/2$ cup light rum	2 cups ice
3 tablespoons coconut milk	Pineapple wedge
5 tablespoons crushed pineapple	1 maraschino cherry

Blend the rum, coconut milk, pineapple, and ice in a blender at high speed until smooth. Strain into a glass and serve with a straw. Top with a pineapple wedge and a cherry.

Mock Piña Colada

▼　▼　▼　▼　▼　▼

Makes 4 cups

Another nonalcoholic drink. Our daughter likes this one, mostly because it contains ice cream.

One (8-ounce) can crushed
　pineapple, undrained
2¹/₂ cups vanilla ice cream
　or frozen yogurt,
　softened
1 teaspoon rum extract

1 teaspoon coconut
　extract
1 tablespoon confectioners'
　sugar
Ice cubes

Combine the pineapple, ice cream, rum extract, coconut extract, and sugar in a blender. Add enough ice cubes to bring the mixture to make 4 cups and process until smooth, stopping periodically to scrape down sides. Serve immediately.

Pineapple Punch

Ponche de Piña

8 to 12 servings

This is a traditional *calientito* (hot toddy). I remember my grandmother and all the family elders sipping a small glass of this *ponche* (punch) during important family gatherings.

3 pineapples	**³/4 cup sugar**
3 cinnamon sticks	**1 cup coconut milk**
2 teaspoons whole cloves	**1 quart light rum**
2 teaspoons whole allspice	

Peel, core and finely chop or shred the pineapples. Add 3 cups of water and let stand overnight. Mix the pineapple and water with the cinnamon, cloves, allspice, sugar, and coconut milk in a large saucepan. Boil for 5 minutes. Strain the liquid into a large pitcher. Add the rum and serve hot.

Aztec Punch

16 to 20 servings

Aztec Punch looks very pretty in a punch bowl. Why is it called Aztec Punch? Perhaps because of the papayas and guava nectar. These fruits are used more readily in Mexican cookery than apples and oranges giving the recipe a more authentic Mexican flavor. If you want it non-alcoholic, leave out the champagne. It tastes super either way. Fresh fruit always adds a great flavor to any drink.

1 fresh pineapple, peeled, cored, and cut in chunks	2 cups orange juice
3 oranges, peeled and sectioned	2 cups guava nectar
2 papayas, peeled, seeded, and sliced	1 bottle champagne
2 cups strawberries, halved	1 bottle ginger ale
	Ice
	Mint sprigs

Mix the pineapple, oranges, papayas, strawberries, orange juice, guava nectar, champagne, and ginger ale together in a large punch bowl. Add the ice and garnish with mint sprigs.

Rum Eggnog

Rompope

6 servings

You can't have a Fiesta Navideña (Christmas party) without homemade Rompope. There are some traditional drinks that translate anywhere.

4 eggs	**¹/₂ teaspoon ground**
1 (12-ounce) can sweet-	**cinnamon**
ened condensed milk	**1 teaspoon vanilla extract**
¹/₂ cup rum	**Ground cinnamon**

Mix together the eggs*, condensed milk, rum, cinnamon, and vanilla in the blender. Serve in small glasses. Sprinkle with a little ground cinnamon.

*With eggs and other raw foods from animals, there is a small possibility of Salmonella food poisoning. The risk is greater for those who are pregnant, elderly or very young and those with impaired immune systems. These individuals should avoid raw and undercooked animal foods. Healthy people need to remember that there is a very small risk and treat eggs and other raw animal foods accordingly. Use only properly refrigerated, clean, sound-shelled, fresh, grade AA or A eggs. Avoid mixing yolks and whites with the shell. Refrigerate eggs after removing them from the shell, prepared egg dishes and other foods if you won't be consuming them within an hour.

Mexican Eggnog

Coquito

Makes 8 to 10 servings

This drink reminds me of a liquid *Pastel de Tres Leches*. It's deliciously sweet and makes a great after-dinner drink. This one takes a little time but your effort is rewarded with the first sip.

---

2 to 3 cinnamon sticks

1 (12-ounce) can evaporated milk

1 (12-ounce) can of condensed milk

4 egg yolks, lightly beaten

1 (15-ounce) can cream of coconut

4 cups rum

Boil the cinnamon sticks in 2 cups of water. Remove the sticks when the water is yellow and has the smell and taste of cinnamon. Add the evaporated milk, condensed milk, and egg yolks and cook over low heat, stirring so the mixture does not stick to the bottom of the pot. When it has been boiling for a few minutes, add the cream of coconut and rum. Stir well and remove from the heat. Cool. Stored in the refrigerator, it lasts for approximately 4 to 6 weeks.

Sangria

This is a wonderful sangria recipe. It goes quickly, so make plenty. It's perfect for summer gatherings. It kind of sneaks up on you on a hot summer day, so watch out.

3 lemons, sliced	**$^1/_2$ pint brandy**
1 lime, sliced	**1 gallon (about 4 liters)**
6 oranges, sliced	**dry red wine**
1 cup sugar	**Ice**

Place the lemons, lime, and oranges in the bottom of a large punch bowl. Sprinkle the sugar over the fruit. Add more sugar if the oranges are sour. Add the brandy and let the fruit stand at least 1 hour. Add the wine, stir well, and allow to sit for 30 minutes or more. Serve over ice.

Sangria for Kids

About 20 servings

If the grownups can have sangria, so can the kids—without the wine of course. They love the chunks of fruit. This juice mixture is fantastic for brunches too.

1 quart orange juice	2 cups assorted fruits,
1¹/₂ cups white grape juice	such as strawberries,
1 (2 liter) bottle 7-Up,	mango slices, orange
chilled	slices, grapes, etc.
Ice	Mint sprigs

Stir the orange juice and grape juice together in a large pitcher. Add the 7-Up and stir. Add the ice and fruit. Ladle into tall glasses and garnish with mint.

Tequila Sunrise

▼   ▼   ▼   ▼   ▼

You've had your Margaritas, your Piña Coladas, and now your Tequila Sunrise. You're all set for the finest Southwestern barbecue spread of a lifetime. Put on the mariachi music and dance around the patio.

2 tablespoons tequila	**1 tablespoon grenadine**
¹/₄ cup freshly squeezed	**Ice**
orange juice	**Orange slice, for garnish**
1 tablespoon Triple Sec	

Place the tequila, orange juice, Triple Sec, and grenadine in a blender with ice and blend. Serve in a stemmed glass garnished with a slice of orange.

Torito

This is a hot one. Just as with the Jalapeño Margarita, you have to prepare yourself for a different taste sensation. If you like a good kick in the palate, we're sure you'll like this.

---

2 tablespoons Tequila or
rum
1/2 cup orange juice
1/4 teaspoon vinegar

1 pearl onion
1 teaspoon chile pepper
powder

Mix the tequila with the orange juice, vinegar, onion, and chile pepper powder. You can adjust the amounts to find the combination that suits your taste.

Did You Know?

▼ ▼ ▼ ▼ ▼ ▼ ▼

TEQUILA

Margaritas, Sunrises, Shooters—you name it, you can't make it without tequila. It's another one of those wonderful gifts Mexico gave to the world.

What is tequila? Well, it's an alcoholic beverage made from fermented sugars (*agua miel*) derived from the *piña* (core) of the Blue Weber agave cactus-like plant, one of at least one hundred agaves. The agave looks like it would be a cactus, but it is actually related to the lily. Its leaves grow to an average of ten feet tall. At the plant's maturity, approximately eight to twelve years, a center stalk (the flower) grows up from the center to a height of about fifteen feet. Agaves are said to be pollinated by bats.

At maturity, the leaves are cut off to expose the *piña*. After being roasted and crushed, the *piña* produces 98 percent of the agave sugars needed for fermentation.

Tequila is named after the city in the state of Jalisco in Mexico where it is produced. The city of Tequila's origin can be traced back to the Aztecas. The Tiquila Indians established a settlement thirty-five miles northwest of Guadalajara. It is a small hillside town located at the foot of a dormant volcano. This town has more than thirty tequila-producing factories. The first major distiller of tequila was Jose Cuervo, established in Mexico in 1795.

Tequila evolved from *pulque*, a drink that was initially prepared by the Zapotec Indians. They used *pulque* in religious ceremonies and for medicinal purposes. After *pulque* came Mezcal. The Spanish, needing a stronger spirited drink, took the *pulque* and fermented it for several days and then distilled it into Mezcal. The sugars used for fermentation came from the sap of the roots, stalks, and leaves of the wild agave plant.

The different levels of tequila are:

Blanco (Plata): unaged tequila
Gold: unaged tequila with additives to give is its amber color
Reposado: aged in oak barrels from sixty days to one year
Anejo: aged in government sealed barrels for a minimum of one year. (Tequila production is government-regulated in Mexico much the same way Cognac production is regulated in France.)

A few of the more popular tequila brands are: Aguila Blue Agave; Chinaco; El Conquistador; Herradura; Jose Cuervo; Montezuma; Sauza; Constitución. A newcomer on the tequila block is Tequila Nacional; owned by El Paso's own Park Kerr, author and businessman.

So, if you have a special occasion coming up or would just like to have something special to sip on after a long hard day, try tequila. The flavor reflects the very nature of the Hispanic community, warmth, strength, courage, and soul.

Did You Know?

▼ ▼ ▼ ▼ ▼ ▼ ▼

LEGEND OF THE MARGARITA

So far, I have found four different versions of how the most popular tequila drink, the Margarita, was created. If you know of another one, or know which one is the correct story, email Aprovecho and share it with us. Here goes:

First Version: There was a wealthy *caballero* (gentleman) who was totally consumed with the beauty of a young woman named Margarita. So, he had a drink created in her honor by the local bartender. Sadly, he woke one morning to find both Margarita and his money gone. Only her garter remained. (Sounds iffy to me.)

Second Version: A man by the name of Francisco (Pancho) Morales is credited with the creation of the Margarita in 1942. Supposedly he was working at a place called Tommy's Bar when a woman came in and asked for a drink he had never heard of. Not wanting her to think of him as inept (and for fear of ruining his reputation as an excellent bartender), he conjured up a drink mixture of tequila, Cointreau, and lime juice. The woman loved it and asked Pancho for the name of the drink. He told her it was a Margarita. Pancho died in El Paso in 1997. (This one sounds quite convincing.)

Third Version: The Margarita was named for Margarita Sames of San Antonio. The drink was especially created for her for a Christmas party she was hosted in Acapulco in 1948.

Fourth Version: The Margarita was named after Margorie King, a young actress back in the 1930s. She reportedly could not drink any alcohol except tequila. The owner of Rancho La Gloria, Danny Herrera, created the drink so that Margorie would not seem unlady-like by drinking straight tequila.

Which is real? Which is fiction? Don't know. Do you?

Making Tamales

Proverbs
Dichos

An apple a day keeps the doctor away.
La mejor medicina es la buena comida.

Something is better than nothing.
Algo es algo, peor es nada.

A hungry person is an angry person.
Hambre y esperar hacen rabiar.

Knowledge is power.
Saber es poder.

Possession is nine-tenths of the law.
El que se fue a Sevilla, perdio la silla.

Husk Preparation

Cornhusks are usually sold in 8-ounce packages, approximately 50 husks per package. They can be purchased at any supermarket that sells Latin American groceries or a Hispanic or Latin market.

Sort through the husks, removing any corn silk or other materials you may find. Silks are a lot easier to remove when the husks are wet. If you try to remove silks embedded in the husks when they are dry, you will end up tearing the husks.

Place the husks in a large pot and cover with warm water to soften. Weigh the husks down with a heavy object. Leave the husks in water anywhere from a couple of hours to overnight. Separate the husks and rinse once or twice more. Remove any remaining silk strings at this time.

Stand the husks in a large pot or basket (I found that a clean dish drainer works the best) and allow the husks to drain. Pat the husks dry when you are ready to make the tamales.

SOAK

CLEAN

RINSE & DRAIN

Masa

Makes about 1 pound

---

4 cups masa harina
2 teaspoons baking powder
2 teaspoons salt
2²/₃ cups broth, reserved
   from meat

1¹/₃ cups lard, beat until
   fluffy

Mix the masa harina, baking powder, and salt. Add the broth to the masa mixture a little at a time to make a moist dough. Add the masa dough to the lard. Beat until the dough has a spongy texture. A quick test to make sure the masa is light enough is to drop a small ball of masa, about the size of a pea, into a glass of water. If it floats to the top, the masa is ready. Taste just a smidgen of the masa for salt content. This is enough masa for 2 dozen medium to 1½ dozen large tamales, or 4 to 5 dozen small cocktail tamales. To add a little kick to your tamales, try adding some of the red or green sauce into the masa mixture. This will add flavor if you are looking for something a little spicier.

WHIP

MIX

Pork Filling

Tamales can be filled with a variety of meats or other foods, such as chiles. Shredded chicken, beef, or pork are traditional, but I have known people to fill their tamales with chile con queso, beans, or vegetables mixed with chile. Then of course there are sweet tamales. These don't have a filling but the masa is prepared with a sweetened flavor (see recipe, page 317). The following is a simple shredded pork recipe that is the most common filling used in making tamales.

$^1/_4$ cup vegetable oil

4 to 5 pounds pork roast

 (3 pounds, if boneless)

1 large onion, sliced

3 cloves garlic, chopped

1 teaspoon cumin powder

2 teaspoons salt

Heat the oil in a large Dutch oven. Brown the pork on all sides. Add enough water to cover the roast. Add the onion, garlic, cumin, and salt. Boil until fork tender, about 2 to 3 hours. When the meat is done, remove from the stove and cool.

Discard the fat and bones. Remove the meat from the pot, reserving the broth. When the meat is cool enough to handle, shred it with 2 forks or by hand.

Red Chile Puree

Makes 2 cups

> **9 dried New Mexico or**
> **California red chiles, hot**
> **or mild or a combination**
> **(about 3 ounces)**
>
> **1 small onion, chopped**
> **2 cloves garlic, chopped**

Toast the chiles on a large baking pan for about 4 minutes. Cool slightly and then remove the seeds and stems. (Wear rubber gloves when handling chiles.)

Combine the chiles, at least 2 cups of water, enough to cover the chiles completely, the onion, and garlic in a 4-quart pan. Cover and bring to a boil over high heat. Reduce the heat and simmer, covered, until the chiles are soft, about 30 minutes. Remove from the heat and cool slightly.

Whirl the chile mixture in a blender until smooth. Run through a sieve to discard residue and any unprocessed chile skins. The puree can be refrigerated, covered, up to 1 week. (If you want a hotter sauce, try adding 1 or 2 chiles de arbol, stemmed and seeded.)

SEED & STEM

SIMMER & SEASON

PUREE

Green Chile Sauce

Makes 2 cups

2 medium onions, chopped
$^1/_3$ cup vegetable oil
1 (7-ounce) can diced
   green chiles
1 (13-ounce) can
   tomatillos, drained

1 cup chicken broth
3 tablespoons lime juice
2 teaspoons dried oregano
1 teaspoon ground cumin
Salt

Heat the oil and sauté the onions until soft, about 5 minutes. Stir in the green chiles, tomatillos, broth, lime juice, oregano, and cumin. Bring to a boil, reduce the heat, and simmer, uncovered, for 25 minutes, stirring occasionally. Whirl in blender until smooth. Season to taste with salt.

Assembly

Mix the meat with 2 cups of sauce and simmer for 20 minutes, adding broth if needed. If you look closely at the cornhusks, you will see (or feel) that one side of the husk is smoother than the other side, which has ridges. Spread the masa on the smooth side so that the tamales separate more easily from the husk when cooked. Spread 2 tablespoons of masa down center of husk to form a rectangle, 1 inch from the top and 3 inches from the bottom. This should be spread to about ⅛-inch thick. (A cornhusk is usually triangular in shape; the top is the straight edge, the bottom the pointy edge.)

FILL

Spoon 2 rounded tablespoons of filling in the center of the masa.

Fold the husk so that the masa edges meet. Wrap the smooth side of husk around the outside of the tamale and fold the tip. Place seam side down on tray and cover with damp paper towels until all tamales are prepared.

To steam, use a 12- to 14-quart steamer or place a metal rack in a 12- to 14-quart pot. Add 1 inch of water to the pot. Stack the tamales loosely in the steamer, overlapping the edges. Lay them in a circu-

WRAP

FOLD

lar fashion leaving an opening down the center so that steam can circulate and you can add more water during the steaming process, if needed.

Leave 2 inches between the tamales and the top of the pot. Place unused husks over the tamales and cover the pot with a lid. This will keep steam from escaping and will assure adequate circulation.

Bring the water to a boil and adjust the heat to maintain a steady low boil. Continue to cook, adding boiling water to maintain the water level at 1 inch. Cook until the masa is firm and does not stick to husk. Open 1 tamale from the center of pan to test. Be sure to use tongs to pick up the tamale, it will be extremely hot. Cooking time is approximately 1 hour.

STACK TAMALES IN A CIRCULAR FASHION

(Place a coin at the bottom of pot before stacking tamales. As the water boils, you will hear the coin rattling around. When you stop hearing the coin, it's time to add more boiling water down the center of the tamale stack to keep the steam going until the tamales are cooked thoroughly.)

Rule of Thumb: One pound of masa plus one pound of filling equal one dozen tamales.

ENJOY — APROVECHO!

Sweet Tamales

Makes 12 tamales

---

1 pound masa harina	1 cup raisins
1 teaspoon baking powder	1 teaspoon ground
1 tablespoon salt	cinnamon
1 cup chicken broth	$^1/_2$ teaspoon ground cloves
$^1/_2$ pound lard, beat until	$^1/_2$ teaspoon ground allspice
fluffy	$^1/_2$ cup chopped pecans
1 cup brown sugar	corn husks

Mix the masa harina, baking powder, and salt. Add the broth to the masa mixture a little at a time to make a moist dough. Add the masa dough to the lard. Beat until the dough has a spongy texture. A quick test to make sure the masa is light enough is to drop a small ball of masa, about the size of a pea, into a glass of water. If it floats to the top, the masa is ready. Add the remaining ingredients to the dough and mix thoroughly. Place 2 tablespoons of dough in middle of a corn husk, spreading towards the top end and fold over the bottom end. Steam the tamales as you would the hot tamales (see page 317).

Did You Know?

▼ ▼ ▼ ▼ ▼ ▼ ▼

POINSETTIAS

Another gift that Mexico gave to the United States is the beautiful poinsettia or *Flor de Noche Buena* (Christmas Eve Flower). It is said that the Aztecs cultivated the poinsettia and Montezuma himself revered this extraordinary flower. Unfortunately, because of the climate, poinsettias could not be grown near the capital, which is

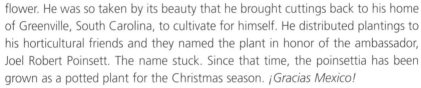

now called Mexico City, but had to be grown and imported from Central and South America.

In the seventeenth century, because of poinsettias' lovely red color and blooming time (Christmas), the Franciscan priests started using them for adornment of the altar during the Fiesta of Santa Pesebre, a nativity procession. It wasn't until 1825, however, that the first U.S. ambassador to Mexico, a botanist, came across the Christmas

flower. He was so taken by its beauty that he brought cuttings back to his home of Greenville, South Carolina, to cultivate for himself. He distributed plantings to his horticultural friends and they named the plant in honor of the ambassador, Joel Robert Poinsett. The name stuck. Since that time, the poinsettia has been grown as a potted plant for the Christmas season. *¡Gracias Mexico!*

Legend of the Poinsettia

The legend of the poinsettia has it that there was once a young Mexican girl named Pepita who was very poor and had no gift to offer the Christ Child at Christmas Eve services. She was terribly sad as she walked to the chapel in her village. Not knowing what else to do, she bent down by the roadside and picked some flowering weeds to take as an offering to the Nativity. As she approached the alter, she remembered the kind words her little friend Pedro had told her, "Even the humblest of gifts, if given in love, are acceptable in His eyes." She felt her spirits lift a little. As she lay the bouquet of weeds down, they burst into a brilliant bloom of red. Everyone at the chapel was certain they had witnessed a Christmas miracle.

From that day on, the bright flowers were known as the *Flores de Noche Buena*, the Flowers of Christmas Eve, and now they bloom each year during the Christmas season.

Did You Know?

▼ ▼ ▼ ▼ ▼ ▼ ▼

LAS POSADAS

A colorful and enjoyable Christmas tradition in the Hispanic culture is *Las Posadas*. This celebration takes place from December 16th to December 24th, Christmas Eve. It is the reenactment of Joseph and Mary's journey from Nazareth to Bethlehem in search of shelter before the Christ Child was born. *Posada*, in Spanish, means lodging. On each of these nights, two children, a boy and a girl, pose as Mary and Joseph. Other children act as angels and shepherds. Candles are held by each and everyone to light the way. Meanwhile parents and neighbors walk behind them as the multitude, singing and saying prayers. If the *Posada* is acted out in a neighborhood, a stop is made in several homes, where Mary and Joseph ask for shelter and they are turned down. At the last stop, they are welcomed, and the party begins. A piñata is provided for the children while special seasonal foods are laid out for all to enjoy. The feast usually includes tamales, *capirotada*, *champurrado*, *buñuelos*, and hot Mexican chocolate. Use the recipes in this book to create your own *Las Posadas* feast.

Submitted Recipes

Mayor Caballero's
Arroz con Pollo y Camarón

▼   ▼   ▼   ▼   ▼   ▼   **6 to 8 servings**

Olive oil as needed for sautéing	$1/4$ teaspoon cayenne
3 to 4 skinless and boneless chicken breasts or thighs, cut into strips	$1/2$ teaspoon paprika
8 ounces chorizo	2 bay leaves
1 large onion, diced	$1/4$ teaspoon ground saffron or turmeric, dissolved in 2 cups boiling water
3 garlic cloves, minced	2 cups chicken broth, boiling
2 red or yellow bell peppers, seeded and chopped	2 cups long-grain white rice
2 medium size tomatoes, seeded and chopped	$1/2$ pound cooked shrimp
$1/2$ teaspoon salt	1 cup frozen peas
$1/4$ teaspoon black pepper	1 (4-ounce) can artichoke hearts, drained, quartered, and lightly sautéed in olive oil

Preheat the oven to 350 degrees. In a large ovenproof skillet or paella pan, heat the oil, brown the chicken and set aside, covered with foil. Brown the chorizo and set aside to drain on paper towels. Sauté the onion, garlic, and bell pepper for 3 to 5 minutes. Add tomatoes, salt, pepper, cayenne, paprika, bay leaves, and saffron-water mixture. Bring to a boil. Add the chicken and chorizo, cover, and simmer for 5 minutes. Add the broth and rice. Cover tightly and bake for 30 minutes. Fluff the rice, push the shrimp under the rice, top with the peas and artichoke hearts, cover, and bake for another 15 minutes.

Raymond Caballero was the mayor of El Paso from 2001 until 2003. Mayor Caballero is an attorney and spent six years in the U.S. Department of Justice. He then entered private practice as a trial lawyer. In addition to handling many civil and criminal cases, Mayor Caballero has presented two cases to the United States Supreme Court.

Some of his priorities as Mayor included the establishment of a Border Health Institute, a Border Trade Initiative, increasing tourism, and revitalizing the downtown area.

Estela Casas' **Pozole Verde**

▼ ▼ ▼ ▼ ▼ ▼   **8 to 10 servings**

2 pounds long green chiles,
   roasted, peeled, and
   seeded
Salt and pepper
1 medium onion, chopped
Cooked jalapeño, seeded
   (optional)
3 pounds cooked shredded
   beef
1 (29-ounce) can hominy

4 cloves garlic, minced
4 bay leaves
$^1/_2$ teaspoon ground cumin
1 teaspoon crushed
   oregano
$^1/_2$ head lettuce or cabbage
12 radishes, sliced
Pinch crushed red pepper

Place the chiles, onion, 1 cup water, and salt to taste in a blender. If the chile sauce needs a little more punch, add a cooked jalapeño to blender. Cook the shredded beef in slow cooker with the hominy, chile sauce, garlic, salt, pepper, bay leaves, cumin, and oregano. Allow to cook for 1 hour. Serve with shredded lettuce or cabbage, sliced radishes and crushed red pepper.

Estela Casas' parents were from Chihuahua, Mexico, and she is a first-generation El Pasoan. She graduated from Burges High School and attended Arizona State. Estela returned to El Paso to pursue a carrer in broadcast journalism. She has been in the profession for over twenty years and is a popular and respected personality as the news anchor for KVIA-TV. Her love of children (she has three) comes across in her special "Estela's Escuelas" features. These are two of her favorite recipes.

Picadillo Navideño

6 to 8 servings

$^1/_2$ **pound medium beets, chopped**	**4 carrots, chopped**
3 pounds ground beef	**3 to 4 potatoes, chopped**
2 tablespoons olive oil	**1 cup raisins**
1 medium onion	**1 cup chopped pecans**
3 garlic cloves, minced	**1 tablespoon ground cinnamon**
Salt and pepper	**1 tablespoon ground cumin**

Cook the beets in water until tender, reserving the cooking liquid. Heat the oil and sauté the meat with the onion, garlic, salt, and pepper. Once cooked, add the carrots and potatoes and cook for a few minutes, then add the beets, raisins, pecans, cinnamon, and cumin. Cook for 10 minutes. Add the reserved liquid if the dish gets too dry at any point, or when re-heating.

Roberto Chacon's
Mole Poblano

▼ ▼ ▼ ▼ ▼ ▼

---

4 dried pasilla chiles, stemmed and seeded	$^1/_4$ cup raisins
4 dried red New Mexico chiles, stemmed and seeded	$^1/_4$ teaspoon ground cloves
	$^1/_4$ teaspoon ground cinnamon
1 medium onion, chopped	$^1/_4$ teaspoon ground coriander
3 garlic cloves, chopped	3 tablespoons shortening or vegetable oil
2 medium tomatoes, peeled, seeded, and chopped	1 cup chicken broth
2 tablespoons sesame seeds	1 ounce Mexican chocolate, or more to taste
$^1/_2$ cup chopped almonds	1 banana (to make it really sweet)
6 corn tortillas, torn into pieces	

Combine the chiles, onion, garlic, tomatoes, 1 tablespoon of the sesame seeds, almonds, tortilla pieces, raisins, cloves, cinnamon, and coriander. Puree until smooth, in batches if necessary.

Melt the shortening or heat the oil in a skillet and sauté the puree for 10 minutes, stirring often. Add the broth, chocolate, and banana and cook over very low heat for 45 minutes. The sauce should be thick. Add this mole to your favorite enchiladas instead of red chile sauce. Use the remaining sesame seeds to garnish.

Roberto Chacon was born and raised in El Paso. He has lived in El Segundo Barrio, Sunset Heights, Northeast, and back to El Segundo. He graduated from Bowie High School (the original one) in 1973 and was an MP in the Army. He came back to El Paso and was persuaded by a teacher friend of his to return to school. He decided on UTEP where he learned TV production. He's been at Time Warner Cable since 1983. Roberto married Gloria Garcia in 1984 and now has three sons: Roberto Jr., Antony, and Carlo Joseph.

Terry Chambers'
Pink Stuff

▼ ▼ ▼ ▼ ▼ ▼ **10 to 12 servings**

1 can cherry pie filling
1 can sweetened
condensed milk
1 can chunky pineapple,
drained and cut into
bite size
1 can mandarin oranges,
drained
1 can pears, drained and
cut into bite size

1 can peaches, drained and
cut into bite size
Chopped pecans
Marshmallows
Strawberries, cut into
bite size
Seedless grapes
Cool Whip

Mix the pie filling and sweetened condensed milk in a large bowl. Add the remaining ingredients, adding the Cool Whip last. Mix well and chill for several hours.

Terry Chambers and her husband, **Rick**, are native El Pasoans. They were married for twenty-six years and have one son, Eric. Terry comes from a large family of three sisters and two brothers. Rick has only one sister. Terry's interests include cooking, sewing, quilting, arts, and crafts. Her career has been in the accounting field. Rick Chambers passed away while this book was in progress. We miss him.

Lily Cordell's **After-school Quesadillas**

▼ ▼ ▼ ▼ ▼ ▼ ▼ **2 servings**

> **2 (6-inch) corn tortillas** **Leftover meat**
> **Butter** **Salt**
> **2 slices asadero cheese**

Warm the corn tortillas in the microwave for 20 seconds or on a griddle to soften them. Melt the butter in skillet. Fill each tortilla with 1 slice of cheese and meat. Fold the torillas in half. Sauté the quesadillas in melted butter over medium-low heat. Turn and cook the second side.

Lily Cordell was born in El Paso, Texas, to proud parents Teresa and Robert Cordell. She is fourteen years old and a freshman at Franklin High School. She is an avid reader and hopes to become a lawyer someday. She says, "My mom tells me I can never starve if I know how to cook, which is why this cookbook is so important and sends out a message to other people my age."

Argelia Cordero's Chile Colorado con Carne

8 to 10 servings

---

8 to 10 dried New Mexico or
   California red chiles,
   seeded and stemmed
2 cloves garlic
Salt
2 tablespoons lard or
   vegetable oil

5 pounds pork roast, cut
   into cubes
1 teaspoon garlic salt
2 large potatoes, cubed

Rinse the chiles and cover them with water in a small pot. Boil. The chiles will turn bright red when cooked. Puree the chiles with about ½ cup of the cooking water in a blender with the garlic and salt to taste.

Heat the lard in a deep pot and add the pork. Brown the meat until no juices are visible. Add the garlic salt, potatoes, pureed chile and 2 cups of water. Lower the heat to medium and cook until the potatoes are tender. Add more water, if necessary to reach desired consistency. Taste for salt.

Argelia Cordero was born and raised in El Paso. Her parents are hard-working, goal oriented individuals who are always available to offer help and advice to Argelia and her two brothers and sister. Her mother was her inspiration to go to college. She is single and has one daughter who is now also attending college.

Mando's **Salsa**

Makes about 4 cups

---

2 pounds jalapeños, rinsed
  and stemmed
2 tablespoons vegetable oil
Garlic salt
$^1/_2$ large onion, chopped

3 medium tomatoes,
  chopped
1 bunch fresh cilantro,
  minced

Place the jalapeños, oil, and garlic salt to taste in a pot and bring to a boil in 4 quarts of water. When the water boils, reduce the heat and simmer for $1^1/_2$ to 2 hours. Periodically check to make sure the water level remains full.

Drain the chiles, reserving the liquid, and set aside. Cool slightly. In a large bowl, mash the jalapeños with a potato masher or pastry cutter. Make sure all the jalapeños are completely broken up. Add the onion, tomatoes, and cilantro. Add enough of the reserved liquid to achieve the desired consistency. Cover the bowl and refrigerate for about 1 hour.

Born and raised in El Paso, in El Segundo Barrio, **Armando Cordero**, or Mando, is a graduate of "La Tech." He is a musician, printer, and computer technician, and worked for the *El Paso Times* and Digital Corp. for thirteen years. He now works for The Albuquerque Independent School System in their Muti-integrated Computer systems department. He is married and has ten (!!) kids.

  "*Consejos* (advice) came from my grandmother (*mi Chita*), my mom, and my brother. They are the ones I have to thank for the successes in life. Words of wisdom came from my *Chita*, words of courage came from Mom."

Jose Cordero's **Caldo** de **Albondigas Segundo Barrio**

▼ ▼ ▼ ▼ ▼ ▼ **6 to 8 servings**

2 pounds ground beef
2 eggs
$1/2$ cup long-grain rice
2 teaspoons ground cumin
2 cloves garlic, minced
Salt and pepper
$1/2$ cup finely minced
   onions
3 stalks celery, chopped
   (about 2 cups)

6 carrots, chopped
   (about 3 cups)
5 potatoes, cubed
   (about 3 cups)
1 (9-ounce) can tomato
   sauce
$1/2$ cup chopped fresh
   cilantro

Mix the ground beef with the eggs, rice, cumin, garlic and salt and pepper to taste. Shape into approximately $1^1/2$-inch meatballs. Bring 3 to 4 quarts of water to a boil. Gently place the meatballs into the boiling water. Add the onions, celery, carrots, potatoes, and tomato sauce. Cover and reduce the heat to a low boil for about 1 hour or until the carrots, potatoes, and the rice in the meatballs are tender. Serve hot. Garnish with cilantro. Serve with tortillas or Bolillos (page 140).

- -

A native of El Paso and of El Segundo Barrio, **Jose R. Cordero** now resides in Mystic, Connecticut. In 1994, he completed a twenty-seven year career in the military, where he served as a professional musician and educational clinician throughout the world. These multicultural settings varied from our nation's capital to the back streets of the French Quarter, from Carnegie Hall in New York City to October Hall in Leningrad, USSR.

Jose is also working on a wonderful project at this time. He is forming the first all Native American Symphony Orchestra

Barbara Já net Cueto's
Sopa de Fideo

▼   ▼   ▼   ▼   ▼   ▼   **6 to 8 servings**

---

1 (7-ounce) package of
Mexican or Italian pasta,
such as La Moderna Fideo
(vermicelli), stars, or
white rice
2 tablespoons vegetable oil
$^1/_8$ to $^1/_4$ cup finely
chopped onion, or to
taste

$^1/_8$ to $^1/_4$ cup fresh tomato
finely diced, or to taste
1 clove garlic, finely
chopped
1 (8-ounce) can tomato
sauce
Salt
$^1/_4$ cup chopped fresh
cilantro

In a medium saucepan heat the oil and sauté the pasta until golden brown.
Add the onion, tomato, and garlic and sauté for a few seconds. Add the
tomato sauce and sauté for a few seconds. Stir in 3 cups water for thicker
sopa or up to 4 cups for a more watery *sopa*.

Bring to a rapid boil over medium-high heat. Add salt to taste and the cilantro
and lower the heat to a simmer. Cover and cook another 15 to 20 minutes, or
until the desired consistency is reached. (You can add julienned celery and carrots for a change with the cilantro.)

Barbara Já net Cueto was born and raised in El Paso, Texas, into an Irish-
Mexican family. She has been involved in music and theater for most of her life,
professionally for almost twenty-five years. In the beginning it was rock, but now
it is mostly Mexican music. She has a deep love and regard for both. She has
sung with artists such as Juan Gabriel, Augustine Pantoja, and Grupo Mazz.
Check out Barbara's CD: "Esta Noche Es Pá Bailar" by Barbara Já net.

Charlie Gallinar's
Sopa de Albondigas

▼ ▼ ▼ ▼ ▼ ▼   **6 servings**

SOUP	MEATBALLS
2 (16-ounce) cans chicken broth	1 pound ground beef
1 medium onion, diced	3 tablespoons rice, uncooked
2 stalks celery	$1/2$ cup chopped onion
3 carrots, sliced	$1/4$ cup chopped fresh cilantro
1 cup minced fresh cilantro	
$1/2$ tablespoon garlic salt	$1^1/2$ teaspoons dried oregano
$1/2$ cup salsa	

For the soup, combine all the ingredients in a soup pot, bring to a boil, and then simmer for 10 minutes.

For the meatballs, mix all the ingredients together and form into small (1-inch) balls. Place the meatballs in the soup and bring to a boil. Cover, reduce heat, and simmer for 30 minutes. Serve with warm corn tortillas and Spanish rice.

A native of El Paso, **Charlie Gallinar** is currently pursuing his master's degree in Urban and Regional Planning at Rutgers University in New Jersey, far away on the East coast. Check out Charlie's website: segundobarrio.com. The *Segundo Barrio Company* is not a company at all, but a nonprofit, nonpartisan effort founded in 2000 to share information on El Paso with El Pasoans. *Segundo Barrio* is intended to evolve into a forum where El Pasoans directly involved with issues can share their information.

Caroline Garland's
Fried Chicken

▼   ▼   ▼   ▼   ▼   **4 to 5 servings**

---

1 whole chicken (5 to 6
    pounds), cut into pieces
Salt
1 cup milk or cream
1 tablespoon Louisiana hot
    sauce

1 egg
2 cups all-purpose flour
Salt or seasoned salt and
    pepper
Vegetable oil, for frying

Soak the chicken pieces in icy cold salted water for at least 1 hour. Change the water after half an hour. Drain the chicken. With a fork, beat together the milk, hot sauce, and egg. Put the flour, salt (or seasoned salt), and pepper in a paper bag.

Heat enough oil to cover the chicken in a deep cast-iron skillet until very hot. Dip the chicken, a piece at a time, into the egg mixture and then shake it in the bag of flour. Place the chicken pieces in the hot oil and fry over medium-low heat. Fry until golden brown on one side, then turn and continue cooking until golden brown on the other side. Drain well.

Caroline Garland's Green Beans and Ham Hocks

Snap off the ends of fresh green beans, pulling off strings. Place a ham hock or two in a deep pot. Cover with the green beans. Fill with water. Tightly cover the pot and cook slowly for 2 to 3 hours, or until the beans are tender.

Caroline Garland's Hispanic background comes from her Cuban mother. She says she's the only *guera*, or fair-skinned person, in her family. Caroline is the Public Affairs Director at Time Warner Cable and, most importantly, a breast cancer survivor. Caroline says, "These two dishes make me think of my mother and grandmother. The chicken won't taste right unless it's fried in a cast-iron skillet. I'm fortunate enough to have a skillet passed down from my grand-mother, to my mother, and now to me."

Julia Gedaly's **Atole**

▼   ▼   ▼   ▼   ▼   ▼   **4 to 5 servings**

$^1/_2$ **cup all-purpose flour**
1 (5-ounce) can
  evaporated milk

$^3/_4$ **teaspoon ground**
  cinnamon, or to taste
Sugar

Toast the flour in a stainless steel saucepan, but do not burn it. The flour has to be stirred constantly for about 1½ minutes. When the flour is toasted, slowly pour in ¾ to 1 cup water. The amount depends on how thick or thin you like your atole.

Continue stirring while adding the water over low heat to prevent burning. When the mixture is the consistency you want it, slowly pour in the evaporated milk. The amount should be according to your taste. Add the cinnamon (more or less to your liking). Add sugar, again to your liking. Some people prefer a sweeter atole. Serve in warmed mugs.

Born and raised in El Paso, Texas, **Julia Gedaly** has been teaching kindergarten for seventeen years. When not teaching, she enjoys being with her family or doing artwork, like designing silk scarves or pencil drawings.

Rosa Guerrero's Ensalada de Nopalitos Estilo Toluca

1 bag fresh *nopales* or
2 (1.86 pound) jars of
nopales in water (see
page 232 for preparation
of *nopales*)
1 medium onion, diced
2 or 3 fresh jalapenos,
diced
1 large potato, boiled and
diced
1 cup chopped fresh
cilantro

4 ripe avocados, diced
1 cup cooked ham, diced
1 cup *chicharrones* (pork
rinds), crumbled
2 ounces diced Monterey
Jack cheese or Chihuahua
menonita, $1/2$ cup
4 slices bacon, fried and
crumbled
Salt and pepper
Warm tortillas

Boil the fresh nopales for 10 minutes. Drain and rinse. Mix the nopales with the remaining ingredients in a large bowl. Serve with hot, fresh tortillas. You can also make taquitos with the nopalito salad.

A native El Pasoan, **Rosa Guerrero** has been dubbed a Cultural Icon—El Paso's Ambassador for the Arts. She founded the Rosa Guerrero International Folklorico. Ms. Guerrero has been a constant contributor to humanitarian efforts in the region and is a pioneer in the development of multicultural programs for the El Paso Public Schools.

Ruben Gutierrez's
Mexamerican Queso

 **Makes about 8 cups**

---

5 pound block Velveeta
  cheese
1 (10³/₄-ounce) can
  Campbell's Cream of
  Mushroom Soup
1 (5-ounce) can
  evaporated milk
1 large onion, diced

1 tomato, diced
6 to 10 fresh jalapeños
¹/₂ cup (1 stick) butter or
  margarine
1 tablespoon garlic salt
Tortilla chips or Lays potato
  chips, for dipping

Dice the Velveeta so it will melt faster. Combine the cheese, soup, and evaporated milk in a crock-pot on high. In saucepan, combine the onion, tomato, and jalapeños. Add the butter and garlic salt. Sauté the ingredients until the onion is golden brown. Add the onion, tomato, and jalapeños to the crock-pot. Stir frequently until the cheese has melted. Serve as a party dip or add to shredded brisket and make some great burritos.

Ruben Gutierrez's professional career includes several levels of music production in El Paso. He recently released a collection of his musical works in a CD entitled "Beveled Facets" (Latin/Jazz Piano).

Corina Heredia's **Biscochos**

6 dozen cookies

1 pound lard	2 teaspoons ground
6 cups all-purpose flour	cinnamon
4 teaspoons baking powder	2 teaspoons ground anise
3 eggs	Pinch ground clove
1 cup sugar	Cinnamon-sugar
1/2 cup rosé wine	

Preheat the oven to 375 degrees. Beat the lard until fluffy. Mix the flour and baking powder. In a separate bowl, mix the eggs, sugar, wine, and spices. Then add the lard to the flour and work in until all the flour has been incorporated. Finally, add the egg mixture and work in well. Depending on the weather, you might need to incorporate more flour if dough is too sticky. Roll into 1/2-inch balls and place on an ungreased baking sheet. Press each cookie with a fork dipped in flour to flatten the dough ball. Bake for 20 to 25 minutes. Remove from the oven and roll in cinnamon sugar.

Now a resident of Sunland Park, New Mexico, **Corina Heredia**, a pastry chef, works for Prologis. Corina says, "This recipe means a whole lot to me. I remember my mom doing these biscochos for *posadas*, *kermezes*, and all of my sisters' weddings, and mine too."

Kati Hunyadi's **Paella** with **Chicken, Artichokes,** and **Red Peppers**

▼ ▼ ▼ ▼ ▼ ▼   **6 to 8 servings**

---

3 cups chicken broth
Pinch saffron threads,
   toasted and soaked in
   $^{1}/_{2}$ cup hot chicken broth
Salt
$^{1}/_{4}$ cup extra virgin olive oil
4 skinless chicken thighs,
   chopped in half and seasoned with salt and pepper
1 red pepper, cored, seeded,
   and cut into 1-inch wide
   strips
1 small head of garlic plus
   6 medium garlic cloves,
   peeled

2 artichokes
3 ounces green beans,
   trimmed
$^{1}/_{2}$ medium onion, grated
   on large holes of grater
1 ripe tomato peeled and
   cut in half
$1^{1}/_{2}$ cups medium-grain rice
$^{1}/_{4}$ cup cooked garbanzo
   beans, rinsed and
   drained (optional)
1 lemon, cut in wedges, for
   garnish

Bring the broth to a boil in a saucepan and lower the heat to a simmer. Add the saffron-infused broth. Taste, the broth should be well seasoned, add salt if necessary. Remove from the heat.

Heat the oil in a paella pan or oven-proof skillet over medium heat. When the oil is hot, sauté the chicken pieces until golden brown and cooked through, 10 to 15 minutes. Transfer the chicken to a platter and set aside.

Reduce the heat to medium-low. Sauté the red pepper and head of garlic and garlic cloves until the peppers are quite soft, but not brown, about 15 to 20 minutes. Meanwhile, prepare the artichokes. Slice off the upper two-thirds of the leaves and trim the stem. Peel away the tough outer leaves, scrape out the choke fibers, and quarter the hearts.

Continued

Transfer the peppers and garlic cloves to a plate (the intact head of garlic always stays in the pan), cover with aluminum foil, and set aside to cool. Sauté the artichokes in the paella pan until tender, about 15 minutes. Transfer to the plate. Sauté the green beans in the pan until soft and wrinkly, 5 to10 minutes.

Meanwhile, peel the peppers, discarding the peel, and set the garlic cloves apart from the peeled peppers. When the green beans are done, remove the pan from the heat and transfer the green beans to a plate. If there is more than 1 tablespoon of olive oil in the pan, pour out excess. Increase the heat to medium and sauté the onion until soft, about 5 minutes. Add the tomato and the reserved garlic to the pan. Season well with salt, and sauté until the water from the tomato has cooked out, the mixture has darkened to a burgundy color, and is a very thick puree, 10 to 15 minutes. If not cooking the rice immediately, remove the paella pan from the heat. (This tomato, garlic, onion mixture, called the *sofrito*, is the flavor base for the paella). You can make the paella several hours ahead up to this point.

About a half hour before you're ready to eat, bring the stock back to a simmer and set the pan with the *sofrito* over your largest burner (or over 2 burners) on medium-high heat. When the *sofrito* is hot, add the rice, stirring until translucent, 1 to 2 minutes.

Stir or shake the pan to evenly distribute the rice, push the head of the garlic to the center, add the simmering stock. As the stock comes to a boil, lay the peppers and green beans in the pan, in a star pattern. Add the artichokes and chicken pieces, and distribute the garbanzo beans, if using, on the top. Do not stir the rice once the water is boiling. Cook on medium-high, rotating and moving the pan over 1 or 2 burners to distribute the heat to cook the rice as evenly as possible. After 8 to10 minutes, when the rice begins to appear above the liquid, reduce the heat to medium-low.

Continue to simmer, rotating the pan as necessary, until the liquid has been absorbed, about 10 minutes more. Taste a grain of rice just below the top layer of rice, it should be al dente, with a tiny white dot in the center. (If the rice is not done but all the liquid has been absorbed, add a bit more hot stock or water to the pan and cook a few minutes more.) Cover the pan with aluminum foil and cook gently for another 2 minutes to help ensure that the top layer of rice starts to caramelize, creating the *socarrat*. The rice may crackle somewhat, but if it starts to burn, remove the pan from the heat immediately. Let the paella rest off the heat, still covered, for 5 minutes. Remove the foil and set on the table. Guests may eat directly from the pan, starting at the perimeter, working toward center, and squeezing lemon over their section, if they want.

Kati Hunyadi teaches Spanish and "Exploratory" languages. She has traveled to various Spanish-speaking countries and studied at the Juan Carlos Instituto in Madrid.

Cesar Inostroza's **Discada**

6 servings

³/₄ pound chicken	**¹/₂ pound wieners**
2 pounds beef, such as sirloin	**2 links chorizo**
¹/₂ pound ham	**¹/₂ bottle beer**
2 pounds bacon (unsliced)	**Salt**
¹/₂ pound baloney	**Flour tortillas**

Cut all the meat into ¹/₂-inch pieces. Heat a pan, such as a wok and cook the meats with the beer until everything is well done. Add salt to taste. Serve with flour tortillas and your favorite beverage.

Born and raised in El Paso, **Cesar Inostroza** attended Bowie High School where he painted his first mural at the age of sixteen. He always knew art would be his passion, and art became his life as well as his career. Cesar has painted several murals throughout town: in the lobby of the State Building, the El Paso Natural Gas Company, and Lincoln Center, among others. He says his inspiration comes from music and interacting with people.

Tricia Martinez's
Carne con Papitas

▼　▼　▼　▼　▼　▼　　**5 to 6 servings**

---

2 pounds lean sirloin, cubed
Salt and pepper
1 medium onion, finely
　diced
4 to 6 jalapeños, finely
　diced

1 (8-ounce) can stewed
　tomatoes
2 tablespoons ground
　cumin
4 to 6 medium potatoes,
　cubed

Heat a pan and brown the beef with salt and pepper. Drain off most of the fat. Add the onion and jalapeños and sauté until translucent and soft. Puree the stewed tomatoes until smooth. Add to the cooked meat. Combine ½ cup water with the cumin and stir into the meat. Add the potatoes and simmer until cooked, about 30 minutes. Add more water, if necessary to keep the mixture moist. (If you don't like jalapeños, use bell peppers or long green chiles instead.)

A native of El Paso, **Tricia Martinez** was the host of the cable cooking program: "Local Flavor." Her favorite educational tool: the dictionary.

Pat Mora's Aunt Carmen's Capirotada

▼ ▼ ▼ ▼ ▼ ▼   **5 to 6 servings**

SYRUP

3 cups brown sugar

PUDDING

1 loaf French bread, sliced
   and toasted

3/4 cup raisins

3/4 cup unsalted peanuts

3/4 cup pecans

1/2 cup angel flake coconut

3/4 cup longhorn cheese

1 orange, sliced

3 cinnamon sticks

Butter

Preheat the oven to 350 degrees. Lightly grease an 11 x 7-inch baking dish. Boil the brown sugar with 3 cups of water for 5 minutes. Layer the remaining ingredients in the baking dish, beginning with the bread and ending with the cheese. Pour the syrup over the layers, decorate the top with the orange slices and cinnamon sticks, and dot with butter. Bake for 15 minutes.

Pat Mora is the author of poetry, nonfiction, and children's books. A couple of fascinating books by Pat are *Aunt Carmen's Book of Practical Saints* and *The Bakery Lady: La Señora de la Panadería*. Although a native of El Paso, she divides her time between Santa Fe, New Mexico, and Cincinnati-northern Kentucky.

Check out Pat's website: patmora.com. There are many others books that she has authored or co-authored. Surf through her website, I guarantee you'll find a children's book or "grown-up" book that you will enjoy. Thank you Pat, for sharing your heart and soul with us.

Kenna Ramirez's
Montezuma Casserole

▼ ▼ ▼ ▼ ▼ ▼   **6 to 8 servings**

1¹/₂ **pounds pork roast**
Salt and pepper
Vegetable oil
1 large onion, chopped
1 pound tomatoes, peeled
  and chopped
8 green poblano chiles,
  roasted, peeled, and cut
  into strips

2 garlic cloves, minced
12 (6-inch) corn tortillas
2 eggs, beaten
6 ounces white or asadero
  cheese, grated
Lettuce and radishes, for
  garnish (optional)

Season the pork roast with salt and pepper. Heat the oil in a skillet and brown the meat on all sides. Add enough water to cover the roast and cook until done, preferably in a pressure cooker. When the meat is cooked and cooled, shred the meat.

Preheat the oven to 400 degrees and grease a 9 x 13-inch glass baking dish. Heat a small amount of oil and sauté the onion, tomatoes, chiles and garlic. Add this mixture to the shredded pork with a little water. Fry the tortillas in a little oil and dip in the beaten eggs. Place in the prepared baking dish, add the meat mixture, and top with grated cheese. Bake until browned and thoroughly cooked. Serve with lettuce and radishes, if desired.

Kenna Ramirez was First Lady of El Paso when her husband, Carlos, was mayor from 1997 to 2001. She has served on many local, state and national boards. She organized and was Co-Chair of the First Ladies Summit of the Texas-Mexico Border, an event hosted by First Lady Laura Bush. A proud El Pasoan, Kenna continues to serve the community.

Congressman Reyes's
Red Velvet Cake

8 to 10 servings

CAKE
1¹/₂ cups vegetable oil
1¹/₂ cups sugar
2 eggs
2¹/₂ cups flour
¹/₂ teaspoon salt
1 tablespoon cocoa
1 cup buttermilk
1 teaspoon vinegar
2 (2-ounce) bottles red
   food coloring

**CREAM CHEESE
FROSTING**
¹/₂ cup (1 stick) butter
12 ounces cream cheese
1 teaspoon of vanilla
   extract
1 cup confectioners' sugar,
   or more if needed
1 cup chopped pecans

For the cake, preheat oven to 350 degrees. Grease a 9 x 13-inch baking pan. In a large mixing bowl combine the oil, sugar, and eggs. In a separate bowl, sift together the flour, salt, and cocoa. Gradually add the oil mixture to flour mixture alternating with the buttermilk. Add the vinegar and food coloring. Pour into the prepared pan. Bake for 20 to 25 minutes and then check for doneness with toothpick. Cool completely.

Whip the all the frosting ingredients together and frost the cake.

Silvestre Reyes, Congressman, now in his third term, is the first Hispanic to represent the 16th District of Texas in the U. S. House of Representatives. Born and raised up the road in Canutillo, Texas, he is a Vietnam veteran and former Chief of the Border Patrol in El Paso.

Coach Nolan Richardson's
Homemade Rolled Tacos

     Makes 1 dozen rolled tacos

1 pound ground beef	6 jalapeños
Garlic powder	1 pound cheddar cheese
Salt	12 (6-inch) corn tortillas
6 tomatoes	Vegetable oil, for frying

Cook the ground beef in a small amount of water. Drain the meat. Add garlic powder and salt to taste and set aside.

Boil the tomatoes and jalapeños until soft. Put 5 of the tomatoes in a blender and blend. Pour this mixture into a saucepan with water. Make the mixture as thin or as thick as you want it. Mix all 6 jalapeños with the remaining tomato in the blender. Add 1 tablespoon of the jalapeño mixture to the sauce and add salt to taste. Grate the cheese. Place the meat mixture in tortillas and roll them up. Fry the tacos in hot oil until crispy. Pour the tomato-jalapeño sauce over the tacos. Cover with shredded cheddar cheese.

Nolan Richardson has coached basketball for thirty-eight years. He is the only coach to have won a championship on every college level. Coach Richardson now lives in Fayetteville, Arkansas, on his horse ranch where he enjoys fishing in his private ponds and taking care of a vast array of animals.

Alfredo & Lynn Salas'
Magic Cookie Bars

▼　▼　▼　▼　▼　　　　**Makes about 15 bars**

1/2 cup (1 stick) butter or margarine

1 1/2 cups graham cracker crumbs, about 36 crackers

1 (12-ounce) can sweetened condensed milk

1 (6-ounce) package semisweet chocolate morsels

1 (3 1/2-ounce) can flaked coconut

1 cup chopped nuts

Preheat the oven to 350 degrees (325 degrees for a glass pan). Melt the butter in a 9 x 13-inch pan. Sprinkle cracker crumbs evenly over the butter and pour the condensed milk evenly over the crumbs. Top evenly with the remaining ingredients and press down gently. Bake 20 to 30 minutes, or until lightly browned. Cool thoroughly before cutting. Store, loosely covered, at room temperature.

Both **Lynn and Alfredo Salas** are native El Pasoans. Alfredo teaches accounting at El Paso Community College and Lynn is also an educator. Lynn says, "Like so many other things on the U.S.-Mexican border, our marriage brought together two different cultures. Alfredo learned to eat broccoli and I can't get enough jalapeños. In fact, I am a late-night quesadilla junkie! So with beans and rice on the one hand and mashed potatoes and meatloaf on the other, we have managed to enjoy the best of both cultures. Our children's food preference? Pizza!"

Marge Vallazza's **Chilaquiles**

▼ ▼ ▼ ▼ ▼ ▼   **5 to 6 servings**

---

12 (6-inch) corn tortillas	**2 (14-ounce) cans**
Olive oil	**enchilada sauce**
1 medium onion, chopped	**4 ounces Cheddar cheese,**
	1 cup

Spread the tortillas out on to air dry for a couple of hours. Tear the tortillas into pieces or cut them into squares. Preheat the oven to 300 degrees. Heat a skillet. Flick some water drops into the skillet; if the drops dance, it is hot enough. Add enough oil to coat the bottom of the skillet. Heat the oil and sauté the onion until translucent. Remove the onion from the skillet and set aside. Again, add enough oil to cover the bottom of the skillet, and add the tortilla pieces, turning constantly and adding more oil as necessary to lightly coat the pieces. Add a can of enchilada sauce and coat the tortilla pieces. Remove from heat. Mix in the onion. Layer tortilla pieces, remaining enchilada sauce, and cheese in a glass baking dish until all the ingredients are used up. Bake for 30 minutes, until the cheese is brown and bubbly. Remove from oven and let stand for about 5 minutes.

Chilaquiles can be made with tomato sauce instead of enchilada sauce (then they're called entomatadas).

Marge "Lady Margaret" Vallazza has been writing poetry since she was twelve years old. Her greatest influences are the Bible and her mother, a British war bride from Scotland. Because her Mexican-American father traveled extensively with the U.S. Army, she and her sisters had minimal Hispanic influence as they were growing up. However, in her mid-twenties, she became interested in learning more about her Hispanic background and began to write poetry that reflected this heritage.

Please check out Marge's (Lady Margaret's) website: www.geocities.com/heartland/fields/6919/favourites.html

How to Make CASCARONES

Cascarones are confetti-filled eggs that are enjoyed at Easter and many other holidays and fiestas in Mexico and the Mexican-American communities here in the United States. They have been a tradition for many centuries. It is said that not only will your wish come true if you break a confetti-filled egg on someone's head but it will also bring that person good luck. Here are the instructions on these easy-to-make confetti-filled *cascarones*. Make your own wishes come true and bring someone good luck while having some good old-fashioned fun!

The first step is to prepare your egg shells. My family starts collecting shells about a month before Easter so that we have plenty of them. Each time you use an egg, carefully crack open the pointy end of the egg with the back of a spoon. Lift off pieces of the egg shell and empty the egg into a bowl. Rinse the eggshells and set aside to dry.

The next step, is to color the shells. Use food coloring diluted in some warm water with a teaspoon of vinegar, or purchase one of the commercial egg dyes available around Easter time.

Tissue of various colors adds to the decorative nature of the *cascarones*: purple tissue on yellow-dyed eggs, blue tissue on pink eggs, etc. Have your confetti ready in a clean dry bowl. Gather other coloring mediums to use on the eggs as well. My daughter likes to draw pictures on the dyed eggs with markers once they're filled and covered. This adds a nice, personalized touch. Do this while the dyed eggs are drying.

Set the dried eggs in the egg carton, hole-side up. Fill each egg half to three-quarters full of confetti. If confetti is not available, use a hole-punch on the Sunday morning newspaper comics; it works just as well. When all the eggs are filled, apply a little glue (like Elmer's) to the outer rim of the egg where the hole is. Place a round piece of tissue paper over the hole and press (gently) down on the glue to adhere. Put the egg back in the egg carton to dry.

After the tissue has dried on the eggs, decorate the *cascarones* with markers, paints, stickers, whatever suits your imagination. Fill a large bright basket on Easter Sunday with these colorful *cascarones* and watch the fun begin.

How to Make STAR PIÑATAS

Materials
1. 1 balloon, as large as you want your piñata.
2. Old newspapers, torn into strips, and full sheet newspapers to make into cones.
3. Paste mix: 1 cup of flour and ½ cup water (more or less water to create the consistency desired).
4. 6 feet of strong string or yarn.
5. Various colors of crepe paper streamers to decorate the piñata.
6. 1 small bottle of glue.
7. Masking tape.

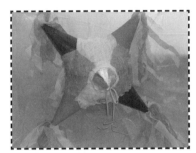

Instructions
A. Inflate the balloon and make a knot to keep in the air.
B. Tie the string to the knot. You will use the string to hang up the balloon to allow it to dry.
C. Dip the strips of newspaper into the paste and cover the balloon with two layers. Let this dry for 24 hours.
D. Make 5 newspaper cones. Attach them to the piñata with masking tape.
E. If you would like to reinforce your piñata a little more, paste another layer of newspaper strips over the shape, including the cones and dry for another 24 hours.
F. When the piñata is completely dry, pull on the string at top to loosen the balloon. Make a small slit in the balloon to deflate. When all the air is out of the balloon, pull out the balloon. Now you're ready to decorate the piñata.
G. Cut the colored crepe paper strips into 10-inch pieces. On the long side of the strip, cut a fringe the length of the strip.
H. Using the bottle of glue, apply a thin line of glue to the crepe paper strip (the side without the fringe), and apply it to the piñata. Experiment. Use your imagination.
I. Allow the piñata to dry for another 24 hours. Attach a piece of wire in the back to dangle the piñata from a rope. Also, carefully make an opening in the back with a craft utility knife to fill the piñata with candies. Then simply tape the opening closed again. Remember: A piñata is an instrument of fun. Always keep smaller children far away from the spot where the piñata is being hit. Accidents have been known to occur in the midst of the excitement. A simple piñata can be made from a brown paper grocery bag or even a box. The point is to have fun making it, with or without your children, and then have fun taking turns trying to break it apart. Enjoy!

Did You Know?

▼ ▼ ▼ ▼ ▼ ▼ ▼

PIÑATAS

They're part of most Hispanic celebrations. From birthdays to Christmas you will see these colorful, candy- and toy-filled creations hanging from a rope ready to be broken open to reveal the delightful surprises waiting to be shared by everyone.

The word *piñata* comes from the Italian word *pignatta*, meaning fragile pot. Originally, *piñatas* came from China and Marco Polo is credited with introducing the idea to Europe in the fourteenth century. When the custom reached Spain, the *piñata* was used on the first Sunday of Lent in a fiesta called the Dance of the Piñata. An *olla* (clay pot), was decorated with colorful papers, ribbons, and tinsel.

The Aztecs also used a form of the *piñata* to celebrate the birthday of the Aztec god of war. Pots were decorated with fancy feathers and filled with tiny treasures. The pots were hung and broken with a stick to allow these treasures to fall at the feet of the god's image as an offering.

With the coming of the sixteenth century, Spanish missionaries used the *piñata* to attract converts to their ceremonies. The clay pot was called a *cantero*, which represented Satan. At the time, the most common design of the *piñata* was a round center, where the clay pot was hidden by the decorative papers, with seven points, like a star, each with dangling steamers. These points represented the seven deadly sins: greed, gluttony, sloth, pride, envy, wrath, and lust. Therefore, the *piñata* reflected *catequismo*, meaning religious instruction or catechism. The blindfolded participant represented a force defying evil: *Fe*, meaning faith. The stick used to break the *piñata* symbolized virtue. Once the *piñata* was broken, the candies and fruits that fell out of the pot were the rewards for keeping the faith.

Colorful piñatas can be found in all shapes and sizes. They can be purchased in Mexican markets or specialty stores. There's even a place in El Paso that will ship a piñata to you. But, you can also make one yourself and design it to your heart's content.

CHILE GLOSSARY

Anaheim: Fresh long green chile. Originated in southern California.

Ancho: Dried poblano chile. Dark red to brown, sweet, fruity, and mild.

Cascabel: Dried chile. Round and very hot.

Chile de Arbol: Dried chile. Small, red, and very hot.

Chipotle: Dried smoked jalapeño chile. Dark red.

Chipotle in Adobo Sauce: Chipotle chile in a hot, tomato-based chile sauce.

Fresno: Fresh chile. The color ranges from bright green to red with maturity. Good substitute for jalapeños. Milder than other small chiles.

Green Chile: Fresh chile. Long green. Most common type known as Anaheim because it was the first large commercial crop grown in southern California. It is very green when picked; red if allowed to ripen on plant. Types include: Anaheim, Española, New Mexico #64, Chimayo, Big Jim, Dixon.

Guajillo: Dried mirasol chile. Brownish-orange and fruity-hot.

Güero: Fresh chile. Yellow-blond, fiery-hot. Use in place of jalapeños or serranos.

Habanero: Ripens from green to red to orange. Extremely hot.

Jalapeño: Fresh or canned chile. Small, hot. Green and/or red.

Mirasol: Fresh guajillo chile.

Mulato: Similar to ancho chiles.

New Mexico: Fresh long green chile.

Pasilla: Dried chile with a wrinkled appearance. Dark red to red-black.

Piquin: Dried red chile, also called pequin. Very small, very hot. Good substitute for cayenne.

Poblano: Fresh chile. Wide, dark green. Mild to medium.

Serrano: Fresh chile. Dark green, up to 3 inches long. Hotter than jalapeños.

Tepin: Dried chile. Tiny, very hot. Used like cayenne or piquin chiles.

MEXICAN COOKING TERMS

Achiote: A paste made from the softened seeds of the annatto tree.

Agua Fresca: A cooling drink made from melon or other fruit.

Aguacate: Avocado

Ajo: Garlic

Albóndigas: Meatballs

Anís: Aniseed

Arroz: Rice

Asadero: Mild white cooked cheese made from half sour/half fresh cow's milk.

Asada: Roasted

Barbacoa: Barbecue

Bebida: Drink

Biscochos: Small cinnamon-anise flavored cookies

Bolillos: Small loaves of French-style bread, also called *Francesitos*.

Budín: Pudding

Buñuelos: round fritters, coated with cinnamon-sugar

Burrito: A filling of meats or beans, often with cheese rolled in a flour tortilla.

Cacahuates: Peanuts

Café: Coffee

Calabaza: Squash

Caldo: Soup or broth

Calientito: Hot Toddy

Camarónes: Shrimp

Camotes: Sweet potato

Canela: Cinnamon

Carne: Meat

Carnitas: Small pieces of fried pork

Cebolla: Onion

Cerveza: Beer

Chayote: A pale green pear-shaped summer squash, sometimes known as mirliton in the United States.

Chicharos: Peas

Chicharrones: Pork skins

Chihuahua: Cheese named for the northern Mexican state where it originated, sometimes called *queso menonita*. Similar to Muenster.

Chocolate Mejicano: Chocolate made in Mexico.

Chorizo: Spicy Mexican-style sausage

Cilantro: Pungent green herb found in Mexican recipes, also known as coriander or Chinese parsley

Comal: Flat cast-iron griddle used for making or heating tortillas

Comino: Cumin

Cotija: Aged cheese. Also known as *queso añejo* or *queso seco* (dry cheese). Grated Romano or Parmesan are good substitutes.

Dulce: Sweet

Elote: Corn

Empanadas: Turnovers filled with either meat or fruit.

Enchiladas: Cheese- or meat-filled corn tortillas in red or green chile sauce.

Escabeche: Pickled

Esparragos: Asparagus

Espinaca: Spinach

Fajitas: Marinated grilled strips of beef or chicken.

Flan: Caramel custard dessert

Flautas: Rolled tacos

Frijoles: Pinto or black beans

Frijoles Refritos: Refried beans.

Galleta: Cookie

Garbanzos: Chick peas

Gorditas: Fried masa shells

Guacamole: An avocado mixture served as an appetizer or as an accompaniment to main dishes.

Helado: Ice cream

Hojas de Maiz: Cornhusks

Hongos: Mushrooms

Huevos: Eggs

Huevos Rancheros: Mexican country-style eggs

Jamón: Ham

Jícama: A root vegetable similar in appearance to a potato, but with a taste similar to water chestnut.

Leche: Milk

Lima: Lime

Limón: Lemon

Maíz: Corn

Manteca: Lard

Mantequilla: Butter

Manzana: Apple

Masa Harina: Corn flour

Menudo: A beef tripe soup made with hominy and red chile.

Molcajete: A mortar made of clay or stone used to grind spices or small seeds.

Mole: A sauce made from a paste of chiles, chocolate, and spices.

Nachos: Tortilla chips usually topped with refried beans, jalapeño chiles, and cheese.

Naranja: Orange

Nopales: Prickly pear cactus pads

Nuez: Nuts

Ollas: Cooking pots

Oregano: Oregano, marjoram can be substituted

Pan: Bread

Panela: Similar to dry cottage cheese.

Papas: Potatoes

Pastel: Cake

Pepitas: Raw unsalted pumpkin seeds, generally ground into sauces.

Piloncillo: Unrefined sugar shaped into small brown cones.

Piña: Pineapple

Pinole: Toasted ground corn; makes a delicious drink with milk.

Pollo: Chicken.

Posole: Specially cooked corn kernels or hominy, also referred to as *nixtamal*. When ground, it is used to make masa for corn tortillas.

Puerco: Pork

Quesadilla: A corn or flour tortilla folded over cheese and other ingredients and heated.

Queso: Cheese

Queso Fresco: Mexican cheese similar in texture to farmers cheese. Mild feta cheese is a good substitute.

Rajas: Strips

Res: Beef

Rojo (Roja): Red

Salsa: Sauce generally made with onions, tomatoes, and chile

Sopaipilla: A square of puffed deep-fried dough, served warm with honey or a cinnamon-sugar coating.

Taco: Folded-over corn or flour tortilla with a variety of fillings.

Tomatillo: Small, green tomato-like fruit covered with a papery husk.

Tortilla: A thin pancake-like bread made of wheat or corn flour.

Tostada: A corn tortilla, served flat and crisped (baked or fried) and layered with a variety of fillings and cheese.

Verde: Green

The Border Pantry

We know that not everyone can find all of the ingredients for the recipes in our book, but we felt that it would be helpful to give you a list of staples used in Border cooking. Of course, making everything from scratch with the freshest of ingredients is always best but we realize, from our own life experience, that it's not always possible to do that. With both parents working, and with hungry kids waiting, there will be occasions when time is a more important consideration than anything else. That said, if you don't have the time to make your own enchilada sauce, use a prepared sauce. Keep some canned chopped chile on hand for when you're in a hurry. Some bottled salsa is actually pretty good. Use a cake mix if there's one you particularly like. We won't tell.

Also, we encourage experimentation! No recipe is set in stone. If we tell you to use asadero cheese and you prefer another kind, go for it. Your tolerance of spices (and jalapeños) will also be an important consideration. We like spicy, but everyone will need to find their own comfort and taste level.

Listed below is what we think that you'll need in addition to what you already have on hand in the preparation of many of the Border recipes. You probably have sage, vinegar and corn starch already. Many of our recipes call for Kahlúa and that's simply because we like Kahlúa. Use whatever liquor or liqueur you prefer.

We made this cookbook as a family project to put down in writing the dishes that we want to hand down to future generations of Corderos and Cordells. May you and your family enjoy and share them, any way you'd like.

Spices
Black Pepper
Cayenne Pepper
Chili Powder
Chipotle Powder
Cinnamon (Mexican/Sticks)
Crushed Red Pepper
Cumin
Garlic Salt/Powder
Onion Salt/Powder
Oregano

Mexican Spice Mix

2½ tablespoons chile or chipotle powder

2 tablespoons salt

2 tablespoons garlic powder

1 tablespoon black powder

1 tablespoon onion powder

1 tablespoon cayenne pepper or red pepper

1 tablespoon crushed oregano

1 tablespoon ground cumin

Combine all the ingredients and store in an airtight container. Makes about ⅔ cup.

Liquors and Liqueurs

Amaretto

Grand Marnier

Kahlúa

Margarita salt

Mexican Beer (Pick one!)

Rum

Tequila

Triple Sec

Breads

Bolillos

Corn Tortillas

Flour Tortillas

Meats & Cheeses

Asadero

Cheddar

Chorizo

Lard

Monterey Jack

Queso Blanco

Dry Goods

Barbecue Sauce

Bottled Salsa

Boullion Cubes

Conchitas (Pasta Shells)

Cornbread Mix

Cornmeal Flour

Dry Corn Husks

Enchilada Sauce

Fajita Marinade

Fideo (Vermicelli)

Masa Harina

Mexican Chocolate

Mole Paste

Olive Oil

Piloncillo (Brown Sugar)

Pinto Beans

Rice

Tomato Sauce and Paste

Vegetables

Cilantro

Garlic

Jalapeños (fresh and canned)

Jicamas

Lemons

Limes

Long Green Chiles (fresh and canned)

Mangoes

Onions

Potatoes

Red Chiles (fresh and canned)

Tomatoes

Index

Indicio Español